The *Real* Terror Network

The *Real* Terror Network
Terrorism in Fact and Propaganda

Edward S. Herman

SOUTH END PRESS   BOSTON

Table of Contents

ABOUT THE AUTHOR

Edward S. Herman is professor of finance at the Wharton School, University of Pennslyvania. In addition to co-authoring *The Political Economy of Human Rights* with Noam Chomsky he has written the highly acclaimed *Corporate Control, Corporate Power*.

Acknowledgements

I would like to thank Paul Getman, Joseph Lim and Michael Marchino, graduate students at the University of Pennsylvania, for their assistance in the preparation of this book. Among the many others who provided valuable comments on the manuscript, or other forms of aid, Philip Agee, Benedict Anderson, Richard Arens, Lawrence Birns, Jan Black, Noam Chomsky, Richard DuBoff, David Felix, Michael Klare, Jack Malinowski, Elizabeth Petras and Ellen Ray deserve special mention. John Schall and Michael Albert of South End Press also made many useful suggestions and extended other forms of help in all phases of the production of this volume. The responsibility for the contents of this work, however, rests entirely with the author.

I would also like to express my great debt to the numerous authors and publications that deal with Third World conditions, often with great competence and humanity, but without effective access to the populations of the west, and, most particularly, the United States. It is one of the themes of this book that information is selected and rejected by the U.S. mass media on the basis of principles related to power and interest, not truth and human relevance. Every Latin American country has produced dissident and refugee groups that issue a steady stream of "samizdats," full of information and passion concerning serious violations of human rights. For all practical purposes these messages are "blacked out" in this country. For a taste of the scope of these unheard voices, the interested reader should consult the *Human Rights Internet Reporter*, an annotated bibliography published five times a year in Washington, D.C. (1502 Ogden Street, N.W., Washington, D.C. 20010) and running to several hundred pages of references per issue.

Relatively accessible sources and publications that I have found valuable in studying the "real terror network" of Latin America, and which describe a world far removed from that portrayed in the U.S. mass media, would include the following:

American Friends Service Committee, numerous short reports (most recently, "Militarizing Central America"), slideshows and activity information (1501 Cherry Street, Philadelphia, PA 19102).

Amnesty International, many publications, including newspapers (*Labor News, Matchbox*, both useful), *Annual Reports*, and important country studies and special reports, many cited in the text (304 West 58th St., New York, NY 10019).

Anthropology Resource Center, *ARC Newsletter*, four times a year (59 Temple Place, Suite 444, Boston, MA 02111).

Center for International Policy (CIP), *International Policy Report*, periodic (120 Maryland Ave., N.E., Washington, D.C. 20002).

Counterspy, five times a year (P.O. Box 647, Ben Franklin Station, Washington, D.C. 20004).

Covert Action Information Bulletin, 5-7 times a year, (P.O. Box 50272, Washington, D.C. 20004).

Council on Hemispheric Affairs, *Washington Report on the Hemisphere,* biweekly and invaluable (1900 L Street, N.W., Suite 201, Washington, D.C. 20036).

Ecumenical Program for Inter-American Communication and Action (EPICA), valuable special reports, including most recently Philip Wheaton, *The Iron Triangle, The Honduran Connection* (1470 Irving St., N.W., Washington, D.C. 20010).

Guatemala Information Center, *Between the Lines*, bimonthly (P.O. Box 59027, Los Angeles, CA 90057).

Institute for Policy Studies, updates of materials on U.S. aid and arms flows to Central America and other useful reports (1901 Q St., N.W., Washington, D.C. 20009).

LADOC, bimonthly publication of Latin American Documentation, mainly important materials from Latin America generally ignored in the United States (Apartado 5594, Lima 100, Peru).

Latin America Weekly Report and *Latin America Regional Report* (five separate issues covering the Andean Group, Brazil, Caribbean, Mexico and Central America, and the Southern Cone countries.) Much valuable detail on business, political and social developments (91-93 Charterhouse St., London, DEC 1M 6LN, England).

Latinamerica Press, invaluable weekly news analyses (Apartado 5594, Lima 1, Peru).

Multinational Monitor, important monthly with wide coverage of world business developments of social relevance (Corporate Accountibility Research Group, P.O. Box 19312, Washington, D.C. 20036).

News from Guatemala, monthly (P.O. Box 335 Station R, Toronto, Ontario, Canada M4G 483).

North American Congress on Latin America (NACLA), *NACLA Report on the Americas*, invaluable bimonthly (151 West 19th St., 9th floor, New York, NY 10011).

Solidaridad, Boletin Internacional, important publication of the Archdiocesan Legal Aid Office in El Salvador (San Salvador, El Salvador, C.A. Apartado Postal 06-294).

U.S. Committee in Solidarity with the People of El Salvador (CIPSES), useful reports (1718 20th St., N.W., Washington, D.C. 20009).

Washington Office on Latin America, *Latin America Update*, bimonthly, plus important special reports (110 Maryland Ave., N.E., Washington, D.C. 20002).

These are accessible and useful sources, and interested students of the terror network addressed in this book will find them a good starter for inquiries, even though they only scratch the surface for Latin America alone. The *Human Rights Internet Reporter* provides further references not only for Latin America but for other parts of the globe. Some of the messages which the numerous and valuable underground samizdats are trying to convey are transmitted in the book that follows.

"If we have learned anything this century, it is that respect for the individual, democracy and the rule of law are essential to progress..."

(Alexander Haig, Dec. 4, 1981)

Basic civil liberties, including the right to life, liberty and the freedom of personal and political expression, suffered a drastic setback in 1981. In more than a dozen regional nations, even the most fundamental rights—life and the inviolability of the person—were transgressed by the government-condoned practice of harassing, torturing and murdering political opponents of those in power....These reverses can be linked to policies adopted by the Reagan administration...[which] has allied the U.S. with the most violent regimes in the hemisphere. He has sanctioned atrocities and human rights abuses by providing those governments with essentially unconditioned U.S. support.

(Council on Hemispheric Affairs, Jan. 12, 1982)

Preface

The philosopher-statesman George Savile, first Marquess of Halifax, wrote in the 17th century that "A man that should call everything by its right name would hardly pass the streets without being knocked down as a common enemy." A wise observation. People have a lot to hide, from themselves as well as from their neighbors. Countries also have a lot to hide, more from their own people than from outsiders. In each country a web of myths evolves that allows the loyal citizenry to feel good about their nation, that depicts it and its people as generous, progressive, decent to a fault in its international behavior. People who question these myths, whether myths about a beneficent past, or the myths currently employed to put today's actions and policies in a favorable light, are thus highly offensive to good taste and basic feelings of right and wrong. These doubters of myths may even pose a threat to communal integration and policy, which rest on this foundation of myths, and societies therefore usually have methods for containing or squelching critics who raise such questions.

1

To use an offensive illustration appropriate to this work, which is in the offensive tradition, consider the treatment of those who took an uncompromising position against human slavery before the Civil War. Slavery was an important economic institution and had majority support in the United States. Thus, according to Charles and Mary Beard,

> In the North, where abolitionists naturally carried on most of their work, the ordinary engines of resistance to criticism were supplemented by mob action. Garrison was beaten and dragged through the streets of Boston in 1835 by a maddened crowd, "including many gentlemen of property and influence," and escaped death only because the police seized him and put him in jail. One of his disciples, the Reverend Samuel May, was set upon at least six times in Massachusetts and Vermont. In Philadelphia, an attack on the abolitionists assumed the proportions of a riot. At Alton, Illinois, Lovejoy, a preacher and publisher, after suffering the loss of three presses at the hands of a mob, was shot to death while attempting to protect the fourth.[1]

This work is written in the spirit of Garrison, May and Lovejoy, impelled by a sense of identification and sympathy with the tens of millions of Third World peasants being pushed off the land under a system of "supply side economics with machine guns."[2] In country after country in the U.S. sphere of influence "dominoes" have been falling, with military regimes and other dependent tyrannies coming into power in virtually all of Central and South America, and in Thailand, Indonesia, the Philippines, Zaire and elsewhere. These regimes have almost uniformly displayed the following characteristics: (1) they represent a small elite interest, including the multinational corporation, which they treat kindly; (2) they all use terror, including modern forms of torture, to keep the majority unorganized, powerless, and as means to local elite and multinational corporate ends; (3) the leaderships of these states are almost invariably venal; (4) they have allowed already highly skewed income distributions to become still more unequal, and have caused a large fraction of their populations to be kept in a state of extreme deprivation.

There is, in short, a huge tacit conspiracy between the U.S. government, its agencies and its multinational corporations, on the one hand, and local business and military cliques in the Third World, on the other, to assume complete control of these countries and "develop" them on a joint venture basis. The military leaders of the Third World were carefully nurtured by the U.S. security establishment to serve as the "enforcers" of this joint venture partnership,[3] and they have been duly supplied with machine guns and the latest data on methods of interrogation of subversives. The impoverished and long abused masses of Latin America, as Penny Lernoux observes, "will not stay quietly on the farms or in the slums unless they are terribly afraid. As in Stroessner's Paraguay, the rich get richer only because they have the guns."[4] The "rich" include a great many U.S. companies and individuals, which is why the United States has provided the guns, and much more. Labor costs have been kept low under this system. The "side effects" in the form of widespread hunger, malnutrition, diseases of poverty and social neglect, millions of stunted children, and a huge reserve army of structurally unemployed and uncared for people are the regrettable but necessary costs of "growth" and "development." These side effects have not been heavily featured in the western mass media.

The terror employed by the enforcers, which helps produce these side effects, has been of fearful quality and frightening scope. In its 1974 *Report on Torture*, Amnesty International (AI), pointed out that human torture, for several centuries largely a historical curiosity, "has suddenly developed a life of its own and become a social cancer."[5] It became a major phenomenon during the reigns of Hitler and Stalin, but in Germany it disappeared with the collapse of Nazism; and, following the death of Stalin, torture sharply declined and in many forms disappeared altogether in the Soviet Union and in the Soviet sphere of influence.[6] But it has grown by leaps and bounds in the Third World client states of the west, most notably in the U.S. sphere of influence. More than ten of the U.S. clients in Latin America are National Security States (hereafter NSSs), Third World fascist clones, directly controlled by military elites whose ideology combines elements of Nazism with pre-Enlightenment notions of hierarchy and "natural inequality."[7] These military elites and their cadres have been trained to find "subversion" in any effort or idea that would challenge the status quo in any way—Bible classes, organizing peasants, unions, proposals for land reform or tax increases on property, and the like. They have also learned that subversion, which is the same thing as Communism, is an evil that must be rooted out and destroyed in a permanent holy war. The result has been a system of self-sustaining and ruthless violence, with behavior patterns strongly reminiscent of those of the Nazi secret police.

For example, there has been a steady flow of reports coming out of Argentina, Brazil and Chile of real and simulated torture of children in front of their parents as a method of eliciting "information." For one woman "they made her son Facundo, cry in the 'operating theatre' next to the one in which she was being tortured...For another, they made her listen to her daughter's screams while they interrogated her."[8] That is Argentina. In Brazil, among the large body of first-hand evidence of the torturing of children is one case of a three month old baby tortured to death in front of its mother by police in Sao Paulo's Tirandentes Prison.[9] In Santiago, Chile, to deal with a woman already tortured but still refusing to talk, "Her torturers brought in her one-year-old son and used flat-nosed pliers to jerk out his fingernails."[10] This method was effective.

The sadism of the "security services" of the NSSs is pervasive and institutionalized. The personnel who are delegated to pick people up and deal with them in the detention centers of Argentina, for example, automatically torture prisoners, but they will also take into custody and torture chance associates of a person whom they wish to intimidate or question. Penny Lernoux describes the experiences of a worker priest in Argentina, Father Patrick Rice, arrested on the street simply because he was working and living with the poor. A 21-year old part-time maid, who came to him seeking medicine for a sick sister, was walking down the street with him when he was taken into custody. *Both* were subjected to extreme torture.[11]

As in Nazi Germany, the institutionalized violence of the NSSs has attracted into the coercive apparatus people who have given it increasingly sexual-pathological properties. Rape, and violence directed to sexual organs, is commonplace. The wife of an international lawyer, one of the thousands of murdered victims of state terror in Argentina, in her last view of him, "could see evidence of the use of the electric prod on his face and also that he had been severely tortured around his testicles."[12] She and her husband were picked up at home as follows:

> On November 10, 1976, at 8:30 in the morning, six men dressed as civilians, heavily armed, broke into my house. They used extreme violence with my husband and me and took away books and personal papers, some of which were extremely important to us, such as his university titles, and everything else that one needs in Argentina.
>
> I was in bed at the time they came in. I had only a nightgown on. They forced me to take off my gown, and put on my street clothes, while they watched with obscene looks and a lot of joking....They took us in a Ford Falcon, which is the most common police car, blindfolded. Immediately when we arrived at our destination, they separated my husband and me, and began the brutal treatment.
>
> It is hard to describe what happened to me there, but it will give you an idea of the mentality of these people, when I make some descriptions.
>
> Naturally, in the situation that I was in, with the great nervousness that hit me, I frequently needed to go to the bathroom. The first two times, they took me upstairs, two flights up, to the bathroom. There was not one right there. Every time I would pass the guards that were standing in the hallway there, they would hit me, kick me, insult me, handle me, and hurl every type of obscenity at me.
>
> So finally, whenver I needed to go to the bathroom, I asked them to bring a bucket, assuming that the people who were in the room with me were in the same situation that I was in.
>
> They brought a bucket that had already been used, and I had to do my necessities with my handcuffs on, and I was wearing trousers at the time. I think you can

imagine what I went through, the long time that it took
me every time to lower and raise my pants with my
handcuffs on, with the guards watching and laughing.

This is a calculated way that they have, among others,
to throw even the person who is most balanced mentally
completely out of balance. This is part of their system
not only of physical but also of psychological torture....

They said they were absolutely sure that neither my
husband nor I belonged to any illegal organizations.
This I did not even have to prove to them. But they said
that despite the fact that we were not involved in an
illegal organization, his work as a lawyer in defending
political prisoners, and especially the fact that he was
well known and could do damage outside the country,
made him a dangerous person to them....

The guards treated all of us violently, some more than
others. One of the worst parts was feeling—I will not
say hearing—the cries of pain of some of the people
who were being abused....I could hear the cries of a
young girl who was being brutally tortured with blows
and an electric prod beside me. Suddenly all ceased and
I clearly heard "Che, the blond has gone out of our
hands."[13]

This gives only the smallest flavor of the new "social cancer"
and the quality of the states whose favor is being actively sought
in Washington. The documentation on the extensiveness and
innovative cruelty of torture in these client states is immense,
although as I shall discuss later the U.S. public is largely spared
the pain of having to confront this horror either in its gruesome
details or in meaningful context. Meaningful context would, of
course, involve disclosure of the enormous degree of U.S.
complicity in the origination and servicing of this form of Third
World fascism, a fact I will document throughout this book.
Instead of facts, people in the United States are assured by their
leaders that those countries are in basically good hands—as
General Haig has pointed out, the rulers of these "moderately
authoritarian" states believe in God, as he does. There is some

confirmation of Haig's faith in the Christian qualities of the Argentinian leaders—the exclusive reading matter provided in many of that country's torture centers is *The New Testament*.[14]

Another extremely important reflection of a resurgence of terrorism has been the growth of "disappearances," a phenomenon mentioned by Hannah Arendt as one of the last and most terrible phases in the evolution and degeneration of totalitarian states.[15] The term refers to cases where individuals are seized by military, paramilitary or police agents of the state, who secretly murder and dispose of the bodies of their victims, often after torture, always without legal process, and without acknowledgement and admitted responsibility of the state. Disappearances, as described by a recent report on this subject by AI, is "a particular government practice applied on a massive scale in Guatemala after 1966, in Chile since later 1973, and in Argentina after March 1976."[16] It was a tactic used by the Nazis in the occupied territories in the 1940s under the Nacht und Nebel (Night and Fog) Decree to dispose of those resisters "endangering German security" by means of what Field Marshall Wilhelm Keitel described as "effective intimidation." The victims, in Germany as in Chile, were subject to an often violent arrest, torture, secret imprisonment and usually death. As noted by AI,

> The discovery of mass graves of peoples previously believed to have "disappeared" and the testimony of survivors of secret detention camps have helped not only to fill in the factual vacuum left by each individual "disappearance" but also to refute denials of accountability on the part of government authorities in countries where the practice has become widespread.[17]

Clearly in this new proliferation of the "disappeared" in Latin America we are confronted with something monstrous: AI notes that "making people 'disappear' is an especially abhorrent method of government repression, one which violates a broad range of human rights, and inflicts widespread and continuing physical and/or psychological suffering. A government seeks thereby to ignore its responsibility to its citizens and the international community."[18] This is an understatement, given the fact of severe torture and mutilation as a commonplace in Latin

American disappearances, as well as death and offical silence. We are also dealing here with a phenomenon that is quantitatively significant, the number of disappeared in Latin America in recent decades numbering several score thousands. At the First Latin American Congress of Relatives of the Disappeared, held in San José, Costa Rica, January 20-24, 1981, the estimate given for disappeared men, women and children in Latin America over the past two decades was 90,000.[19] By contrast, the CIA's most recent (newly inflated) estimate of the total number of deaths resulting from "international terrorist" violence for the period 1968-1980, numbers 3,668,[20] or about 4 percent of the number of "disappearances" for Latin America alone.

To take one further case, or set of cases, indicative of the scope and frightfulness of terrorism in the NSSs, we may consider the tiny country of Guatemala. On June 21, 1980, 30 Guatemalan labor leaders were seized by para-military forces at their various headquarters, packed into trucks, and have not been heard from since.[21] A small matter, not worthy of the attention of Lane Kirkland or the U.S. mass media. In the middle of a *New York Times* article on Guatemala in May 1981, it was noted rather matter-of-factly that "Seventy-six leaders of the Guatemalan Christian Democratic Party, which is associated with the Christian Democratic Party of President Napoleon Duarte in neighboring El Salvador, have been slain in the last 10 months. Ten officials of the left-of-center Social Democratic United Revolutionary Front have been killed."[22] Ordinary citizens and peasants in the countryside of Guatemala have been subjected to a much larger diet of massacres by government forces in recent years. The Council on Hemispheric Affairs estimated in mid-1981 that over 7,000 people had been assassinated by the Guatemalan government and its various para-military affiliates since mid-1978.[23] Toward the end of 1981, the Central American correspondent of the London *Economist* reported that "So far this year some 4,000 Indians have been murdered; thousands more have fled their villages."[24] This figure for murder victims in less than one year in a single small country exceeds the previously mentioned CIA estimate for "international terrorists" over a 13 year period.

It is difficult to avoid a sense of outrage not only at the realities of this real terror network but also at western hypocrisy.

An important element in that hypocrisy is the pretense of western non-involvement. Thus, while the killings and torture in the NSSs are sometimes mentioned in the news media—as inexplicable background facts, like cosmic radiation, and for some reason not deserving indignation remotely proportional to the crimes in question—the U.S. role in establishing and maintaining the NSSs in power is generally suppressed altogether. This pattern of hypocrisy, aversion of the eyes, and absence of indignation at extensive and serious crimes can be rationally explained only in terms of a structure of interests. The Third World clients that dispense the terror in Guatemala and throughout the NSSs serve very specific groups, including important elements of the parent western states, who pursue their naked self-interest with a single-mindedness that overwhelms any conflicting value. But in the mouths of spokesmen for these "lands of the 'disappeared'," words like "growth," "development," and even "freedom" are bandied about as if there were some high moral purpose underlying the joint venture operations built on a base of repression. The preferred word for the favorable conditions provided by terror is "stability;" which is sometimes translated into euphemistic operational language, such as that Mussolini "made the trains run on time."

The use of "freedom" in reference to the client states of the west is especially noteworthy, as in country after country political freedom and basic civil rights have been thrust aside in order that privileged elites can more effectively do what they see as advantageous to themselves. "Freedom" in its application to the Third World in this post-Orwellian age, *means* the ability of the larger economic interests to operate without constraint. As democracy and other legal rights for ordinary citizens might be constraining, freedom requires non-freedom in a political-social-economic sense for the majority. Of course a dispossessed and unemployed peasant is perfectly free to strike a hard bargain with Liquigas, Socfin, or Gulf and Western, to hire lawyers to defend his land claims, and to mobilize his influential friends and use his resources to lobby for special tax, subsidy and legal rights. This very special form of freedom brought by the west helps explain why Third World client states do so poorly in meeting basic human needs, and why such states rarely make much advance on the problems of acute poverty and misery that they inherited and which they often enlarge (see chapter 3, especially Table 3-2 and the accompanying text).

As immiseration of the majority is an integral part of the Free World package for the Third World, the unsavory aspects of the package—the terror, the direct spoliation of people and resources, and western complicity—must be rationalized and, as far as possible, kept under the rug. Part of the rationalization consists of the stress on growth and development, whose benefits will allegedly trickle down to the majority "in the long run." Another part of the apologetic involves an appropriate rede-fining and reordering of concepts of freedom and human rights—that is, *economic* freedom is raised to preeminence, where this really means the absence of any constraints on large local and multinational interests; political and civil liberties are pushed into the background; the basic economic needs and rights applicable to the majority, such as jobs, economic security, nutrition and essential health care, are entirely ignored; and the human rights significance of torture and other forms of direct violence are sharply downgraded.

A second facet of this semi-intellectual defense of state terrorism has been the attempt to distinguish between regimes that are "totalitarian" and those that are merely "authoritarian." Commenting on this distinction (which is addressed further below in chapter 1), Charles Maechling, a former State Depart-ment advisor in the Kennedy-Johnson era, writes:

> Right-wing ideologues devised a specious distinction
> between totalitarian and authoritarian regimes. Their
> approach threw a mixed bag of political and economic
> freedoms, nearly all illusory in the Latin American
> context, onto the scale of human rights and assigned
> these freedoms an arbitrary weight exceeding the most
> bestial practices of torture and official murder.[25]

In the new rightwing apologetics totalitarianism is, of course, equated with Communism. This being the ultimate evil, anything we support that is bad but hostile to Communism—such as fascism—is a "lesser evil." This argument was used to justify continuing friendly relations with the Nazis before World War II, and Maechling notes that since 1976 the arguments given for warmer relations with Argentina by a number of multinational banks, corporations, and business groups like the Council of the Americas "have borne an uncanny resemblance to those of their predecessors for Hitler and Nazi Germany."[26]

There is also an uncanny similarity in the tendency of the leaders of the NSSs and the U.S. business and political elite to assume a hostile stance toward parties and organizations representing the working class and peasantry. These elites are comfortable only with elite rule. Genuine pluralism frightens them. This was a lesson learned by Juan Bosch, who retained power in the Dominican Republic less than a year, and it was demonstrated quite clearly to the democratically elected leaders of Guatemala during that country's brief experiment with pluralism and constitutional government. (That experiment was terminated by U.S. intervention—the Ubico dictatorship which preceded it, and the terror regimes which have followed, were never destabilized by the United States.)[27] Blanche Wiesen Cook points out that "The United States' attitude toward democracy in Guatemala changed perceptibly in 1947, when Arévalo introduced a work code affirming the right of workers to organize and strike."[28] Similarly, the crushing and dismantlement of workers' organizations in Turkey in 1980-1981 under a martial law regime, with collective bargaining terminated and the top leadership of the trade unions arrested and threatened with trial for treason, was greeted warmly in the U.S. business community, and U.S. economic and military aid in support of the new regime was substantially increased. This was, of course, the same period during which martial law in Poland, the arrest of trade unionists, and setbacks to union power and democratic rights in Poland were evoking frenzied cries of outrage and demands for action in the United States—a manifestation of hypocrisy, self-deception, and bifurcation of the mind that would be hard to match.

In carefully playing down or ignoring martial law in Turkey, while carrying out a hysterical campaign of moral indignation over Poland, the U.S. mass media have been displaying what we might call their "fundamental laws of motion" as a propaganda system—which may be summed up briefly as: avert the eyes from the terror of friendly fascists; locate and devote full attention to the abuses of the enemy. This is an extremely important task, given the size and human costs of the real terror network. The function of the mass media, as servants of the dominant power interests of a country whose nominal values are liberal, is therefore to obfuscate reality—to pretend that the NSSs and other dependent tyrannies (like the Philippines) are not extremely well arranged to serve western interests; to play down the crucial western involvement in the emergence and spread of this Third World fascist mafia; and, most of all, to avoid and distract public attention from the details about what is happening to several hundred million peasants and other victims of this joint venture. Putting these ugly facts right out on the table would make citizens of the west quite uncomfortable, and might even interfere with the positive support given official terrorists by the leaders of the Free World. A focus on socialist abuses and on the terror of the left and the dispossessed, relatively trivial by comparison, has been found immensely helpful as a diversion from the quantitatively more significant terror that must be protected as functional. The lesser terror is doubly helpful if it can be tied in with Soviet and Communist plots and machinations. Since this tie-in is useful to powerful interests, the western media do not ask much in the way of rigorous proofs of a Red Menace. Where there is a demand for Red terror in the west, a supply is quickly forthcoming.

The reader will already have noted and perhaps been surprised by the remarkable fact that the CIA concept of "international terrorism" does not include those responsible for the 90,000 "disappeared" in Latin America, nor the leadership of the Garcia regime in Guatemala, the direct managers of the murder of thousands in the last few years.[29] I will examine more closely in the following chapter the ways in which establishment scholarship and propaganda, as displayed in the writings of Walter Laqueur and Claire Sterling, also carefully ignore the official terror and focus on the terror of selected individuals and small groups on the left—subsets of what may be called "retail" (as opposed to "wholesale") terror.[30] The political establishment naturally follows the same course. In the world of Jeane Kirkpatrick, the *Sandinistas* are "promoting terrorism" in El Salvador, "terrorism" referring to the actions of the rebels, who are possibly being given some marginal assistance by Nicaragua.[31] Local church sources and independent observers have uniformly contended that the daily murders and mutilations by government and government-sponsored paramilitary forces account for well over 80 percent of civilian killings. These forces were, and still are, armed, trained and given crucial support by the United States, either directly or through one of its client states. Kirkpatrick excludes the massive official murders of civilians from the category of terrorism partly by arbitrarily removing government from the category of terrorist; but she also resorts to the tired NSS cliché that much of the official violence is by irregular forces who are "out of control." It will be shown in Chapter 3 that the death squads of Latin America are under very good control, one of their prime functions being to kill without restraint while allowing the NSS and its sponsor to "plausibly deny" responsibility. This system of distributed functions has worked so well that the death squad has now spread to ten different U.S. client states (see Table 3-3). In chapter 1, it will be shown, further, that Kirkpatrick's system of apologetics is "complete," in the sense that no level or form of murder or torture, or degree of unpopularity, would justify non-support of our "friends."

In short, we have been living not only in an age of escalating "terrorism" but in an age of Orwell, where words are managed and propaganda and scholarship are organized so that terror *means* the lesser terror—the greater terror is defined out of existence and given little attention. With the accession to power of Reagan, Haig, and Kirkpatrick we have entered the *post-*Orwellian era. Claiming a new dedication to fighting "terrorism," this administration has rushed to the support of the world's leading terrorists, including the rulers of the most torture prone NSSs and assorted other rightwing governments with a marked proclivity to violence. In their turn, the governments of Argentina, Chile, El Salvador, Guatemala, Israel and South Africa (among others), greeted the arrival of Reagan with enthusiasm. For some reason they felt that with his team in place any prior constraints on violence were no longer operative. Intensified repression in Chile and other NSSs, Begin's raid on the Iraqi reactor and bombing of Beirut, and an escalation of South African violence against its neighbors all quickly ensued. The irony of this rapidly expanding *real* terrorism accompanying Washington's pronouncement of a new concern with something called "terrorism" was lost on the western mass media.

Following an initial period of bold and open *displacement* of "human rights" by "terrorism" as the alleged soul of U.S. foreign policy, in November 1981 the Reagan administration decided to reorganize the soul further and reintroduce "human rights." More accurately, it was decided that this rhetorical adjustment would not interfere in the least with business as usual; i.e., warm support for any mass murderer-torturer in our sphere of influence. If Carter could establish a reputation for being a human rights zealot by an occasional qualification in his general support of friendly state terrorists, why shouldn't Reagan get away with reconciling human rights with an unqualified support? A recent State Department memo outlining the new commitment indicates just how this may be accomplished,[32] through application of what may be called "The Three B's." (1) *But,* human rights "must be balanced against U.S. economic, security and other interests." (2) *But,* "we must take into account the pressures a regime faces and the nature of its enemies." (3) *But,* human rights are not advanced by replacing "a corrupt dictator with a zealous Communist politburo." The Three B's would seem to cover all contingencies and preclude any restraint on friendly state terror but "quiet diplomacy" (i.e., doing absolutely nothing).[33] As noted earlier, and as discussed in detail in Chapter 3, many of the NSSs are in place precisely because they serve U.S. interests in a joint venture with local torturers, at the expense of their majorities. It follows that on first "But" grounds alone, therefore, U.S. policy-makers can reasonably look the other way while Third World fascists do their thing. Just in case there might be any other loopholes, the second and third "Buts" allow still more leeway for supporting friendly terror. If, as was the case in Nicaragua, over 90 percent of the population is opposed to a "corrupt dictator," who has been armed to the teeth by the United States and its clients, this 90 percent will have to seek arms elsewhere to dislodge the tyrant. The United States and its allies will not supply them. If they buy arms from any Communist power, as may well be necessary, this will be interpreted as evidence that the corrupt dictator's enemies are sinister (But 2). It also raises the spectre of a "Communist Politburo" (But 3)—the worst—so that we must stand firm with the corrupt dictator.

Given the willingness to manipulate facts on the source, volume and meaning of arms flows (so conspicuous in the case of El Salvador in 1981), our continued warm support of fascist dictators will be perfectly compatible with the new "human rights" principles.

I pay considerable attention in this book to the ways in which the mass media of the United States—which I will also refer to as the Free Press—play a strategic role in diverting attention to the lesser terror. In chapter 4, I deal explicitly with the questions of why the media play this role, and the devices used to serve the dominant interests of the state. I do not resort to any conspiracy theories in explaining these processes, which flow from basic structural facts, relationships, and resultant values, the internalization of these values on the part of media personnel, the importance of government and business as information sources and sponsors, and the interplay of all these forces in generating systematic bias via self-censorship.

Because the media do disclose *something* of an unpleasant reality that some leaders of the state would suppress altogether, their massive subservience to larger state and corporate interests is frequently denied, obscured or greatly under-rated. This confusion is sufficiently important to deserve a few remarks and illustrations here. The first step in understanding the reality of mass media subservience is simply to observe carefully what they select, what they suppress, and what arouses their indignation. Take a hypothetical case, to get a feel for systematic bias. Let us suppose that back in the spring of 1980, Polish labor leader Lech Walesa had called a strike. Suppose further that he and 12 of his associates had been arrested and thrown in jail for a month, then released but scheduled for a military trial on grounds of "incitement to collective violence." Because of the threat of observers from abroad, who insisted on a presence at the trial, its scheduled occurrence was put off for a week; but in fact Walesa was tried in secret and sentenced to three years in prison. Would this be newsworthy? Substitute for Walesa, Luis Ignacia da Silva ("Lula"), the 35-year old president of the Sao Bernardo metal-workers union and chairman of the Workers Party, P.T. of Brazil. It is to Lula that the above facts apply, and these facts were barely mentioned in the U.S. mass media—nothing on national TV; and only by the most careful examination of the best national newspapers would the U.S. reader know who Lula is or be aware of his position. Why is the mistreatment of Walesa newsworthy and the abuse of Lula virtually suppressed? Suppose Walesa and 29 of his labor leader colleagues had been seized by the Polish authorities and "disappeared," as the 30 Guatemalan labor leaders mentioned earlier—imagine the uproar and the furious denunciations of Communist iniquity. Ask yourself why serious crimes in Guatemala are suppressed and why the very much alive Walesa is given enormous attention. I offer the following explanatory hypothesis—that the 30 murdered Guatemalan labor leaders were killed by friendly terrorists, favored and supported by important U.S. interests, whereas a focus on the live Walesa allows many points to be scored against Communism.

A systematic dichotomous treatment can be found across the board, whereby huge crimes by state terrorists within the U.S. sphere of influence are either suppressed or given brief and muted treatment, abuses attributable to enemies are attended to repeatedly and with indignation and sarcasm. When enemy abuses are serious, as in the case of Pol Pot's Cambodia, the mass media follow events on a daily basis, accept or freely disseminate claims without the slightest attempt at critical evaluation, and wax hysterical with humanistic concern. Devotion to the victims knows no bounds, although during the period 1969-1972 when the Kissinger-Nixon team was killing Cambodians on a large scale, and helping to set the stage for the Pol Pot era, the mass media showed not the slightest interest. But lesser enemy abuses (as well as retail terror) also attract steady mass media attention and deep concern. In contrast, the reign of terror in Latin America is being treated only occasionally, with antiseptic brevity, without context, and devoid of human detail and touches that might be conducive to sympathetic feeling.

Noted earlier was the brief mention in a press article of the murder of 76 Christian Democratic leaders over a 10-month period in 1980—no indignation was expressed, no sarcasm about this happening in a member of the "Free World," and no mention of the background of U.S. intervention in that state. Editorial comment on these 76 murders has been negligible, and the details of the individual murders have been essentially suppressed—no pictures, no interviews with widows; just a cold statistic that expresses a media coverup. The same treatment was given the AI volume, *Disappearances: A Workbook*, published in April 1981 and greeted with an almost total blackout in the U.S. mass media despite the distinction of AI and the human importance of the subject matter.

Even more striking was the media's response to the First Latin American Congress of Relatives of the Disappeared, which was held in January 1981 in Costa Rica. This was a tremendously dramatic event, with heart rending testimony presented by many of the 55 delegates gathered from 12 different countries of Latin America. Isabel Letelier, widow of the murdered former high official and Chilean economist Orlando Letelier, was present, as well as representatives of the Mothers of the Plaza de Mayo in Argentina. This Congress did not rate mention in the *New York Times, Washington Post,* or any other mass circulation newspaper, magazine or TV broadcast. If there were a Congress on the Disappeared in the Soviet sphere that met in Paris, with mothers from many socialist countries gathered to testify on the disappearances of their children, and relating their personal agony and experiences with the Soviet bureaucrats of death, would the media look the other way?

As it is, they search hard, as befits a Free World Free Press, and come up with matters less shattering. On May 3, 1981, Anthony Austin had an article in the *New York Times* entitled "Soviet Writer Beaten Years Ago, Still Can't Work." Although the heading implies that this resulted from official action, and the article reports an earlier street attack on the same writer, as well as the failure of the Soviet press to report the incident, plus rumours of a "plot" based on Valentin Rasputin's candid writing—it turns out in the end the Rasputin is an establishment figure, who received a state award for literature in 1977; that his attackers were apprehended and imprisoned; and that "there appears to be no evidence that either attack was anything more than the work of ruffians who picked on him by chance." Clearly we have here a news item of sufficient value to justify neglect of the 10-20 Guatemalan victims of official murder that occur on an average day. Less misleading is the item in the *New York Times* of April 13, 1981 entitled "Mother of Jailed Soviet Dissident

18   THE REAL TERROR NETWORK

[Anatoly Shcharansky] Says He Is Being Denied Visitors." On October 13, 1980 the *New York Times* also gave space to a UPI report that "Shcharansky Reported Ill After Fall." Shcharansky was the subject of still another article by Anthony Austin on March 5, 1981. Shcharansky, one individual, has received more attention in the *New York Times* during the past three years than the aggregated several thousand "disappeared" in Latin America during the same time period. So has Andrei Sakharov. Both are genuine victims of injustice and oppression, and I do not denigrate their personal bravery and victimization. But thousands of humans of comparable bravery and worth have been tortured and murdered—have been victims of terror in its ultimate form, which Shcharansky and Sakharov have not—but without hue and cry in the United States. I return to my original hypothesis: that the Free Press *selects* according to the preferences of domestic power interests, which are pleased to air and wax indignant over Soviet abuses, but wish to keep the now far more extensive violence of our client fascists under wraps.

The broad purpose of this book is to show the nature, roots and vast scope of the real terror network, and to examine the ways in which the magnificent propaganda machinery of the west has covered this over and substituted in its place a lesser, and frequently concocted, network that includes—by careful definition and selectivity—only those terrorists who are challenging important western interests or who can be plausibly linked to its enemies. In chapter 1, I describe the new semantics whereby the terror of mass murderers and torturers is defined as off-the-agenda, and I review briefly the history of the use of terrorism and Red Scares as a long-standing means of keeping labor and dissidents politically impotent.

In chapter 2, following a brief discussion of the reasons why a Red Scare was needed in the late 1970s and early 1980s, I examine the recent popular writings and government claims that try to support the notion of a Soviet-based network of international terrorism. It is shown that by the most elementary scientific standards these analyses not only disintegrate, but that they are also quite crude as pure propaganda. It is shown also that, even ruling out internal state terror and confining ourselves to cross-border terrorism, rightwing and state terrorism of the

Free World (which includes Chile and South Africa) is far more important than left and Soviet-linked terrorism. In chapter 3, I describe the vastly larger network of state terror of the NSSs, which does not require resort to logic-chopping, guilt-by-association, and sources that should make the most gullible choke, for demonstration of an openly expressed common interest, purpose and central (U.S.) support for the Big Terror. In chapter 4, the means whereby the mass media of the west have provided a cover for the real terror network are examined. Chapter 5 provides a recapitulation, followed by a brief discussion of the causes of and remedies for terrorism.

I have tried in this book to state my views straightforwardly and without the usual gentility of language. This is because the issues are urgent, the cruelty and hypocrisy discussed here are mind-boggling, and I want these views to be heard. If this is not possible, for those who do read this book I want my position to be "perfectly clear." Since the message is not one appealing to the mass media, according to my own analysis (and experiences) it will not be allowed to reach a mass audience in any recognizable form. The highest probability is that it will be ignored. Where not ignored it will be shown to be unscholarly (evidenced by calling things by their right names, instead of using a pedantic apparatus that would have justified suppression on grounds of tedium); or it will be dismissed as unbalanced on the implicit principle that while it is appropriate to write about Gulag without mentioning the U.S.-sponsored set of torture-prone clients, each critical work on the United States must take Gulag fully into account. This principle reflects pure political bias, and it manifests itself in a system of bias whereby criticism of the enemy can be unconstrained, criticism of ourselves must be mealy-mouthed.

The United States, as the only true superpower after 1945, has had a greater impact on postwar evolution and deserves more credits and debits than any other country.[34] As the world's greatest power, with exceptional influence over the flow of messages, its debits have (in my judgment) been played down. I present a major set of debits in this book. Let them be confronted squarely.

ONE

The Semantics
and Role of Terrorism

The New Semantics:
"Terrorism," "Totalitarianism," "Communism," "Security"

In his "Politics and the English Language," George Orwell pointed out that "In our time, political speech and writing are largely the defense of the indefensible," which, as he notes, creates a reaction analogous to "a cuttlefish squirting out ink."[1] One part of this ink is the use of "euphemism, question-begging and sheer cloudy vagueness [of language]..." This is nowhere better illustrated than in the evolving usage and reworking of words like "terrorism," "totalitarianism," "communism," and "security."

Terrorism and International Terrorism

"Terror," according to the dictionary definition, is "*a mode of governing*, or of opposing government, by intimidation."[2] The "problem" for western propaganda arises from the fact that the dictionary definition inconsiderately encompasses in the word "terrorist" Guatemala's Garcia or Chile's Pinochet, who clearly govern by the use of intimidation, but whose kindly ministrations in the interest of "stability" and "security" are best kept in the background. This calls for word adaptations that will exclude state terrorists and capture only the petty terror of small dissident groups and individuals. All the establishment specialists and propagandists do in fact ignore Garcia, Pinochet and the South African government and concentrate on the lesser terror, by explicit or implied redefinition of "terrorist."

Walter Laqueur, who has academic ties and must therefore confront this problem directly, admits that terror has a wider meaning, and he titles his book *Terrorism*, not just the terrorism of dissidents, or the terrorism of the left. But he says: "My concern in the present study of terrorism is with *movements* that have used systematic terrorism as their main weapon; others will be mentioned only in passing."[3] The state he excludes from the class of objects called "a movement," so that state terror is thereby defined away. He doesn't try to justify this in terms of importance in the whole spectrum of terror—he just happens to be interested in studying the same thing that the *Reader's Digest, Time,* David Rockefeller, and Generals Haig and Pinochet think is an appropriate subject. One might argue on purely technical grounds, however, that on Laqueur's definition, the National Security States (NSSs) represent the triumph of a "movement" or "movements," given the extensive interconnections between them, their linkages to the U.S. military-intelligence apparatus, their common ideology, and the frequency with which they have been products of rightwing conspiracies within national military establishments. The idea that all the lesser terrorists are properly designated "movements" whose "main weapon" is terror is also absurd, but Laqueur has his political purposes and the examination of smaller bits of illogic in his propaganda exercise need not detain us.[4]

The CIA is also obliged to define terrorism in its annual enumeration of "Patterns of International Terrorism." How does it cope with the need to exclude Garcia and Pinochet? It does this by concentrating on "international terrorism," not just plain terrorism. The CIA concept of terrorism itself is close to the dictionary definition cited above, and would include the state-organized violence of Guatemala and Chile. "International terrorism," however, is defined as follows: "Terrorism conducted with the support of a foreign government or organization and/or directed against foreign nationals, institutions, or governments."[5]

In short, if you use "death squads" to kill 7,000 of your own citizens, this is "terrorism" but not "international terrorism." Unless, of course, you do this with "the support of a foreign government." Now, in point of fact, U.S. government aid to, and support of, the police states of Brazil, Chile and Guatemala, among many others, measured by role in origination, police training, military training, provision of military supplies, diplomatic and economic sustenance, and even the provision of the names of individuals to be picked up and "interrogated" as subversives,[6] exceeds by a huge margin Soviet support of the Irish Republican Army, PLO or the Red Brigades. It will be shown in chapter 3, and is suggested by a cursory inspection of Tables 3-3 and 3-4, that this is a *real* and substantial terror network. How does the CIA deal with this? By simply assuming, without the slightest discussion, that the United States is not supporting any official terrorists—only Libya and the Soviet Union do this sort of thing; the United States only supports independent governments, protecting them against terrorists, by definition. This is a patriotic lie of enormous dimension, even though one which every government employs—and of course the CIA is an arm of government, long engaged in lying acording to perceived "needs of state." What is more interesting is that when the government propounds these lies in CIA reports (or White Papers), or when they appear indirectly in the writings of Claire Sterling, or the disinformation team of Robert Moss and Arnauld de Borchegrave—who move without noticeable change in authenticity between dispensing handouts of intelligence agencies in the role of "news analysts" and as authors of explicitly fictional tales of Communist conspiracies (e.g. in their novel, *The Spike*)—the mass media accepts and dispenses them without question.

Another analyst of terrorism, J. Bowyer Bell, also concentrates on the lesser terror, although in contrast with the purer extreme right propaganda of Moss and Sterling, Bell calls attention to the great diversity of motivation of the retail terrorists, distinguishing between psychotic and self-dramatizing individuals and those who are desperate because of social oppression, with legitimate grievances unfulfilled and possibly beyond fulfillment under unjust systems. Bell has the integrity to note in a book published in 1975 that "Others asked if the more recent use of American B-52s over Hanoi was an appropriate military exercise, while the Palestinian use of incendiary grenades in Rome was not."[7] Why then *are* B-52 raids and state terror in the end excluded from Bell's analysis? He is never very clear. In part, it is a matter of definition; as with the CIA, Bell is interested in "transnational terror" and is therefore prepared to ignore internal state assaults on their own people. B-52 raids are transnational, but Bell also arbitrarily excludes warfare between states, even when based on aggression, and he shows a strange myopia in failing to see the extensive sub rosa transnational terror long perpetrated by strong states (e.g. South Africa) against weaker neighbors. In the end, he is making a political choice of subject matter identical with that of Laqueur and Sterling, and one which makes his writing worthy of sponsorship by the American Enterprise Institute for Public Policy Research and the Hoover Institution on War, Revolution, and Peace.

Bell also defends this choice on the ground that state terror has always been with us, and that somehow or other "attention has usually focused on the lone assassin or the tiny band of conspirators"[8]—in other words, the mass media define what is important and justify Bell's focus. What makes this especially noteworthy is that Bell has been sharply critical of how the media's publicity has "played into the hands of" retail terrorists, giving them unreasonably elevated status and thus encouraging their activities.[9] I have pointed out elsewhere that Bell makes a big mistake in failing to see how the media use the petty terrorists for their own purposes, and rarely if ever convey a message that puts the terrorists in any kind of favorable light.[10] But here Bell justifies his *own* focus in terms of a media attention that he himself has condemned as unjustifiable! Bell completes his rationale for ignoring state terror by arguing that, apart from open war, which he has ruled off the agenda, "Remarkably, such authorized [state] terror on a transnational basis has rarely been employed. At least there have been few highly visible or highly successful operations."[11] This was written after the Bay of Pigs affair and 15 years of small and large assaults on Cuba, just to mention one set of cases that Bell has succeeded in excluding from his vision—he has made a major error of fact here, and I will show in the next two chapters that cross-border *state* terror (exclusive of open warfare) is substantially more important than the terror preferred by Bell and the western mass media.

Claire Sterling, Robert Moss, Senator Jeremiah Denton, and General Haig are less concerned with the nuances of definition. In Red Scares past and present, for the less intelligent and more demagogic ideologues and propagandists, bad words like "communist" and "terrorist" become synonymous with anything repugnant to the demagogue. Denton, chairman of the Senate Subcommittee on Security and Terrorism, is clearly in this tradition, with "terrorism" including "youth gangs snatching purses in Philadelphia, but it can be like the takeover of Afghanistan by the Soviet Union."[12] The only thing the word *cannot* encompass is something done by us or by a friend. This "if-I-don't-like-it-call-it-terrorism" definition is used by Alexander Haig and by many others as well. Terrorism is never explicitly defined by Claire Sterling, but in her book, *The Terror Network*, Pinochet, Videla, South Africa, and the death squads of Latin America are simply excluded without explanation, and in fact the intelligence services of these really major terrorists are primary sources for Sterling's stories regarding the lesser terror. (This, despite the overwhelming evidence that they will lie, forge and plant documents, and murder, without the slightest scruple.) Carefully excluding all terrorists of the right, retail as well as wholesale, Sterling throws all other lesser terrorists into a single pot, and without giving any numbers, or analysis by type, she employs a few facts, many unsupported claims of fact, and a steady flow of third-rate literary embellishments a la James Bond, to create an aura of foreboding suitable to a *Reader's Digest*-Haig propaganda end. I will return to Sterling's semisubstantive discussion of the Red terror network in the following chapter.

Totalitarianism, Authoritarianism, and Moderate Autocracy

Another set of semantic adjustments developed to meet the current propaganda needs of the state is in the use of the words "totalitarian" and "authoritarian." Totalitarian is a bad word, and cannot be used in reference to our "friends;" accordingly, the mass media and the terrorism specialists permitted access to the mass media never apply it to allied Third World fascists—for these, more benign words are used, like "authoritarian" or "moderate autocrat."

The irony of this bit of word management is that totalitarianism fits the NSS more snugly than it does enemy states such as Cuba and the Soviet Union. In Hannah Arendt's analysis, the use of secret police, informers, and systematic terror—including torture and disappearances—to intimidate and destroy all vestiges of organized resistance to elite rule, is a primary feature of totalitarianism.[13] So too is a simplistic and complete ideology which denies the rights of the individual, subordinated to a higher state purpose, and which postulates a permanent state of war between the forces of good and evil.[14] These are prominent characteristics of the contemporary NSS and National Security ideology, which reads like it was taken from a Nazi primer.[15] One important element of classical (German and Italian) fascism missing in the NSS is the strong effort to mobilize the masses to get them to identify with the state and its objectives. Classical fascism had a popular base, which Hitler and Mussolini tried to enlarge by public ceremonies and displays, patriotic orgies, and the like. The NSS, in contrast, has no popular base and rests on a groundwork of pure force and external support. Its occasional efforts to rally popular support have been half-hearted and ineffectual precisely because the ideology and organization of the NSS aims at depoliticizing a restive and threatening majority. Jorge Nef points out that repression and state violence in Chile, for example, were part of "a carefully planned strategy to reduce the internal constituency in Chilean politics" and to replace it by "the functional incorporation of external constituencies—foreign consortia, the U.S. defense establishment and 'Free World Allies'—into the support system of the Chilean state."[16] It is for this reason that I have called the NSS a *subfascist* system— Jaguaribe calls it a system of "colonial fascism"—in recognition of its lack of the popular roots of classical fascism, its external support base, and its perfect design for the unconstrained exploitation of the majority of the population.[17]

The concept of totalitarianism was crudely serviceable before the mid-fifties as a means of distinguishing Soviet Russia under Stalin from some of the lesser tyrannies of the west,[18] but with the death of Stalin state violence diminished markedly, arbitrary terror declined, and there was a lessening of "institutionalized anxiety."[19] The Soviet Union is still a one party and oppressive state, with a conservative and self-serving bureaucracy that severely restricts personal movement, controls the formation and activities of all organizations, and monopolizes all aboveground means of communication. But while the Soviet bureaucracy takes good care of itself, neither it nor the satellite leaderships of Eastern Europe ignore the welfare of the mass of the population as do the NSSs, where an active class exploitation of the majority is part of a system dynamic. As noted, also, arbitrary and extremely violent terror has sharply declined in the Soviet Union. Nowhere in the Soviet sphere is human torture employed on the scale found in a score of NSSs, and "disappearances" are not reported there at all. In the NSSs, on the contrary, terror is widespread in its ugliest forms, and its intent is to intimidate and create "anxiety." Thus, although Brazilian cities are notorious for street crime, a Sao Paulo public opinion poll of 1975 showed that more people were afraid of the police (seven out of ten) than of non-official violence. People's fear of the police diminished, however, as their income increased.[20] The former Mayor of San Salvador, noting the regular use in El Salvador of hundreds of armed security personnel occupying a town, searching all the houses, taking into custody hundreds of people, most of whom are eventually released, says:

> The purpose of these operations is not crime prevention but rather to instill terror in the population as a whole. In this way people come to accept the violation of their human rights as something inevitable, a force that cannot be resisted. When the people are released from jail, the authorities act as if they were giving them a gift by restoring their freedom.[21]

The formerly conservative Catholic Church of Latin America constantly stresses the same point—that

> Security, as a good of the nation, is incompatible with a permanent insecurity of the people...marked by arbitrary repressive measures without possibility of defense,

compulsory internments, unexplainable disappearances, degrading processes and interrogation and acts
of violence done in the easy bravery of clandestine
terrorism and in frequent and almost total impunity.[22]

This captures the essence of the NSS, which is not "moderately
autocratic" or "moderately authoritarian"—it is a fullfledged,
technologically advanced, partly absentee-owned, "immoderately
authoritarian" system that manifests some of the ugliest features
of classic fascism and totalitarianism. That is why the Church, in
a reactive process highly reminiscent of Nazi Germany, has risen
up as the last institutional refuge of the majority against a *system*
of intimidation.

The NSS represents and serves the interests of a tiny elite. Its
economic policies of "trickling-up," enforced by the machine
gun, are rationalized on the ground that growth in the long run
will trickle *down* to the lower orders. This is a self-serving
ideology designed mainly to allow the western public to think
well of themselves and their own country. It obscures the primary
fact that in countries like Brazil, Chile and Indonesia the majority
are *means* to elite ends, they are not ends in themselves. When
Somoza visited Costa Rica and was proudly shown some new
educational facilities for the poor, he was impatiently uninter-
ested: "I don't want educated people, I want oxen."[23] The honesty
of this crude bully and mass murderer is refreshing after a dose of
Jeane Kirkpatrick; and it expressed the true spirit of the NSS,
whose function is to keep 200 million Latin Americans in the
physical and moral state of oxen. As I show in chapter 3, the NSS
carries out this function well.

By what routes do U.S. apologists for the NSS find Somoza,
Pinochet et al to be benign and worthy of our support? Basically,
of course, it is that they are our "friends" and cooperate with us;
and, as a last resort, while they may be bad, the Communists are
worse. Jeane Kirkpatrick's rationale for client fascism, for
example, makes all these points—Somoza was a friend; the
Communists are bad (she suggests that we look at a representative case, Cambodia). But she also puts our fascists in a more
positive and appreciative light, downplaying their dependency
and subservience (this falls under the heading of "friendly") and
their insatiable looting, and essentially suppressing the extent

and quality of their violence and its impact on the majority. On the question of looting, Kirkpatrick acknowledges with scholarly judiciousness that "Somoza and the Shah enjoyed long tenure, large personal fortunes (much of which were no doubt appropriated from general revenues)."[24] Note the absence of any invidious language, the honest and open admission of a naughty finger in the till, and the lack of any details on the size of the personal fortunes. The Somoza family, for example, owned the two dozen largest companies in Nicaragua plus over 8,000 square *miles* of land. The suggestion that this property was "appropriated from the general revenues" is a misrepresentation of fact—it was also obtained by the regular confiscation of peasant lands by military force and by the murder of resisting peasants, the collection of bribe money for state favors, and any form of force and fraud one might want to name.[25]

According to Kirkpatrick, the traditional autocrats observe "traditional taboos." But in countries like Uruguay, Chile and Brazil, there had long been taboos constraining military intervention in public life. These were undermined under strong and deliberate U.S. influence, which encouraged the Latin American military to look upon themselves as a political elite of "nation-builders."[26] There had also been traditional limits on the violence imposed on incarcerated prisoners, taboos and limits that were stripped away during the fascist counterrevolutions of the past 30 years. Amnesty International (AI) noted in 1974 in its *Report on Torture* that "There is a marked difference between traditional brutality, stemming from historical conditions, and the systematic torture which has spread to many Latin American countries within the past decade."[27] This is a *new* condition, which *violates* traditional taboos. Kirkpatrick notes that both the Shah and Somoza "occasionally, it is alleged, torture their opponents," and their police forces "were said to be too harsh, too arbitrary and too powerful." In short, they were "traditional rulers of semi-traditional societies."[28] Again we may note the extreme judiciousness—only "occasional" torture was "alleged"—Kirkpatrick has not established to her scientific satisfaction that even occasional torture and "harshness" were actual facts. No numbers, no details, no mention of "disappearances" or the fact that "harshness" may involve killing and multilation of men, women

and children in large numbers. Kirkpatrick is a female Podsnap—
"I don't want to know about it; I don't choose to discuss it! I don't
admit it!; Mr Podsnap had even acquired a peculiar flourish of
his right arm in often clearing the world of its most difficult
problems, by sweeping them behind him (and consequently sheer
away) with those words and a flushed face. For they affronted
him."[29]

Kirkpatrick also asserts that the traditional autocrats "do
not disturb the habitual rhythms of work and leisure, habitual
places of residence, habitual patterns of family and personal
relations;" thus the miseries are bearable and people "learn to
cope." Such societies "create no refugees."[30] "Habitual patterns"
and "family and personal relations" would seem to be rather
seriously affected when paramilitary forces knock on the door at
3 a.m., remove a family member by violence, and no further word
is heard about this "disappeared." On April 30, 1981 nearly 2,000
grieving women, the "Mad Mothers of the Plaza de Mayo,"
appeared to conduct their silent vigil outside the Argentinian
Government House for their missing children. They are among
the hundreds of thousands of victims of random or calculated
NSS violence who contest Kirkpatrick's benign picture. The
claim that people "learn to cope" is in many cases demonstrably
untrue—the thousands of children each year who die of malnutrition or untreated diseases did not "cope"—and it is partly a
meaningless synonym for "managed to survive," as in the phrase
"many Jews learned to cope in Buchenwald."

The statement that such societies "create no refugees" is a
blatant falsehood—the numbers that have fled from the NSSs of
Latin America and the Caribbean in the last two decades are far
in excess of a million, including, among others, some 250,000-
500,000 from Argentina, 75,000-150,000 from Chile, over 200,000
from the Dominican Republic and 500,000 from Uruguay.[31] The
fraction of the population that has left Uruguay is more than
twice that for Cuba, although the publicity differential—con-
forming to my hypothesis on press coverage of negative events in
socialist and fascist states—is such that many people are unaware
of the huge exodus from Uruguay. A large fraction of the refugees from the NSSs have been scientists and other academics and

professionals. The Latin American journalist Hugo Neira contends that there has been a deliberate and continent-wide "lobotomization of intellect" as the NSSs consciously encourage the exit of intellectuals with any tendency toward independence of political and social thought and not purchasable as subservient technocrats.[32] According to Uruguayan scholar and expatriate Mario Otero, "one may fairly say that research in the natural sciences has disappeared in Uruguay."[33] The U.S. physicist Joel Primack suggests that retrogression in all intellectual fields is acceptable in the NSSs, in part, because "the only research necessary was for development and this could be obtained from abroad through multinational companies."[34]

These are cross-border refugees, and their numbers are large. But the *specialty* of the NSS and the really large numbers are to be found in the form of *internal* refugees. In Paraguay, Ecuador, Brazil and elsewhere, literally millions of peasants have been dispossessed by force since 1964. Church sources estimate 7 million peasants forced off the land in Brazil alone since 1960.[35] The NSS especially victimizes the poor, who are not able to afford external migration and would not be admitted abroad in large numbers anyway. In Nicaragua, for example, Lernoux points out that with the spread of cattle ranches, peasants were forced off the land in brutal military campaigns, always waged on the basis of claims "that the peasants were collaborating with a group of left-wing guerillas."[36] Pushed in this fashion into jungle areas of Zelaya, many were left alone till roads were constructed making this land interesting to those with power—"the pattern of land evictions that had occurred elsewhere was repeated in Zelaya—and the same excuse: 'Communist subversion.' By mid-1978 some six hundred peasants in Zelaya had been killed by government forces, according to the Capuchin missionaries."[37] Near a river front area long occupied by peasant families, a National Guard commander arbitrarily authorized a large cattle rancher who was in favor to take over this land. The peasants were simply destroyed or dispersed by force of arms. "Of the original one hundred peasant families living on these lands, only eighteen remained, the rest having fled or 'disappeared'."[38] This is the reality of the respect for "habitual places of residence" in the NSS. What Kirkpatrick calls "traditional auto-cracy" or "moderate authoritarianism" is neither traditional nor moderate—it has added modern methods to the most retrograde elements of traditional modes of spoliation and oppression. Thus, it has worsened a system long immoderate in both ends and means.

With Jeane Kirkpatrick, the rationalization of support for fascist terror is "complete," by the following route—if somebody like Somoza is willing to be our friend, we have an interest in supporting him, as friends are desirable. It is possible that he is our friend because he behaves so outrageously to his own people that they would like to get rid of him—this may be so, but we cannot afford to be moralistic. ("Moralistic" means applying morality to our friends, or ourselves; "morality" is applying moral values to our enemies.) If Somoza is especially vicious and alienates his *entire* population, he becomes totally dependent on us and thus even more reliable as our "friend," thereby deserving more support. If the population under siege by our friend, and his U.S.-trained National Guard, expresses a certain amount of hostility toward us for our long support of his looting and vio-lence, this is ominous and ungrateful. If, furthermore, they have the audacity to seek weapons elsewhere, to offset those we pro-vide Somoza, and which we deny to them, clearly they have provoked us beyond the point of endurance.

If it is argued that he represents something close to the limit of terror plus abusive exploitation of the majority, which he regarded as "oxen," Kirkpatrick has a further reply. We must be sympathetically tolerant of Somoza's terror right now, as he is under siege; in the long run, however, we may expect warm-hearted humanists like Jeane Kirkpatrick, who represent the Judeo-Christian tradition, to exercise "quiet" diplomacy that will eventually strengthen the forces of decency that Somoza is unfor-tunately unable to display right now (in a tradition that dates back to 1935). He must use force now because people who take up arms against him, and who accept them from those abroad who will give them to them, are "terrorists" who are linked to Mos-cow. As Communism is the worst, and we will work for humane values in the long run, it is regrettably necessary to help Somoza kill for the time being. As noted, this argument not only amounts to apologetics for unlimited terror, it is "complete" in the sense that the worse the villainy, the less the indigenous support of our fascist "friends," the more the consequent dependence on us, the greater the justification for our support. It is also "complete" in that any indigenous upheaval not under our control is by definition a case of "terrorism"—and if it reaches outside for protection, this helps support the original suspicions that it was not really indigenous but is yet another illustration of Communist expansionism.

"Communism" and "Security"

Among Latin American elites, a peasant asking for a higher wage or a priest helping organize a peasant cooperative is a communist. And someone going so far as to suggest land reform or a more equitable tax system is a communist fanatic. There is no word or act suggesting the desirability of elite generosity toward the poor, or the need for education, organization or material advance for the majority, that has not been branded communistic in Latin America in recent decades. The Pope himself, having urged both greater generosity and significant reforms on the local elites, was also denounced in Latin America as a tool of communism.[39]

Since communism is the enemy, and peasants trying to improve themselves, priests with the slightest humanistic proclivity, and naturally anyone seriously challenging the status quo, are communists, they are also, by definition, enemies. In the National Security State, "enemies" are evil, a threat to "security," and must be treated accordingly. No form of violence is excessive in a war between the forces of good and evil. This is why in every NSS in Latin America, Church people having any dealings that involve trying to elevate the status of the poor are suspect and potential victims of unlimited violence, as with Father Rice, described in the Preface. Or as in the case of the Jesuit priest Rutilio Grande, a forthright supporter of peasant rights in El Salvador, who thereby aroused the furious hostility of local landowners. Rutilio Grande was shot to death, along with a teenager and a 72 year old peasant, by bullets of standard police calibre, at a time when communications to the area of the triple murder were cut and police patrols were inexplicably absent.[40]

Church people supportive of elementary rights of peasants have been murdered in every NSS. According to Church sources, between 1964 and 1978 the Latin American Catholic Church suffered 935 politically-based arrests, 73 cases of physical torture, 116 murders and disappearances, and 288 cases of forced expatriation.[41] The Church *is* a threat—to the unconstrained and undemocratic power of a completely ruthless elite.

U.S. businessmen and other members of the U.S. elite have a similar tendency to use communism as a "Linus blanket" to justify any action suiting their interest. I recently encountered a U.S. business leader at a church discussion of the transnational corporation—a liberal business leader, who, while expressing the view that productivity enhancement was the primary business contribution to human welfare, nevertheless contended that businessmen should treat those around them "with loving care." Asked about the NSS in Brazil, where he has a plant, he was regretful of the lack of loving care dispensed there, but the coup of 1964, he asserted, "prevented communism." Wonderfully convenient! Naturally, the United States has a right to "prevent communism" wherever it rears its ugly head. Also, the term being a bit fuzzy, standards of proof here have an elasticity that stretches exactly according to need. The number of communists in Brazil in 1964 was small; communism had no significant organizational base; and the contention that Goulart was a "communist" is demagogic nonsense.[42] The fact is that U.S. officials were involved in talks with military conspirators about the "threats" posed by Goulart's predecessors, Quadros and Kubitschek, who were already asserting some small degree of independence from local elites and U.S. business and its support elements, and who therefore would have been found after the fact of a coup to have been "communists."

Communism is an enormously serviceable tool for achieving morally dubious goals under a morally acceptable cover. It is not acceptable to destabilize a country, overthrow its democratically elected government, and institute a reign of terror in order to lower taxes and wages for one's own multinational firms. It is necessary to put forward a higher moral imperative. When United Fruit was faced with the threat of a serious land reform, unionization and higher taxes under the Arbenz government of

Guatemala in 1952-1954, it mounted a huge publicity campaign in the United States that carefully and deliberately played down its material interest, stressing instead the menace of the "international Communist conspiracy." The claim that Arbenz was subject to external Communist discipline was a pure and cynical propaganda fabrication, but that did not interfere with its virtually unopposed institutionalization by the U.S. mass media.[43] The Kinzer-Schlesinger study of the 1954 coup shows how the U.S. government and the press suppressed the inconvenient fact that the Arbenz government voted in the UN as a U.S. client; that despite a number of low level officials and a small minority status in the Arbenz coalition that gave it access to Arbenz' ear, the internal Communist faction was viewed by State Department analysts as possessing "relatively trivial" power; that Guatemala maintained no diplomatic links with the Soviet Union or Eastern Europe; and that "No shred of evidence ever turned up after the coup establishing a secret tie to the Soviets."[44] The real worry of United Fruit—and the U.S. officials that ran interference for this influential company[45]—was serious reform; Communism was the fabricated propaganda vehicle that mobilized public opinion for the huge subversive effort that was then in process.

Juan Jose Arévalo, who preceded Arbenz as president of Guatemala, has even suggested that we distinguish between "Communism," spelled with a C, and "Kommunism," spelled with a K—the former referring to a real linkage to the international Communist movement; the latter, advocacy of serious reform that would encroach on privilege.[46] "Communism" is the handy cover for legitimizing intervention to prevent "Kommunism." A closely related service of "Communism" is that it can be used as a proxy for exacting submission from a government and country that have acted contrary to our will. In the McCarthy era, individuals were compelled to "name names" as an act of humiliating surrender, in which error was acknowledged and integrity and political autonomy were compromised. The constant harping and focus on "Communism" as regards Arbenz and Guatemala served the same role. He was invited to submit—to denounce the Communists, to sever his political connections with them, and to throw all of them out of office (although none had cabinet rank or important posts).[47] Despite the fact that the

Communists were only a small component of the Arbenz coalition, giving way on this point would have hurt Arbenz internally, signalling defeat and loss of independence, fracturing his coalition, and weakening his support base. What is more, his submission would never have been quite enough for the United States without major programmatic adjustments—especially as regards the land reform that was the main object of United Fruit's efforts. The Communist label was first attached to Arévalo and Arbenz merely by their legalizing unions. Arbenz would have been a "Communist" just so long as he persisted in his mildly radical threats to United Fruit and otherwise failed to submit to the substantive demands of the superpower. It was a useful proxy for "Kommunism."

"Security" is another beauty for rationalizing anything one wants, serving as a morally pure and highly elastic cover for more mundane interests such as the desire to obtain favorable terms on contracts to exploit resources, or the preference for non-union labor. The NSSs have the merit that, since the military elites that rule them have a weak or non-existent local base, and rely heavily on their external supporter (the U.S. = the Godfather), they must be very cooperative with the Godfather and its multinational corporate progeny. They provide "security"—to Godfather and progeny—but, regrettably, "insecurity" to the majority of the population. As Church observers in Latin America reiterate about the NSS,

> Security should not be the privilege of systems, classes and parties;...the State cannot sacrifice rights to guarantee private interests. Security, as the good of the nation, is incompatible with a permanent insecurity of the people.[48]

As this pattern of security-insecurity requires keeping the majority in a subservient and miserable condition, to the advantage of a small elite, it is possible that this quietly seething cauldron will one day explode. But the Godfather, progeny, and the local elites—who invest heavily in Miami real estate and elsewhere abroad—take a short view, hoping that the ultimate result of their lack of loving care applied to the multitude can be put off by terror—or that they can get out before the deluge.

The Red Menace and Its Role

"Terrorism" and "Red scares," separately or in combination, have been long-standing features of the U.S. political landscape, recurring in roughly 25-30 year cycles from the Haymarket affair of 1886 to Haig's demagoguery of 1980-1982. They have served an important role at home and abroad in helping the business community and national elite in their struggle against effective labor organization and reformist political threats, and in favor of unconstrained business domination, enlarged arms budgets, and imperial expansion.

Red scares have all been created and/or stoked by conservative interests and have served conservative ends. In all of them an attempt has been made to deny the indigenous roots of democratic upheavals (union organizational efforts, strikes, protests against government domestic and foreign policies) and to smear them as foreign imports. Red scares have all had the effect of weakening labor and reform movements by unleashing irrational forces that divert attention from real issues and cast doubts on the patriotism and purposes of unionists and reformers. Especially in their union busting phases, the Red scares have often featured violence and agents provocateurs, which have been used to justify draconic government intervention (troops, deportations, jailings of radicals and union leaders, loyalty and union control legislation). Red scares have all featured alleged radical conspiracies usually linked to some foreign power, whose existence and importance are "proved" by evidence that is partially or wholly fabricated. This evidence may be easily demonstrated to be false or defective, but during the "age of terrorism" the national media disseminate the required line without serious criticism, feature the fabricated and inflated claims as news, and contribute to the hysteria and "cleansing" of the dissident elements. Subsequently, and long after the Red scare has taken its toll, it is discovered that the conspiracies were a mirage; that, as Levin remarks about the scare of 1919-20, millions of people had been induced to believe in and take drastic actions to counter a massive conspiratorial threat "when no such threat existed."[49] As in the case of the "gaps" in our military arsenal—of bombers, missiles, "throwweight," and vulnerable "windows"—discovered by the arms lobby whenever there is a perceived opportunity for a killing, the repeated discovery that weapons gaps and terrorist conspiracies were fraudulent never interferes with the media playing the same role in the next phase of elite need for a gap or terrorist scare.

Late nineteenth century Red scares, such as the Haymarket affair of 1886 and the Pullman strike of 1894, were offshoots of business-labor conflict and the business struggle to prevent unionization. The Pullman strike involved significant violence, most of it carried out by thugs hired by the railroads, but, with the aid of the press, successfully attributed to the strikers.[50] The press not only exaggerated actual and threatened striker violence, it disregarded the extreme intransigence of the railroads and their use of agent provocateurs; and the *New York Tribune* and other papers swallowed easily an "anarchist plot to blow up the Capitol."[51]

The great Red scare of 1919-1920 was less exclusively directed at the threat of union organization, but that was still a central feature. The war and inflation resulted in a great deal of turbulence, with labor seeking to maintain and improve its economic status by aggressive bargaining and strikes and by enlarging its organizational base. Business, on the other hand, wanted a return to prewar or nineteenth century conditions of freedom from government interference (unless helpful), and, especially, freedom to deal with labor on a man-to-man basis (corporation to individual worker). The steel and coal strikes of 1919 were broken with very powerful assists from well stoked public fears of non-existent "Communist" domination of unions. One historian of the Red scare, Robert Murray, noted that the strategy of the steel industry was to convince the public "that 'bolshevism' was the *only* strike issue."[52] Similarly, the coal strike was converted by a well organized propaganda campaign into a virtual Communist insurrection, and "Government officials, both state and federal, soon took up the cry of 'radicalism'."[53] The union itself was the real concern and object of attack of the business community, and it was by the effective equating of unions with radicalism "that employers really made their devastating raids on the power of organized labor."[54] By means of a huge propaganda barrage, "The general public was finally brought to believe that almost every union man was opposed to the American way of life and was the unworthy, if not deliberate, dupe of dangerous radicals."[55]

It is interesting to note that this equating of unions and radicalism occurred despite the fact that John L. Lewis, the leader of the coal miners, was bitterly anticommunist, and the union movement in general was dominated by individuals like Samuel Gompers, who believed in capitalism, the divine mission of the United States and the evils of communism. Gompers and other top labor leaders actively supported the postwar patriotic crusade and the campaign against domestic radicalism; but by the fall of 1919 they found that their vociferous anticommunism had produced a political environment in which "even the wildest antiunion charges seem believable."[56] This would hardly be the last time the anticommunism of the U.S. labor leadership helped consolidate the power of forces inimical to labor's interest.

The media contributed greatly to the 1919-1920 hysteria by news bias, gullibility and blatant support of the business-superpatriot attempt to discredit and injure labor. In the case of steel, the power of the steel companies allowed them to "assume charge of the law enforcement agencies in many local communities," and the increasing violence was "often the result of police belligerency or of insidious action on the part of steel representatives," including the extensive use of labor spies and strike-breakers.[57] Planted documents were also put to good use, with labor spies reproducing copies of *The Communist Manifesto* and distributing them among the steel workers, for "capture" by the Department of Justice to demonstrate a Red conspiracy.[58] According to Murray:

> The ruthless methods employed by the steel companies were not described to any extent in the press. Instead, reports of riot disorders were written in such a manner as to make it appear that steel officials were always on the defensive against those who were attacking law and order. Newspapers dwelt mostly on the evidence of radicalism involved and related all other factors to it. The public, therefore, received a completely biased picture of the strike situation.[59]

The major newspapers also disseminated without serious question the most outlandish claims of conspiracies emanating from and controlled by Moscow. According to Attorney General Palmer, the radical alien movement dominated domestic radicalism and was itself a Moscow surrogate,[60] receiving orders directly from Lenin and Trotsky. This and similar rubbish was taken at face value, the *New York Times* reporting on January 4, 1920, with an objectivity applied sixty years later to equally cogent pronouncements of Haig and company, that

> Radical leaders planned to develop the recent steel and coal strike into a general strike and ultimately into a revolution to overthrow the government, according to information gathered by federal agents in Friday night's round-up of members of the Communist parties. These data, officials said, tended to prove that the nationwide raids had blasted the most menacing revolutionary ploy yet unearthed.[61]

Business played the same game: as Murray notes, "T.T. Brewster, chief spokesman for the coal operators, released to the press wholly untrue reports which claimed the coal strike was being undertaken on direct orders from Lenin and Trotsky and that Moscow gold was financing the whole project."[62] These tactics were successful—unionism and reformism as well as any radical tendencies suffered major setbacks and the groundwork was set for the "age of normalcy"—and the Great Depression!

The Red scare of 1947-1955, whose most famous symbol was Senator Joseph McCarthy, was less conspicuously oriented to the weakening of the union movement, but that was one of its major consequences. The forces underlying McCarthyism were complex, but it was part of an anticommunist campaign that served elite interests well. The business community had lost power and prestige during the depression and Second World War; it was disturbed by the rise of the CIO, New Deal pro-labor legislation, and other acts directly serving the interests of the working classes. In *The Great Fear* David Caute notes that "Within the business community were elements that could never come to terms with the New Deal and saw in anticommunism a convenient weapon with which to smear progressive legislation and to weaken the power of organized labor."[63] In fact, at the end of World War II, the top business trade and lobbying organizations, the National Association of Manufacturers and U.S. Chamber of Commerce, were both very preoccupied with the menace of unions, socialism and communism, which were looked upon as a continuum. External threats and opportunities also called for a more business-oriented government. Anticommunism could serve, as it did in 1919-1920, to weaken the New Deal coalition and unions, and provide an ideological underpinning for a more aggressive foreign policy.

Truman, Forrestal, Acheson and a great many elite power interests got the post-World War II Red scare rolling; McCarthy was the most notable representative of a later phase of this process, which from the viewpoint of some members of the elite got temporarily out of hand. McCarthy was originally sponsored by a group of Wisconsin businessmen, and he was always a hero for a sizable fraction of the business community, who appreciated the fact that his anticommunism was not contaminated by any vestige of reformism. His support from business waned when he began to attack the military establishment and the strongly pro-business administration of Eisenhower, which threatened to split the Republican party. By then the predominant business view was that he had "served his purpose" in bringing anticommunism to the fore and "Keep[ing] the albatross hung around the neck of the New and Fair Deals."[64] As if by a miracle, at that point McCarthy's pronouncements ceased to be reported as front page news and fact.

The union movement was hard hit by the Great Fear, suffering from purges of members and its leftwing unions and party leaders, splits within unions (from the formation of scab "anticommunist" unions like the IUE), a general discrediting and suspicion of unionism in spite of its "housecleaning," and the passage of anti-union legislation that served to contain the growth of unions in succeeding decades. In 1919-1920 the Red scare, although of shorter duration, contributed to more serious defeats for unionism—the unionization of the steel industry was forestalled till the New Deal era, and the union movement was kept in a completely impotent state during the twenties. In the Truman-McCarthy-Eisenhower era, the cleansed and somewhat weakened unions maintained their position as an interest group of some weight, able to extract political concessions as a junior partner in a new Cold War consensus. The dominant union leadership even served an active role thereafter in close collaboration with the CIA and business firms such as Grace and M.A. Hanna in infiltrating and splintering Third World labor organizations and setting them up for (and even participating in)[65] rightwing coups that terminated both independent unionism and any labor voice in national affairs.

The Red scare of 1947-55 also decimated the ranks of dissenters in the mass media and strengthened pressures toward conformity of opinion in the culture at large. The FBI, HUAC, McCarthy, the Legion, and the various blacklisting services that arose in "the time of the toad" served as "enforcers," with the cooperation of employers, unions and the press, in insisting on loyalty to a particular anticommunist ideology (*not* to any principles of democracy, civil rights, equality, or spirit of humanity or brotherhood) as the condition for acceptability and sometimes employment. Under this assault, many liberals who did not already accept anticommunism as *the* criterion and value—and many already did—were either cowed into submission or opportunistically became anticommunists with a fervor that often exceeded that of the enforcers. Thus, when the last democratic government of Brazil was swallowed up by a coup, the Kennedy liberals in Washington were ecstatic at the triumph of "democracy" over "Communism." The Great Fear, in short, helped institutionalize an aggressive anticommunism that could convert every popular upsurge in the Third World into a "Communist threat" and make a totalitarian overthrow of democracy a triumph of "democracy" itself.

The Truman-McCarthy era was also notable for the rise not only of the informer, but the *lying* informer.[66] It was important to the enforcers to show that certain hated individuals (e.g., the liberal Asia specialist Owen Lattimore, and liberal black diplomat Ralph Bunche) were Communists or "linked to" Communists; and, as in all Red scares, Moscow gold and orders, and Moscow's plans to conquer the world, had to be put on the record. Eventually, informers were produced who would provide the desired information, spun out of the whole cloth. As their lying was useful, the growing number of perjurers for the FBI were regularly protected by the government. Recanting witnesses became numerous and demonstrated perjury extensive in 1954, but prosecution for perjury of government witnesses was confined almost entirely to those who claimed that they lied on government instruction. Marie Natvig, who had been a witness for the FCC in a case involving a broadcasting license for Edward

Lamb, originally made the outlandish claim that Lamb had told her in 1936 of his plans to seize the communications industry and create an insurrection of the armed forces! In early 1955 Natvig recanted, alleging that her lies had been provided by the FCC prosecutor. She was convicted of perjury and jailed. Two other FCC witnesses retracted evidence, claiming coached lying. Harvey Matusow, who had provided numerous and convenient details on conversations involving alleged Communists who were under government attack, also recanted, and he also got a stiff jail sentence—for lying that he lied! As David Caute points out

> The informers as a group made a living out of pretending to an encyclopedic knowledge of the communist movement across the face of a vast country. On a nod from prosecutors, they sold hunches or guesses as inside knowledge, supporting their claims with bogus reports of conversations and encounters.[67]

Caute also notes that

> Invention was in any case the specialty of renegades, who traded heavily on mounting American popular fears of Soviet military aggression. Crouch ["one of the most brazen and colorful liars in the business"] was full of detailed Soviet invasion plans. During the Foley Square trial Charles W. Nicodemus, who had left the CP three years earlier, testified that the Party planned to coordinate its revolutionary putsch with a Red Army invasion through Alaska and Canada. Soviet emigres like Victor Kravchenko, Alexandre Barmine and Igor Bogolepov (a Soviet colonel who had defected to the Nazis in 1941 and operated a radio transmitter on their behalf) were always ready to delight Congressional committees with the wildest 'inside stories' of diabolical Kremlin plots.[68]

It took the Free Press years to start lifting the lid on outright perjury and coached disinformation, and the assumptions of the Red scare were never seriously questioned. Thus, the Great Fear was effective in creating an ideological groundwork for rearmament, Vietnam and the spread of the National Security State in the U.S. sphere of influence.

Terrorism and the Red menace never die, they merely ebb and flow in accordance with the propaganda requirements of the moment. The era of McCarthy and the Great Fear was associated not only with a need to roll back union power and welfare state advances, but also with perceived elite needs for rearmament and a forward policy abroad, most vividly expressed in the Truman Doctrine, with its Orwellian complement in the concept of "Containment." The United States was "containing" somebody else as it established 3000 overseas bases and made one of the most dramatic external advances in power since the era of the Roman Empire. In the late 1970s and early 1980s new terrorist networks and Red menaces were called into play once again to serve the traditional functions, as we shall see in the next chapter.

The U.S. Role in the Third World

The United States was uniquely powerful in 1945, in sole possession of nuclear weapons, its leading rivals defeated or devastated in victory. It moved quickly and steadily into the power vacuum left by receding colonialism, engineering the displacement of European and Asian colonial powers by clients and strenuously resisting radical changes and nationalistic movements threatening western control. This conformed exactly to the demands of major U.S. economic interests, long desirous of an "open door" to sales and investment and access to raw materials and other economic opportunities.

One difficulty quickly apparent was that anti-colonial, democratic and nationalistic movements within the Third World were not reliably cooperative about "opening doors," permitting easy western access to markets and raw materials, and accepting integration into the western political economy. The result was very extensive and systematic U.S. and other western support of more amenable regimes designed to meet western criteria of "stability." But the very process of installation of these regimes as well as their subsequent behavior contradicted each element of the conventional U.S. ideology, which claimed our devotion to democracy, self-determination and human rights. How are the value claims and the reality to be reconciled? As we saw earlier, the conventional reconciliation takes the form of a negative—we do not actively pursue our interests in the face of threatening indigenous reform and social change which must be fended off (Kommunism); rather, we simple oppose an alien international conspiracy (Communism). While this kind of self-serving rationalization can impress those needing balm to salve their consciences, and has great propaganda value, the real answer and true reconciliation lies in a priority system in which the liberal and humane values rank low. To be more precise, the *operative* principles dictating U.S. support and hostility in the Third World have been business criteria first, military convenience second, and any humanistic considerations third *and thus effectively irrelevant*. In fact, they are less than irrelevant—they are in conflict with the first two criteria, and therefore when we get to practical situations, as in Brazil 1960-1964, humanizing forces like Church activists, educators and union organizers become "threats." The evidence is overwhelming that political violence in all its worst forms has grown enormously under U.S. auspices since 1945, exactly as would be expected on theoretical grounds. I describe this in some detail in chapter 3, on the real terror network. Since these ugly facts fly in the face of the ideology of U.S. benevolence, the ideologists have had to run hard to provide cover, as is described in chapters 2 and 4.

TWO

Contemporary Terrorism (1): The Lesser and Mythical Terror Networks

The Demand for a New Red Scare

A new Red Scare in the form of a "Soviet-backed international terror network" has been vigorously pushed in the United States during the past decade, reaching new heights in 1980-1981. It was badly needed by the forces of the right. One effect of the Great Society and Vietnam war was to stimulate populism—the belief on the part of many formerly apathetic people that they had legitimate claims that could be pursued both in private bargaining and in the political arena. Protest and demands extended from civil rights marches and war protests to more material claims on the part of the poor, the disabled, the old, women, Indians and others. Establishment spokesmen expressed open dismay at the weakening of traditional restraints on the masses, and their assertive demands to share political power with the elite. We saw in the last chapter that a durable method by which the U.S. business and upper class contends with such problems is by means of a refurbished Red Menace.

The threat of a democracy working too well was strongly felt by the business community during the 1960s and early 1970s in its inability to contain either the steady growth of social regulation

(EPA, OSHA, consumer safety) or the tendency to use public expenditures and taxes for broadly based social ends. Leonard Silk and David Vogel described in their 1976 survey *Ethics and Profits: The Crisis of Confidence in American Business* the extent to which the business community was in rebellion against its perceived "loss of control," the "rising tide of entitlements," and the painful hand of government as regulator and redistributor of income *downward.*[1]

A second factor influencing the U.S. elite has been the "Vietnam syndrome."[2] The effect of the Vietnam war debacle, and the closely associated Watergate affair, was to discredit the anticommunist ideology and the military establishment and thus to inhibit U.S. freedom to intervene abroad by military force. This was reinforced by relative economic decline and economic problems that brought home the economic burden and limits of U.S. military power. Soviet military advances toward parity also threatened U.S. freedom of action as the only global policeman and hegemonist. These developments were anathema to important sectors of the national elite, who have been fighting hard since the last helicopter took off from Saigon in 1975 to reverse a public psychology that has limited our willingness to do elsewhere what we have "done for freedom" in the Philippines, Guatemala, Chile and Zaire.

With the 1980 election of a rightwing business "surrogate," an acceleration of Red Scaring was assured. Given the Reagan program of massive transfers of benefits from the poor to the rich, and the great expansion in government outlays for high technology waste (i.e., "defense"), there is only one foolproof means of inducing the victimized population to accept such losses: showing a need for us "all" to sacrifice in the face of an implacable aggressor. Reaganism has also meant a sharp elevation in the status of a "new class" of rightwing ideologues spawned by the Cold War, militarization and anticommunism. It is these elements, long dominant in the military-intelligence apparatus and in rightwing think-tanks and journals, that have been spiritually close to the National Security States (NSSs), their ideology and leadership, and most understanding of the need for wholesale terror. The liberal establishment has been actively involved in U.S. sponsorship of the NSS, and has provided an important cloak of respectability to this system of state terrorism; but it has done this to some extent under the pressure of unyielding political-economic and anticommunist ideological imperatives, and with qualms.

The forces now in power actually *like* the torturers, and rush to their defense as a hen runs to protect her chicks. We must therefore expect not only a more aggressive policy of arming and otherwise supporting the NSS—whose leaders and cadres will now be much freer to rip out fingernails—we must expect an intensified ideological cover. The classic ink thrown out by the pro-fascist cuttlefish is the Red Menace—the implacable aggressor. The Soviet Union is the best available implacable aggressor, and the Reagan-Haig-Pinochet-Viola team is making a determined effort to show that all communists under the various beds are "linked" to Moscow, directly or through "surrogates." The disinformation specialists have long since gone to work and produced the required linkages and surrogates, and they have been given enough space by the Free Press, with criticism kept sufficiently in the distant background, to clear the ground for a greater "defense" establishment to meet the implacable aggressor.[3] I turn now to a brief look at some of these disinformation efforts.

The Protocols of the Elders of Moscow

Claire Sterling's *The Terror Network* can be examined at two levels—as a cynical and opportunistic piece of propaganda that serves a classic Red Scare purpose, or as a document to which rules of scientific evidence may be applied. It is highly significant that a book which cannot be taken at all seriously at the second level—as I will show below—is, nonetheless, a best seller, heavily and uncritically featured by the leading media enterprises, both liberal and conservative, and allowed to define reality for the general public. In each important historical case of institutionalization of Red Scare myths, intellectual rubbish proclaiming the myth has been pushed front and center, and contrary opinions and serious attacks on the myth have been kept in the background or suppressed. Red Scare analysts have pointed out that this near unanimity in the mass media and vocal support by prestigious government and business sources has been critically important in making myths believable to the general public.[4]

As James Cory notes, Sterling's "*The Terror Network* is essentially a rightwing fairly tale," that no more proves a Soviet controlled terror network than it proves the existence of an Easter bunny.[5] The style is of a work of propaganda, breathless, smug, mainly working over individual episodes with full dramatics, each stripped of any historic or political context, with knowing little touches added of "coincidences" from which large inferences can be hinted at. The terrorists are always "precision-tooled," everything is "carefully engineered," with "colossal" weaponry, "inexorably advancing" toward "single-minded" objectives—they "dominated the world scene" between 1970 and 1980, "Fright Decade I"—yet for all this Sterling's terrorists are almost always wiped out, for reasons unexplained.

In what sense did the "terrorists" dominate the scene? In numbers of people killed? In seriousness of abuses committed? In bringing about political change? In receiving media publicity? Sterling does not say. In speaking of the colossal weaponry and precision-tooled methods of the retail terrorists of the left (to whom she confines her attention) she says that they even have "ground-to-air heat seeking missiles that can knock a moving plane out of the sky from six miles away...[as] part of their working kit."[6] Who has these? Where? How many? Where have they been used? How does their technology compare with that of the police? Not a word that would give this phrase substance. We learn that the retail terrorists got intensive training in "prisoner interrogation." Do they use torture? Do people die under torture by retail terrorists? How do their interrogation methods stack up with those used in Chile by the police? Nothing—just a passing phrase on "prisoner interrogation" that constitutes a lie by indirection.

Sterling has this remarkable property—that if you take a sentence virtually at random and analyse it, you find that if she tries to make a substantive point, that point is either false or misleads by suppression of relevant context. "It was three years before the opening of the terrorist decade when Fidel Castro's companion in arms died in wretched obscurity in the Bolivian Andes." Apparently the "terrorist decade" started precisely on January 1, 1970—but note the suppression in this rhetorical flourish: Guevara did not just die in obscurity; he was taken prisoner and then murdered in cold blood. A small point, but a display of Sterling quality. She then quotes Guevara, inaccurately,[7] on the need to become cold but selective killing machines, suppressing a large context of fact—this was 1966 with the *U.S.* killing machine working full blast in Indochina—and ignoring Guevara's analysis and careful explanation of why the repressive forces led by the United States are likely to continue their brutalities and will simply not permit Latin America to liberate itself through peaceful means. (Although this was before the Chilean events of 1973, Guevara was very closely acquainted with the Guatemalan intervention of 1954, which clearly demonstrated how far the United States would go to prevent socialization via use of the democratic process.) On Guevara's lack of success in Bolivia, she says not a word about conditions in Bolivia, but remarks that the peasants "ran away at the sight of Guevara."[8] Now why should peasants run away from him and his tiny band, who were not reported to have committed the slightest violence against peasants? Sterling does not say, but implies that it was because of the direct threat posed by Guevara. But it was the *indirect* threat that bothered the peasants. Throughout Latin America, counter-insurgency has frequently led to wholesale massacres of peasants who have anything to do with guerillas, or even those in their general vicinity. Peasants are, with very good reason, far more often scared of their Free World "protectors" than of guerillas.[9]

Sterling protects the official torturers of Latin America mainly by massive suppression, but the small tricks she uses when these must be mentioned are illuminating. One is to make the military merely responsive to the influence of others. A second is the rationalization that, well, that's what military people always do, ho-hum—what do you expect torturers to do but torture? Why should we get moralistic about such matters? A third device is straightforward lying. She argues, for example, that in Uruguay and Brazil, the military were "called in" or were provoked; they never took any initiatives, never had interests of their own that they were pursuing; and they themselves never provoked anybody. She mentions the murder of Dan Mitrione in Uruguay, failing to point out that he was an instructor in torture and a torturer, that death squads were already in existence killing dissidents regularly, and that the Tupamaros, who she says, "murdered with increasing clarity of intent," were being tortured and killed with increasing clarity of intent. Langguth points out, moreover, that in their early years the Tupamaros "did not try to maim or kill. Their bombs were only noisy public-relations devices to introduce themselves...When the Tupamaros did appear in public, they took the guise of public benefactors."[10] An excellent case can be made that Tupamaros *killings* followed and were provoked by U.S.-sponsored torture and counterinsurgency operations.

The Tupamaros "deliberately killed democracy" according to Sterling—the army merely "did what armies do in such situations...and got results."[11] Of course the only fact that is clearly observable, and the only one that Sterling knows, is that the *army* killed democracy—that the Tupamaros *wanted* such an outcome (rather than serious reforms) and that they were not themselves reacting to increasing provocations of the military-security establishment, is a premise of the fairy tale. It is a curious fact that the Tupamaros wanted something that destroyed them, and that the purely responsive army happened to do that which served their advantage quite nicely. Sterling never mentions that the merely "provoked" intelligence-military establishment didn't stop killing and torturing after the Tupamaros were completely eliminated. Just a bunch of little old torturers doing their thing.

Sterling on Brazil involves even more brazen lying, even though she touches on Brazil very lightly. She mentions it only because she repeatedly asserts that Marighela's Mini-Manual on urban terrorism was "revolutionary scripture" during the Fright Decade. What about Marighela himself? She notes, finally, that he was killed, and that his urban revolutionary efforts in Brazil failed. "He never got past the stage of provoking the militarists into intensified repression, whereby [sic] they have retained power ever since."[12] In this small masterpiece of deception, Sterling fails to mention that Marighela's manual was written— and that his resort to guerilla warfare occurred—only *after* a military coup and savage repression and after all democratic options had been totally foreclosed, and in an environment previously quite free of any "terrorism" of the left. But having suppressed the facts on the original source of terrorism in Brazil, this dishonest person has the audacity to make Marighela the provoker of *further* repression. Notice the phrase "whereby they retained power ever since." The generals would presumably have given up power if only the terrorist Marighela, appearing for unexplained reasons, hadn't "provoked" them to do what generals and torturers always do when provoked.

Most of Sterling's book consists of assertions and generalizations of the sort just discussed, loaded with distortions by omission and with a great deal of psychologizing based on nothing but Sterling's say-so. Periodically she throws in quotations and references that attempt to give a scholarly aura to her work. As Levin describes the famous Lusk report, and other classic works in the pseudo-science of terrorism,

> The data is presented without any effort—serious or otherwise—to evaluate its validity or relevance. Generalizations and conclusions, unsupported by data, are sprinkled throughout....The pseudoscholar proceeds to laboriously accumulate vast numbers of "details" and documents...Some of the details and documents refer to facts. Some of the details are fiction. Nothing remains unexplained...Simultaneity is taken as proof of cause and effect...[V]ast historical forces [are assumed to be] set in motion by the mere will of a few monstrously evil but brilliant men. They pull puppet strings and duped and compliant millions act out their will. [13]

This describes Sterling's book, with its details and coincidences, its footnotes, and its conclusions based on a great leap of the imagination from the prior assumptions and the scattering of real and concocted fact.

A great many of Sterling's details come from "intelligence sources," and a large fraction of the remainder are from right-wing propagandists like de Borchegrave, Michael Ledeen, Moss, Michael Crozier and others, who all rely heavily on one another or on "intelligence sources." Conor Cruise O'Brien observes that this intra-rightwing citation process may involve a great many nominally different sources tracing back to only one, "producing a cumulative effect on the unsuspecting reader through a kind of echo chamber." [14] Even more important is the high probability that this one source may be contaminated—may be a product of an agency whose function is imaginative lying to create a desired disinformation result. O'Brien points out that Sterling "consistently assumes that anything she is told by her western intelligence sources must be true. Her copious but naive footnotes often refer to unnamed intelligence sources, whose veracity she simply takes for granted."[15] This is not quite correct. She only assumes that those facts and allegations were correct that fit her fairy tale. She complains, in fact, that intelligence sources throughout western Europe, in cowardly fashion, possibly themselves infiltrated by the KGB (as in *The Spike*), steadfastly *deny* the Soviet terror network. But she can always rely on the more atavistic intelligence sources of Chile and South Africa for agreement with her big picture and for provision of any required details. Diana Johnstone contends that Sterling (and presumably Robert Moss and the rest of the disinformation crowd) are not simple products of the CIA, but, on the contrary, represent the more rightwing elements of the western intelligence community, close to DINA and BOSS (the Chilean and South African CIAs), elements which are striving for greater freedom of action and possibly control of other intelligence agencies.[16]

Sterling's methodology also has this pseudoscientific property, as described by Diana Johnstone:

> The more important an alleged "fact" is to her argument, the more mysterious and unreliable its source. For example, the very keystone of her "terror network" is a "Tucaman Plan," supposedly drafted "under KGB supervision" in Argentina's Tucuman province in May 1975 and discovered by Argentinian police the following winter "in a safehouse of the ERP, a Trotskyite terrorist band." The Plan called for rounding up the Tupamaros and three other Latin American guerrilla bands to create a "Latin American Europe Brigade" of "1,500 qualified Latin American terrorists" to go off to Europe for "an orchestrated assault on the continent." The "usual documented footnote" for this whopper explains that the contents of these incriminating reports discovered by Argentinian police "were told to me by one of the best-informed intelligence analysts in Europe."[17]

Johnstone shows that this "best-informed analyst" is surely Robert Spike Moss, the prince of disinformation, and that there is no evidence anywhere that she got the information from anybody else. Johnstone then points out the still more fundamental fact that,

> ...even if she heard it from a hundred "analysts," the original source was the Argentinian police, the same police whose death squads were then in their heyday, kidnapping and murdering countless unionists, lawyers, Peronists and liberals, members of parliament and Catholic nuns—all of the victims promoted to "terrorists" for the occasion. And these murders and disappearances were so numerous and so blatant that European officials were growing uneasy and even critical. To forestall such criticism, Argentine authorities took the line that they were "defending the West" from a "terrorism" that also threatened Europe—the "Tucaman Plan" would seem to offer much-needed evidence to support this line. Sterling accepts this politically utterly implausible story, leaked from a notoriously motivated and unscrupulous source, as gospel.[18]

The other major piece of evidence of a Soviet "plot" to sponsor a retail terror network is the claim made by a Czech defector, General Jan Sejna, who according to Sterling, fled Czechoslovakia in 1968 "a jump ahead of the invading Soviet army."[19] According to Sejna, the KGB set up camps in Czechoslovakia starting in 1964 to train terrorists for European operations, including members of the Red Brigades and others whose names he provided to Michael Ledeen in an interview in 1980. Curiously, although this would seem important information if true, Sejna never got around to mentioning it till the 1980 interview, which was published in a rightwing Italian journal. Also, contrary to Sterling, Johnstone points out that Sejna got out of Czechoslovakia *well* before the Russians—he was implicated in a top level corruption scandal and left the country in the process of a democratic cleanup *during* the brief "Prague spring!" This evidence is vintage terrorist pseudoscience.

Whenever Sterling tries to show the subservience to (or

control by) Moscow of specific retail terrorist groups of the left, the closer one looks the less the plausibility. In Italy, the flimsy "links" of the Red Brigades to Moscow through Czechoslovakia (based on the usual Sterling sources) run up against the indigestible fact of furious hostility between the Red Brigades and the large Italian Communist Party (presumably also a Moscow "surrogate"). The Red Brigades actually preferred Enrico Berlinguer, head of the CP, as a kidnapping victim, but settled for Aldo Moro as second best. Moro himself was an important figure in Italy at the time of his kidnapping and murder partly because he was central to on-going negotiations for a Great Compromise that would have reintegrated the Italian CP into mainstream politics. That the Soviets would be managing, or even giving substantial aid and comfort to, a group trying to discredit and weaken the largest "fraternal" party in western Europe is extremely implausible: farfetched even for terrorism pseudo-science. Given the continuing hostility of the U.S. leadership to all such efforts at legitimizing the CPs of Europe, a CIA role in Red Brigade shenanigans would at least be more rational than Moscow support.

A close look at Sterling's methods as applied to a specific terrorist group is given by Conor Cruise O'Brien in his examination of her "proof" that the Provisionals of the Irish Republican Army are Soviet proxies. The Provisionals got some arms from Eastern Europe—but O'Brien points out that they got some from the United States as well. The Provos also have some ties with other terrorist organizations. But how does Sterling show that the Provos are ultra-left Marxists? By putting forward a few selected quotations of statements made by two fringe members of the Provos while in Italy, as quoted by an Italian revolutionary journal. There are many other statements that could have been quoted that would convey a quite different impression, but Sterling locates the few that convey the message she prefers. O'Brien comments:

> Claire Sterling assumes that the Italian interview constitutes the real, the esoteric doctrine, while Provo statements in America etc. are merely exercises in deception. This is a gratuitous assumption, and a false one. The Provos, like other people in similar positions,

choose horses for courses, so when they want support from foreign reds they send someone who can present the Provo cause in terms foreign reds are likely to fancy. To New York, on the other hand, they send a good Irish Catholic Republican. But—and this is the fact that Claire Sterling gets inside out—it is the good Catholic who is for real. The people who are being conned are the foreign reds.[20]

As one who knows a great deal about, and has little sympathy for, the Provos, O'Brien's further and closing remarks on Sterling are worth quoting:

> In short, as far as the Provisionals are concerned, Claire Sterling has got it all hopelessly wrong. She could only fit the Provisionals into her pattern by misunderstanding them, and she *has* misunderstood them, comprehensively. Instead of trying to understand the phenomenon first—in its own peculiar historical and local context—and then seeing how it may relate to the rest of her subject matter, what she has done is to jump at quotations and other bits that seem to suit her thesis, and then assume that these handy bits constitute the key to understanding the phenomenon as a whole. Sometimes she bends a particular bit to fit another bit. Thus she claims (with sources of the type described above) that Irishmen and others were trained in Libya by Cubans and East Germans in, among other things, "underwater warfare" and how to be frogmen. And she goes on: "Whether a coincidence or not, the IRA used frogmen to blow up Lord Mountbatten on his fishing boat." It is neither a coincidence nor not a coincidence; it is just plain wrong. Frogmen were not used for that murder.[21]

The Soviet-network propagandists all rest their case heavily on the Soviet's use of "surrogates" or "proxies." Libya, Cuba and the PLO are Soviet "surrogates," so that whatever they do is done on behalf of their master. Sterling, Moss and company use these terms with great assurance, but never stop to define them or to discuss the details of why and how the Soviet controls these alleged proxies, if they control them at all. Are Libya and the PLO as closely linked to the Soviet Union as Brazil and Chile to the United States? The question does not arise for a Moss or Sterling (or in the mass media). One obvious difference— Kaddafi was not installed in power with significant or decisive assists from the Soviet Union.

If the Soviet Union does not control these surrogates, but supports them because of some common interest, their terrorism may be carried out independently of, possibly even contrary to, Soviet desires. Thus the question of degree of control or influence is important and worthy of discussion. None of the three major surrogates allegedly controlled by the Soviet Union are controlled to the degree it controls, say, Czechoslovakia—where, as in the case of Brazil and Chile, the external power played an important role in the counterrevolution—and Soviet influence declines from Cuba to Libya and the PLO. Cuba, driven into Soviet arms by the U.S. boycott and continuous U.S. hostility and intervention, is economically dependent, but still retains at least some autonomy while trying to maintain warm relations with its benefactor. Western propaganda always presumes that Castro's actions abroad are a response to Soviet "discipline" (an assumption rarely made in reference to the actions of western satellites). But even in Angola, for example, the former head of the CIA's operations there, John Stockwell, stated that "After the war we learned that Cuba had not been ordered into action by the Soviet Union. To the contrary, the Cuban leaders felt compelled to intervene for their own ideological reasons."[22] Stockwell points out that

> Moreover, the Cuban policy in Angola was consistent with Cuba's ideology and its international stance. Our Angola program, like the previous Bay of Pigs and *Operation Mongoose* war against Castro, was a direct contradiction of our public policies, making it essential that we keep the American public from knowing the truth. The Cubans weren't ashamed of their program and they didn't need to hide it from their own people, or from the world press.[23]

As regards Latin America, the Castro-as-Soviet-surrogate theory has been contradicted for years by the fact that Soviet Latin

American policy has accommodated quite cynically to an ugly status quo, in sharp contrast with Castro's hostility to that status quo.

Libya is far more independent of the Soviet Union, and its classification as a "proxy" or "surrogate," implying that its behavior is a function of Soviet orders, is unsupported and implausible propaganda. Libya has bought a lot of weaponry, for cash, and has received some military training and diplomatic support from the Soviet Union. (It turns out that Libya has also gotten a lot of support, logistical, training and operational, from former CIA agents now in the business of servicing terrorists who are well heeled.) Kaddafi has, however, denounced the Soviet invasion of Afghanistan, even during his visit to Moscow (a point not discussed in the Free Press—possibly because it disrupts the "surrogate" view), and he has not only rejected Soviet requests for naval bases, he has also claimed territorial water rights inconvenient to Soviet as well as to U.S. maritime interests. His militant Islamic ideology is anathema to the Soviet leadership. He seeks Soviet support with reluctance, under the pressure of open U.S. threats. If the Soviets are willing to support him it is because he splinters a hostile Arab bloc of states and because his own isolation pushes him into a tentative reciprocal relation with them. Only an enormously biased press could convert this marriage of convenience into a control-surrogate relationship, with his terrorism accepted as a product of Soviet orders. The same point may be made as regards the PLO—a splintered group, whose supporters include Saudi Arabia as well as the Soviets, and whose more extreme groups espouse aims in the Middle East different from those of the Soviet Union (which favors a settlement that would include and ratify the existence of Israel). The Soviets support the PLO partly on ideological grounds as self-proclaimed leader of the oppressed, partly to build support among Arab nationalists and preserve a slim and weakened position in the Middle East.

In the Sterling view, the international terrorists controlled from Moscow are trying to "destabilize western democracies." As many of these retail terrorists are extremely nationalistic and would appear to be pursuing local ends, the idea that they all have the global objective of "destabilizing western democracy" is classic terrorist pseudoscience, resting, as in the Lusk report and other Red Terror constructs of the past, on carefully selected "facts" and the final imaginative leap. The Provos case illustrates the data selection process. The imaginative leap is to a mysterious Soviet power of discipline and control that produces the common destabilization purpose. But even ignoring the false assumption of Soviet control, is this objective of destabilization compatible with Soviet methods and interests anyway? There is a long tradition of Leninism that regards terrorism as a form of infantile leftism, and Stalin went far in extracting any revolutionary teeth from foreign Communist parties. The Soviet Union has been opportunistic in its relation to left parties and groups abroad, but its main external thrust, as manifested in the behavior of the Communist parties closest to Moscow, has been conservative. These parties have increasingly striven to work within the system and have opposed destabilization tactics and disruptive groups rather consistently. The French Communist Party fought the student-based upheavals in France in 1968, and the Italian Communist Party, as noted, has been furiously hostile to the Red Brigades (who have reciprocated in dislike). As a general proposition it can be said that retail terrorist groups in the west have been splinters from orthodox Communist parties or have been otherwise contemptous of and hostile to the CP. If these conservative CPs are reflecting Moscow's interest, how can one claim Moscow's connivance in general destabilization? Of course, Moscow could be pursuing detente-stabilization at one level and destabilization at another, but since the latter weakens the force of the former—and is contrary to traditional Soviet hostility to adventurism—the destabilization strategy requires solid evidence.

This scepticism is strongly reinforced by the fact that destabilization of democratic societies in the west appears to be quite contrary to Soviet interests. Destabilization would most likely bring into power rightist regimes more violent and more hostile than their predecessors. The Soviet leadership has been pressing for detente for many years because the military burden of the arms race is extremely heavy to the poorer country. Furthermore, it has been technologically backward in many fields and has been seeking trade and technological exchange for urgent economic reasons. Efforts to destabilize would damage Soviet efforts along these lines.

In the Third World, Soviet interests and intentions are more ambiguous. Part of the Soviet moral resources in the world arises from its claim, as the leading socialist state, to leadership and support of the oppressed. It can justify aid to the NLF in Vietnam, SWAPO in Namibia, and the indigenous Neto-led rebels of Angola, to take just three examples, on the grounds that the movements supported were popular, were resisting an oppressive old order, or were fighting against aggression from without. If the Soviets failed to support such movements they would lose face and status as leader of the anti-imperialist bloc.

Of course, the bias of the western media is so huge that Soviet and Cuban aid to an indigenous movement against an ancient colonialism in Angola, or against South African efforts to destabilize the successor regime, is a priori aggressive and evidence of Soviet "expansionism." U.S. journalists like Hugh Sidey can blandly infer Soviet aggressive intent by merely noting its audacious provision of aid to Vietnam in the face of our decision to smash that distant country into submission.[24] Laqueur even refers to Polisario, a liberation movement indigenous to a land which they want to control, as "terrorists" in relation to an invading Morocco that has been supported by the United States![25] These premises of the natural right of the west to intervene anywhere on its own terms, and the inappropriateness of any Soviet moves beyond its borders (even in defense of people resisting external aggression), makes it easy to demonstrate enemy "terrorism."

Even with this reliance on manipulated definitions and the premise of different natural rights to intervene as between us and them, the Soviet network analysts never provide numbers. This is because if they were obligated to get specific, the numbers would be relatively small and would reveal that Guatemala by itself is more of a terrorist problem than the entire (mythical) Soviet network. But the little stories of liberal-left middle class youth, with good intent, becoming cold-blooded killers, feeds well into western biases and helps rationalize the needs of the multinational corporation. By tying together resistance movements in the Third World and seemingly arbitrary and wanton hijackings, kidnappings and murders in Italy, and making them all part of a Soviet plot to undermine western democracies, a lot of needs are met—we turn attention away from western support of official terror in the National Security State, and we put pressure on the Soviet Union and Cuba to halt their support—not for the Baader-Meinhof gang or Red Brigades—but for the peasants of El Salvador, Guatemala and Namibia.

Anticommunist Terror (Retail and Smaller State Networks)

Claire Sterling begins her *Terror Network* with an eerie description of a recent, major terrorist attack, the Bologna, Italy railway station bombing which left 82 dead and many more injured. Having extracted some emotional capital from this event, she notes quickly that this was a *rightwing* terrorist act, which is outside of her province (she deals with rightwing terror only "obliquely," she says—an appropriate malapropism), as it was "receding" and left terror "dominated" the 1970s. This ends her discussion. Nowhere does she make the faintest attempt to prove this bland assertion, which is contrary to fact. The Bologna act caused a new record number of retail terrorist casualties; but the previous record, in the 1970s, was set by another rightwing terrorist act, the bombing of a Cuban airliner in 1976 that resulted in 73 deaths.

I will show in this section that anticommunist ("Black" or fascist) terror, including western state terror across borders, was vastly more substantial than terror from the left during Sterling's "Fright Decade," and remains so in the early 1980s. This means, of course, that a Reagan-Haig shift from a concern for "human rights" to "terrorism" would involve addressing an unchanging set of fascist and other client networks (ignoring for the moment that this is Orwellian rhetoric as regards both "human rights" *and* "terrorism"). On the Haig-Sterling-Moss logic of "surrogates," also, the Reagan administration would be in the remarkable position of chasing its own tail: the surrogates of Washington are the primary retail and state terrorists. As we penetrate below this smokescreen of rhetoric in the pages that follow, it will be seen that this allegedly "antiterrorist" administration is stoking up the fires of international terrorism to new heights by encouraging its most brutal and active state and retail practitioners.

Orlando Bosch, for example, a far more impressive killer than "Carlos the Jackal,"[26] is never referred to by Haig or Kirkpatrick. He was directly implicated in the 73 deaths in the Cuban airliner bombing of 1976, and his group of Cuban refugee anticommunist terrorists is credited with several hundred bombings and scores of murders (some under contract with DINA or BOSS). Bosch and most of his close associates were trained by the CIA in connection with the secret and illegal war on Cuba; and in recent years Bosch has had close relationship with (and has been on the payroll of) the secret police of Chile and Venezuela.[27] These secret police, in their turn, were tutored by the CIA and maintain close relationships with it today. Is Bosch a CIA "surrogate"? If an individual was trained in Libya, Cuba, or the Soviet Union, or visited there, in the Haig-Moss-Sterling world they would be forevermore "surrogates"—but for some reason such a rule does not apply for CIA training and DINA affiliation. In any case, Bosch outdoes Carlos, and the Cuban refugee network as a whole (discussed below) is probably the largest retail terrorist network in operation now and active during the "Fright Decade." The Fright Decade, in which rightwing terror was "receding" according to Sterling, was also the period in which Operation Condor—a unique conspiratorial network of cross-border murder—was started by six subfascist states in Latin America. On the state level, Begin's Israel in its Lebanese invasions and Botha's South Africa in regular assaults on their neighbors each kill more civilians across borders during an average month than Libya does in a year. Indonesia has been engaged in a murderous assault on East Timor since 1975 that has resulted in the death of possibly a quarter of the Timorese population, over 200,000 people. Other western client states like South Korea have been abducting nationals from Western Europe, Japan and the United States, bribing foreign politicans, and intimidating people in places like Los Angeles on an extensive scale for several decades.

Claire Sterling and Walter Laqueur claim, as evidence of the Communist root of terrorism, that terrorists concentrate on the democracies and rarely disturb the Communist sphere. This is a major error of fact, made credible to the uninitiated only by grace of the major biases of the western mass media. South Africa's assaults on Angola and Mozambique during the past five years are cross-border terrorist attacks beyond anything suffered by any western democracy. But as South Africa is part of the Free World, and Angola and Mozambique are left-oriented states, these attacks are played down and are not called terrorist. Since 1959 Cuba has been subjected to many more terrorist acts than any western democracy, very possibly more than all of them put together, including many assassination attempts directed at the head of state. Sterling and Laqueur can pretend that Communist powers are terror-free only because of the patriotic bias of the propaganda system of which they are a part. With Cuba having been officially declared bad, and the enemy, acts that would be designated terroristic if taken against Free World states like Paraguay or Indonesia lose that character in the propaganda system when taken against Cuba. Furthermore, the manager and sponsor of this terroristic assault on Cuba has been the United States, the leader of the Free World in its struggle against "terrorism."

It is the ultimate double standard, and a tremendous testimonial to the biases and power of the Free Press, that the United States could hire members of the mafia, and other assassins, in an *admitted* eight attempts on the life of Castro,[28] and carry out a secret war of sabotage, murder and political blackmail of quite considerable scope,[29] and come out of this as Uncle-Sam-The-Clean, Fighter-Against-Terrorism. I ask two rhetorical questions: If Colonel Kaddafi had admitted to eight attempts on the life of the President of the United States, what would be the world reaction? Why are small crimes by Kaddafi proof of evil and larger crimes by the United States proof of nothing? I offer a rule applicable within the west: for a given state crime, criminality is inversely related to GNP, firepower, and strength of western affiliation. On this rule it is clear why discovery of a cache of arms from Castro in Venezuela (possibly planted by the CIA), is far more sinister than extended plotting with civil and military leaders for the overthrow of constitutional governments (Brazil, Chile), or the organization and management of literal invasions (Guatemala, Cuba) by the United States.

Sterling and Laqueur can only get away with playing dumb on the assault on Cuba because the mass media play dumb, in this case often pretending that the secret war and assassination attempts were merely comic failures best forgot—so we can get on with the serious business of coping with Carlos. The media's biases on this point are shown once again in the reception given the book by Warren Hinckle and W. W. Turner, *The Fish Is Red, The Story of The Secret War Against Castro* (Harper and Row, 1981). Like Claire Sterling the authors spell out a terror network, and do so in equally popular and more readable and less pompous style. This book differs from Sterling's in two substantial respects, however. First, its documentation is more compelling and the existence and characteristics of the secret war and the associated terrorist network is not subject to serious question. (The brief review in the *New York Times* on September 13, 1981 devotes only one sentence to the secret war core and themes of the book, dismissing this as already proven and stale!) Second, it is a terror network sponsored by the wrong party. The demand is for a Soviet-based network or PLO or Cuban villainy, not any old terrorism. I feel that it is a safe forecast that the Free Press will not give *The Fish Is Red* the red carpet treatment accorded the less well written, less truthful, and less important terror network dealt with by Claire Sterling.

The Cuban Refugee-DINA-CIA Connection

The Cuban refugee terrorist network has been responsible for a large fraction of the sensational and seriously destructive terrorist acts in the western hemisphere, and substantial numbers in Europe and Africa, over the past decade. Consisting of an elite of 100-200 or so hard-core exiles, many of them hoodlums, dispersed to New York, New Jersey, Miami and Puerto Rico, and operating under names like Alpha 66, Omega 7, Brigade 2506, CORU (the Commandos of United Revolutionary Organizations) or CNM (Cuban Nationalist Movement), but with overlapping membership, they have bombed and killed, and intimidated the Cuban exile community, with virtual impunity over this period. The intensity of Cuban refugee terrorist network violence may be indicated by the 25-30 bombings alleged by police officials for Dade County, Florida, in 1975 alone.[30] In March 1980 the FBI itself declared that Omega 7, which claimed credit and responsibility for 20 bombings in New York City between January 1975 and January 1980, is "the most dangerous terrorist organization in the United States." The seizure of its members was said to be a matter of the "highest priority" for the federal government;[31] but its members have not been seized, and the assumption of power by the "antiterrorist" forces of Haig and Reagan will surely give this "most dangerous terrorist organization" a new lease on life.

Throughout the 1960s many of these terrorists were in the employ of the CIA, who taught some 2000 of them the arts of bomb construction, demolition, and efficient murder as part of the secret war against Cuba. Ever since, the CIA-trained cadres have not only maintained a continuing flow of attacks on Cuba, they have become an international mercenary army, serving in the Congo, in Vietnam, in combatting the Puerto Rico independence movement, in Watergate operations, and as members of murder teams sent out by DINA, BOSS and other intelligence services. Watergate burglar Bernard Barker claims that he recruited 120 Cuban exiles for Operation Diamond, the Nixon administration's program for subverting domestic opposition to its policies. The Watergate break-in was a part of Operation Diamond.[32]

The network has assassinated Cuban diplomats in Lisbon, Mexico City and New York City. It has been implicated in the murder of exiled Chilean General Carlos Prats and his wife in 1974; in the attempted assassination of exiled Chilean official Bernardo Leighton and his wife in 1975; in the murder of Orlando Letelier and Roni Moffitt in Washington D.C. in 1976; and in the murder of South African economist Robert Smit and his wife in 1977.

A compilation of incidents attributed to the Orlando Bosch group alone published in *Granma*, October 19, 1980, included, in addition to some of those just mentioned, 85 bombings, one bazooka attack, a number of shootings and unsuccessful murder attempts, and the 1979 murders of Carlos Muniz Varela, a Puerto Rico dissident, and of Eulalio J. Negrin, a Cuban living in New Jersey who supported a dialogue between the Cuban exile community and the Castro regime. The killings attributable to this group are numerous—73 in the Cuban airliner; more than a dozen murders of Cuban officials and citizens; numerous murders within the Cuban exile community in infighting and efforts to intimidate; and unknown numbers of murders as agents of DINA and similar official terrorist bodies.[33]

The Cuban government publishes lists of terrorist acts carried out against it, in which it gives specific details of time, place, methods, damage inflicted, and participants. These are often verifiable, and Cuban refugee groups frequently proudly claim responsibility. Table 2-1 shows a breakdown of this data for the years 1973-1979, derived from a partial tabulation and

Table 2-1

Terrorist Attacks Against Cuba Attributable To
Cuban Refugee Groups in the United States, 1973-1979

	Number of Bombings	Numbers Injured	Numbers Killed
Attacks on Cuban Embassies and Missions	28	3	6
Attacks on Cuban Economic Facilities (Airlines, Power Lines, Sugar Refineries...)	14	0	80
Attacks on Individuals	40	1	8
Totals	82	4	94

confined here to attacks on Cuban facilities and persons. The years included omit both the period of the Kennedy-CIA secret war and several years of the reescalated Nixon-sponsored assaults on Cuba. Cuban refugee terrorist network acts of terrorism increased in 1977 and then escalated sharply again in 1979-1980, on both occasions in response to Castro's more vigorous efforts at rapprochement with the United States. This was a threat from the standpoint of the refugee-fascist-right, which unleashed campaigns of intimidation directed at the Cuban community in the United States that were virtually unchallenged by U.S. authorities.

The Cuban refugee network, armed and trained by the CIA, was never *disarmed*. As Jeff Stein observes, the members of the network are "comfortably into their third decade as America's first and only home-grown international terrorist group."[34] Its members continue to deal in and hold explosives and weaponry, and they use them to bomb, kill and intimidate. Although this group violates the law in one way or another every day of the week, its members hold press conferences and publish many newspapers in which they announce their intentions to commit violence, and they move around freely. Despite the avalanche of violence for which they are responsible, they rarely go to jail, and if they do go they do not stay long. William Schaap pointed out toward the end of 1980 that

> Of the eight terrorists in jail—the only people charged after hundreds of bombings, shootings, and murders— one is out on bail already, two more may be out on bail shortly, one will be out on parole in a few months, and four more will be released in Venezuela in a matter of weeks. All of them, especially Orlando Bosch, the mastermind, have vowed consistently to continue their murderous careers.[35]

Bosch served a brief jail sentence for a bombing attack in which he was caught red-handed, but he was paroled in 1972, after serving only four years of a ten-year sentence. In violation of his parole he went abroad and was allowed to move freely from Venezuela to Chile, Nicaragua, Costa Rica, the Dominican Republic, and back to Venezuela. In 1974 he was arrested in Caracas, Venezuela, implicated in two bombing attacks. Although long in violation of his parole, the U.S. government declined Venezuela's offer to send him back to the United States.[36] In 1976, again implicated in a bombing plot, and still in violation of his parole, the United States once again declined an offer (this time by Costa Rica) to put him in U.S. hands for rearrest and incarceration.[37] Bosch was shortly thereafter taken into custody in Venezuela once more for his confessed part in the bombing of a Cuban airliner in which 73 lives were lost. The newly elected leaders of the rightwing Social Christian movement of Venezuela shifted his trial to a military tribunal, which found him innocent of anything but faulty identification papers. While in a Venezuelaₙ jail, Bosch was paid a salary by the Venezuelan secret police, DISIP. The treatment of this world class terrorist by a government that is now openly and warmly pro-Reagan tells us a great deal about the meaning of Reaganism and the new campaign against "terrorism." I wonder whether Carlos would have been given similar treatment in a Soviet or Hungarian court following a confession (and other compelling evidence) of participation in a bombing attack that left 73 dead? If so, what would have been the response of the western media?

The Cuban refugee terror network has been the most important retail terror network operating anywhere during the past decade. In contrast with organizations like the Baader-Meinhof gang and the Weathermen, the Cuban network continues to function, year after year, without serious legal impediment. For Sterling, Laqueur, Haig and the U.S. mass media these terrorists either do not exist or are not included in the category terrorist. They are apparently killing the right people *for* the right people (DINA, the CIA perhaps), in which case the law ceases to function and the Free Press does its thing. Dinges and Landau cite a Miami policeman's claim that the CIA organized a meeting of the various Cuban refugee terrorist groups in 1976 in the Dominican Republic (with Orlando Bosch in attendance) for the purpose of channeling their terrorist activities outside the United States, particularly against enemy states such as Cuba.[38] It is possible that the Cuban refugee terrorist network operatives know too much, and that U.S. officials must go easy for fear of seriously embarrassing disclosures. Whatever the reasons, we see here a major terrorist network sponsored by the west, still durable and extremely active, but denied its rightful place in the Fright Decade by the Free Press.

Operation Condor

In 1976 six National Security States of Latin America—Argentina, Bolivia, Brazil, Chile, Paraguay and Uruguay—entered into a system for the joint monitoring and assassinating of dissident refugees in member countries. The program was directly initiated under the sponsorship of Chile and its head of the secret police (DINA), Manuel Contreras. Chile provided the initial funding, organized a series of meetings in Santiago, and provided the computer capacity and centralized services.[39] However, the United States deserves a great deal of credit for this important development, partly as the sponsor and adviser to DINA and other participating security services, but also because Operation Condor represented a culmination of a long sought U.S. objective—coordination of the struggle against "Communism" and "subversion." In 1968, U.S. General Robert W. Porter stated that "In order to facilitate the coordinated employment of internal security forces within and among Latin American countries, we are...endeavoring to foster interservice and regional cooperation by assisting in the organization of integrated command and control centers; the establishment of common operating procedures; and the conduct of joint and combined training exercises."[40] Condor was one of the fruits of this effort.

Under Operation Condor, political refugees who leave Uruguay and go to Argentina will be identified and kept under surveillance by Argentinian "security" forces, who will inform Uruguayan "security" forces of the presence of these individuals. If the Uruguayan security forces wish to murder these refugees in order to preserve western values, Argentine forces will cooperate. They will keep the Uruguayans informed of the whereabouts of the refugees; they will allow them to enter and freely move around in Argentina and to take the refugees into custody, torture and murder them; and the Argentinians will then claim no knowledge of these events. Under this system, two former Uruguayan Senators, one a former President of the Senate, Zelmar Michelini and Hector Gutierrez Ruiz, were kidnapped and murdered in Buenos Aires. We also note, just to keep the reader abreast of the quality of this cooperative enterprise, that both Michelini and Ruiz were tortured before being murdered, and that Michelini's daughter Margarita was also seized and "disappeared."

By July 1976 some 30 Uruguayan exiles, registered as refugees with U.N. officials in Buenos Aires, had been taken into custody and disappeared, surely murdered. Subsequently, several hundred more Uruguayans were picked up and have not been heard from since. Argentine authorities did not acknowledge these arrests, in conformity "with the policy of the security forces to withhold information on arrests involving investigation of subversion" (Juan de Onis of the *New York Times*, parroting the language of fascist terrorism).[41] Many other cross-country disappearances have also occurred. As reported by de Onis,

> Chilean exiles also were handed across the border to Chilean secret police and have not been heard of since. Gen. Juan Jose Torres, a former President of Bolivia, was kidnapped in Buenos Aires and found dead in an automobile trunk. Gen. Carlos Prats Gonzalez, commander-in-chief of the Chilean Army under the late President Salvador Allende Gossens, was killed by a bomb in Argentina. A similar network of intelligence [sic] operations has also worked between Brazil and Uruguay. Persons abducted in the southern Brazilian state of Rio do Sul, with cooperation from local political police, wound up in Uruguayan jails.[42]

Data are sparse, but the six country murder network toll starts with abduction-murders of Uruguayans alone numbering in excess of two hundred. This terror network threw fear into the hearts of the many thousands of political refugees who had resettled in the Operation Condor states, as they saw themselves now without a safe haven or any protection by legal process. They were now benefiting from that "coordinated employment of security forces" that General Porter described earlier as one of the prime objects of U.S. efforts in Latin America. As this extensive and terrible form of transnational terrorism flowed from U.S. policy efforts and perceived interests, it has not received much notice in the U.S. mass media.

This murder network soon extended its operations beyond the borders of the six participating countries. A secret report of an FBI agent assigned to Buenos Aires, describing Operation Condor, called attention to "a more secret phase" which "involves the formation of special teams from member countries to travel anywhere in the world to non-member countries to carry out sanctions, [including] assassinations, against terrorists or supporters of a terrorist organization from Operation Condor member countries."[43] It is worth noting that the FBI agent reporting on this matter not only approves the enterprise (which he thought "a good operation") but falls easily into accepting the notion that the victims of its murder squads are "terrorists." Data are lacking on the scope of this global phase of Operation Condor, which is difficult to distinguish from unilateral international terrorism carried out by the Argentine or Chilean secret police or one of their contract agents, often members of the Cuban exile terrorist network. Kidnappings, murders and attempted murders in Mexico and Italy have been proclaimed by the Cuban Squad Zero from 1975 onward, some surely under contract with DINA, although others were apparently to divert attention from the real (DINA) killers. [44] Orlando Bosch has worked for and been protected by DINA. The Letelier-Moffitt murders in Washington, D.C. were carried out by a Cuban-Chilean agent team that may have been part of Operation Condor.

The CIA was well aware of the internal (member country) use and global extension of Operation Condor and headed off its activities in several allied countries like France and Portugal by informing the authorities.[45] The CIA did not head off the Moffitt-Letelier murders, although it knew that DINA triggermen had entered the United States. Why? It is possible that the CIA knew of the prospective murders, and let them happen because it was murder of the right people—people such as Operation Condor and the Free World's secret police kill daily. It is also conceivable that the CIA suspected something fishy about to happen, but chose not to inquire, because of their "faith" in the choice of their fascist counterpart. It is also possible that the CIA bungled and made no inquiry, and that Pinochet and DINA murdered on the streets of Washington, D.C. assuming that Washington would not mind; after all, both DINA and Operation Condor are U.S. offspring. How was Pinochet to know that bringing his death squads right into the heart of the Free World was unseemly?

With its hand forced, and obligated to proceed in the case of a well-publicized murder in Washington, the U.S. government did a great deal to subvert the case. Documents were leaked to the press which linked Letelier to Cuba, effectively smearing him and creating a false red herring that was used both to justify murder and to divert inquiry away from our warm friends in Chile. Although the CIA knew from the day of the murder that DINA agents had come in to do a job, this was hidden from the press and from other parts of the government as long as possible, and the false trail of suggestions of a left-terrorist murder was pushed by people who knew this was a lie.[46] Thus the prosecution of the murderers was carried out by a government that was so compromised by its own lies and suppressions and hamstrung by its own involvement and collaboration with the Cuban and Chilean assassins, that it was inevitable that the case would be conveniently "lost." The United States government chose not to interfere with the death squad at work on U.S. soil before the fact—and it was therefore not going to be *able* to prosecute successfully after the fact. The United States was one of the sponsors of Operation Condor, had trained the Cuban terrorist triggerman, and had been instrumental in bringing into existence the Pinochet regime. This set of relationships, with its potential for "greymail," and its connection with our "security interests," means that the terrorists of Operation Condor, like the Cuban refugee terror network are our progeny. We are not likely to hurt our own.

South African Transnational Terrorism

South Africa, by itself, has very probably killed more people in the course of its "secret" warfare on its neighbors during the 1970s than the PLO, Red Brigades, Baader-Meinhof gang, Carlos, Cuba and Libya taken together. In a single raid on the Namibian refugee camp of Kassinga on May 4, 1978, South African forces killed over 600 people, a large proportion women and children. Many hundreds have been killed in Angola in search and destroy operations aimed at "the deliberate killing and terrorizing of Angolan civilians in any area where SWAPO might find support or help."[47] The ruthlessness of these operations, with the indiscriminate killing of men, women and children, the burning down of all houses, the destruction of mission hospitals, staggers the imagination, although once again the Free Press has kept this largely under cover, preferring to concentrate on Soviet maneuvers on the Polish borders rather than actual invasions of African states by the apartheid regime.

Much of this destruction was carried out by hundreds of mercenaries, although regular South African forces have also been involved. According to one defector, who became "disgusted and tired of killing civilians,"

Our main job is to take an area and clear it. We sweep through it and we kill everything in front of us, cattle, goats, people, everything. We are out to stop SWAPO and so we stop them getting into the villages for food and water. But half the time the locals don't know what's going on. We're just fucking them up and it gets out of hand. Some of the guys get a bit carried away.

[He describes an operation in southern Angola during which two children appeared and started to run.]... They'd taken their clothes off to show they weren't armed. We shot this young girl. She must have been about five. And we shot her father. We shot about nine in all.

I don't know how, but somehow this girl's mother and her sister didn't get shot. Well, we left them there and carried on with our patrol. She followed us: This mother and her little kid. She followed us all day, just walked along about 100 meters behind us. She didn't cry or say anything. This freaked me out.[48]

Other defectors, some of them former white mercenaries from Rhodesia, have confirmed these accounts of merciless killing of civilians and scorched earth policies that have caused massive destruction in southern Angola. The Angolan government itself estimates that just during the 18 month period ending in December 1980, the South Africans mounted 13 major air and land assaults as well as numerous small-scale attacks.

Similar South African operations have been carried out on a hit-and-run basis in Zimbabwe and Mozambique. Their purpose has been clear. South Africa intends to continue its wholly illegal occupation of Namibia, as a buffer and plunder state, and its murderous attacks on the black front-line states are partly to destroy SWAPO bases and sources of assistance, partly to injure and weaken countries on its border and on the border of Namibia that would be likely to aid Namibian independence. As is noted in a *Wall Street Journal* report,

South Africa waits, scuttling peace initiatives like the all-party conference in Geneva last winter and waging a

generally low-level guerilla war that costs it little—
given Namibia's diamond, uranium and copper wealth—
and gives its troops some counterinsurgency training in
the bargain.[49]

This *Journal* report also calls attention to the great "encouragement" given South Africa's escalated violence against Angola by
the new antiterrorist Reagan administration—indirectly in its
obvious toleration/sanction of the Israeli bombing raid on Iraq,
in the new anti-Libyan campaign, and more directly in Washington's warmth and understanding of the "context" that may be
impelling the apartheid regime to occupy Namibia illegally and
to kill black Africans without restraint.[50]

The Reagan administration's role in the recent sharp
escalation of South African terrorism can hardly be overstated.
Only the Free Press and the most supine or reactionary leaders of
the Free World could fail to see that code words like "realism,"
"understanding of the problems," "context," and "quiet diplomacy" mean that "we are behind you all the way; understand that
any criticisms we make are strictly PR, to allow our allies to
pretend that we object to your assaults on your neighbors (or
your own black majority). " Even before Reagan, U.S. business
had found South Africa profitable and therefore good, and our
military-intelligence apparatus has long had the warmest relations
with BOSS; but under liberal administrations, and even under
Nixon and Ford, the loss of national prestige from open alliance
with apartheid and Namibian aggression had a constraining
effect. With the extreme right now exercising significant power in
Washington (sharing it with the traditional conservative business
interests), the bars are down—the formerly muted alliances with
South African racism and Third World fascists have now become
open and warm.

The mass media have played a strategic role in covering up
the massive transnational violence of the apartheid regime. First
and foremost, they have suppressed the facts. These are available,
and can be found in black African, radical, underground, and, to
a lesser extent, liberal-left European publications. Extensive and
horrifying details were given in the British *Guardian* series, cited
above, based on on-the-spot reporting and interviews with a
number of South African mercenary defectors. This series has

not been reprinted in the United States, summaries have not been made available, and similar on-the-spot coverage in Angola is not provided. As in the case of East Timor following its invasion by our client state Indonesia, the Free Press does not go to the victims—government or refugees—it gets its information from the propaganda services of the invader. In connection with this open invasion of Angola, the *New York Times* has carried two front page and two second page articles based on South African handouts, describing "captured Soviet advisers," the view of the war as seen from South Africa, and a portrayal of the loot captured by the South Africans.[51] Nothing from the end of the Angolan victims.

What makes the "Soviet adviser" gambit doubly dishonest is that the Cubans and Russians are in Angola mainly because South Africa's incursions and support of Savimbi pose a serious threat to the Angolan regime. The *Wall Street Journal* account cited earlier points out that

> Both publicly and in private talks with western govern-
> ments, Angola insists it would order the Cubans to
> withdraw if it were assured of an end to South African
> raids. Conversely, it warns that further attacks could
> force it to reach out even further to the Soviets, who
> seek political gain in the turbulence and instability of
> southern Africa.[52]

This highlights once again the monumental hypocrisy of the west in its pretense at concern over terrorism, with its apologetics for preferred terror in terms of a Soviet presence! The preferred terror is also not only large scale and extremely ugly, it is in support of aggression in Namibia and protection of the cruel system of apartheid in South Africa itself.

Israel's Sacred Terrorism

Among the recipients of U.S. military and economic aid and diplomatic support, Israel occupies a unique place. Israel is generally portrayed by the U.S. mass media as the *victim* of terrorism, a characterization that is in part correct. Its own role as a major perpetrator of state terrorism is consistently down-played or ignored, in accordance with the general principle, discussed earlier, that violence employed by ourselves or by our friends is excluded from the category of terrorism, by definition. The record of Israeli terrorism, however, is substantial, far too extensive even to attempt to sample here.[53] A small glimpse into the reality was given by Prime Minister Menahem Begin in a letter published in the Israeli press in August 1981, written in response to what he regarded as hypocritical criticism of the Israeli bombing of Beirut, which killed hundreds of civilians. Begin offered a "partial list" of military attacks on Arab civilians under the Labor governments, which included over 30 separate episodes that left many civilians dead. He concluded that "under the Alignment government, there were regular retaliatory actions against civilian Arab populations; the air force operated against them; the damage was directed against such structures as the canal, bridges and transport."[54] "The picture that emerges," former UN Ambassador and Foreign Minister Abba Eban wrote in response, "is of an Israel wantonly inflicting every possible measure of death and anguish on civilian populations in a mood reminiscent of regimes which neither Mr. Begin nor I would dare to mention by name."[55] Eban is harshly critical of Begin's letter because of the support it gives to Arab propaganda; he does not contest the facts. He even defends the earlier Israeli attacks on civilians with the exact logic which orthodox analysts of terrorism attribute to—and use to condemn—retail terrorists; namely, that deliberate attacks may properly be made on innocent parties in order to achieve higher ends. Eban writes that "there was a rational prospect, ultimately fulfilled, that afflicted populations [i.e., innocent civilians deliberately bombed] would exert pressure for the cessation of hostilities."[56]

Begin's list is indeed "partial." It is supplemented by former Chief of Staff Mordechai Gur, who stated that "For 30 years, from the War of Independence until today, we have been fighting against a population that lives in villages and cities," offering as examples the bombardments that cleared the Jordan Valley of all inhabitants and that drove a million and a half civilians from the Suez Canal area in 1970, among others.[57] The Israeli military analyst Zeev Schiff summarized General Gur's comments as. follows: "In South Lebanon we struck the civilian population consciously, because they deserved it...the importance of Gur's remarks is the admission that the Israeli Army has always struck civilian populations, purposely and consciously...the Army, he said, has never distinguished civilian [from military] targets... [but] purposely attacked civilian targets even when Israeli settlements had not been struck."[58]

There are other examples that might be cited, among them, the terrorist attacks against civilian targets (including U.S. installations) in Cairo and Alexandria in 1954 carried out in an effort to poison relations between the United States and Egypt; the murderous attacks on the villages of Qibya, Kafr Kassem, and others; the shooting down of a Libyan airliner in 1973 with 110 killed as it was attempting to return to Cairo after having overflown the Sinai in a sandstorm; and many others. Lebanon has been a regular target of Israeli terrorism, including direct invasion and systematic bombardment of cities, villages and rural areas that has caused hundreds of thousands of refugees and many thousands of casualties. Still another dimension of state terrorism is the brutal treatment of the civilian population in the occupied territories, and the murder of Palestinians in the interchange of terror that has been proceeding in Europe for many years.[59] Terrorism in the pre-state period was also extensive, another story that is largely unknown in the United States, where commentators like to pretend that terrorism is an invention of the Palestinians.

The *Diary* of former Israeli Prime Minister Moshe Sharett is a major source of evidence for a conscious policy of deliberate, unprovoked cross-border attacks, in which advantage was taken of superior military power and a servile western propaganda machine, with the intent of destabilizing neighboring states and provoking them into military responses.[60] Sharett was a foot-dragger in these enterprises, often shaken by the ruthlessness of the military establishment—"the long chain of false incidents and hostilities we have invented, and so many clashes we have provoked;" the "narrow-mindedness and short-sightedness of our military leaders" [who] "seem to presume that the State of Israel may—or even must—behave in the realm of international relations according to the laws of the jungle." Sharett himself referred to this long effort as a "sacred terrorism."[61]

Where Israeli state terrorism is acknowledged in the United States, it is almost invariably described as "retaliatory," hence not criminal even if regrettable. To cite only one example, consider the laudatory article by Amos Perlmutter on General Ariel Sharon in the *New York Times Magazine*.[62] Commenting on Sharon's exploits as the commander of Unit 101 in the early 1950s, Perlmutter writes that "Every time terrorists were captured in Israel, they would be interrogated to determined where they had come from. Then an Israeli force would return to the terrorists' villages and retaliate against them, an eye for an eye— or, more often, two eyes for an eye." Perlmutter is a knowledgeable military historian, who certainly knows that this is an outrageous falsehood. The "retaliatory actions" of Unit 101 were characteristically directed against completely innocent civilians in villages that had no known relation to terrorist acts, for example, Qibya, where 66 civilians were massacred in October 1953 in the first major operation of Sharon's Unit 101. There was no known connection between the villagers of Qibya and any terrorist actions against Israel. Israel angrily denied charges that its military forces were responsible for this massacre, pretending that the "retaliation act" was carried out by "border settlers in Israel, mostly refugees, people from Arab countries and survivors from the Nazi concentration camps..."[63] Commenting on this fabrication in his diary, Prime Minister Moshe Sharett observed that "Such a version will make us appear ridiculous; any child would say that this was a military operation," as was tacitly conceded much later. He writes that in the cabinet meeting following the massacre, "I condemned the Qibya affair that exposed us in front of the whole world as a gang of bloodsuckers, capable of mass massacres regardless, it seems, of whether their actions may lead to war. I warned that this stain will stick to us and will not be washed away for many years to come."[64] Sharett was wrong in thinking that "this stain will stick to us." The typical response is falsification of the sort practised by Perlmutter in the *New York Times*. A critical commentary on Perlmutter's whitewash of the bloodthirsty General Sharon in *The Nation* fails to mention this remarkable suppression and distortion of the historical record.[65] This single example is, unfortunately, quite typical of a long and ugly story of atrocities and cover-ups.

Argentine Transnational Intervention in Boliva to Combat the Threat of Democracy

In July 1980, a rightwing military coup led by General Luis Garcia Meza Tejada succeeded in preventing the accession of the newly elected President of Bolivia, Hernan Siles Zuago. The military officers who led the coup were major participants in the drug traffic and were also well known as shakedown men and close allies of organized crime in Bolivia. The coup had a deeper significance, however, in its assault on organized labor and other popular and democratic tendencies, and in the active intervention and participation of the Southern Cone fascist network.

As far as the drug trade goes, one U.S. narcotics official asserted that "for the first time ever the drugs mafia has evidently bought itself a government."[66] *Latin American Regional Reports* claimed that the narcotics business "was the mainspring for the 17 July coup, and that vast amounts of cocaine money have been passed on to the country's new leaders." Garcia Meza reportedly received a direct grant of $100 million to finance his new government. Interior Minister Colonel Luis Arce Gomez was the "leader of a major drug ring," and Minister of Education, Colonel Ariel Coca, developed "one of the biggest cocaine smuggling networks in South America" while serving as head of the Bolivian Air Force at Santa Cruz. This coup effectively joined together cocaine and National Security State thuggery and terror. In the days immediately following the coup "large numbers of convicted traffickers were released by Arce from prisons in Cochabamba and Santa Cruz and absorbed into the interior ministry's paramilitary units."[67] A reign of terror ensued that involved widespread torture, murder and disappearances.[68]

Along with the drug mafia, the other notable participant in the Bolivian coup was the Argentine military regime, which masterminded the takeover strategy, supplied the coup leaders with diplomatic and political advice, and provided more than 200 military and intelligence personnel to help in the direct management of the coup. Newsman Ray Bonner quoted one U.S. military adviser in Bolivia as saying that "The Argentine military did everything but tell Gen. Garcia Meza the day to pull it off..."[69] In Buenos Aires a computerized list of potential opponents of the regime was prepared, and these individuals were imprisoned, exiled, tortured and murdered in the few days following the coup. Argentine advisers were also on hand to instruct Bolivian "security forces" in modern methods of torture, which were used extensively in the post-coup period.

All of this was done fairly openly and on the basis of standard NSS ideology. Argentine President Jorge Videla declared that an elected government in Bolivia posed "a high degree of risk because of the possibility that such a government would promote ideas contrary to our way of life and the permanence of military governments."[70] This is a fine case of chickens coming home to roost. Here is a U.S. ally engaging in open intervention to extend Third World fascism to neighboring states. There was no pretense of a "left" or Communist threat in Bolivia (Bonner quotes a senior U.S. military adviser to the effect that "There probably isn't a Communist guerilla in the entire country.")[71] It was democracy itself that was felt to be threatening to our fascist client. The Carter administration did not like this outcome, having supported the democratic process that resulted in the Suarez victory, and to its credit it protested vigorously and cut off aid. But it should be noted that the Carter administration took no really strong actions; none as regards Argentina, which had engaged in a gross intervention for purposes and with results that the United States theoretically opposes strongly on fundamental principle. Imagine what the U.S. response would have been if Castro had done half as much! But Castro would have been threatening the *real* fundamentals, which, as are described in chapter 3, have nothing to do with democracy.

Concluding Note

In sharp contrast with Castro, our own progeny and assorted other friendly state terrorists are allowed to get away with direct, cross-border murder and numerous other interventions, stretching even to the United States, most of which fail to generate serious publicity or indignation. General Park's South Korea was able to engage in extensive bribery of U.S. politicians without causing significant damage to itself—certainly nothing was done so severe as closing its U.S. Embassy, let alone any major act of hostility. South Africa, also, has been able to expend large sums buying and bribing U.S. newspapers and funding U.S. politicians without significant adverse repercussions. Currently, South Africa is openly propagandizing in the United States on Namibia and campaigning against hostile U.S. politicians through hired law and PR firms and alleged "trade councils," again without real exposure or apparent impediment.[72] We have seen that South Africa can invade its neighbors and murder their civilians at will without arousing Free Press attention or indignation. Sudanese president Jafar el Numeiry can arrest 12,000 at a crack or announce that he is training several hundred men to infiltrate into Libya on suicide missions aimed at removing key figures in Col. Kaddafi's government,[73] again without notice or comment in the west. The principle of "whose ox is being gored" controls news and indignation both.

The rise of the NSS was a product of U.S. planning and strategy, as will be described in the next chapter. Operation Condor was a logical outcome of those efforts. As we have seen, Argentina's security services participated in the overthrow of a democratic government in Bolivia in 1980, and they were actively engaged in aiding the murderous repression in Guatemala during 1981. These interventions have not been seriously objectionable to the United States, so that, in contrast with relatively trivial moves by Castro, these have not been placed in the category of "aiding terrorism." The Reagan administration has gone further, openly soliciting Argentina to extend its valuable services to Nicaragua—in the form of "infiltrating combat forces"—and to El Salvador, by means of direct participation alongside the local death squads.[74] Oberdorfer and Tyler reported in February 1982 that U.S.-backed subversion by force against Nicaragua had already begun "along the Honduran-Nicaraguan border within the last three months."[75] Argentina was reportedly training 1,000 men as part of an action program organized and financed by the CIA, "but the possibility of using American personnel to undertake unilateral action against some unspecified 'special Cuban targets' also was envisaged."[76] This mobilization of members of a sponsored fascist network to do our regional killing and subverting by proxy—an application of the "Nixon Doctrine"—is, like Operation Condor, quite consistent with U.S. ends and notions of acceptable means. With Reagan it appears that the fascist network will be mobilized more extensively and openly along Operation Condor lines, and the United States will be an integral part of the "team." The only step as yet unfulfilled in our cultivation of state terrorism is "bringing the NSS home," but we move steadily closer.

THREE

Contemporary Terrorism (2):
The Real Terror Network

Introduction

The really massive and significant growth of terrorism since World War II has been that carried out by states. And among states, the emergence and spread of the National Security State (NSS) has been the most important development contributing to state terrorism and thus to the growth of overall world terrorism, using the word in its basic sense—intimidation by violence or the threat of violence. Contrary to Sterling's foolish remark about the "colossal" armaments of retail terrorists, state military resources are vastly larger, and the power of even small states to intimidate is much greater than that of non-state terrorists. Only states use torture extensively as a means of intimidation, and if we use as our measure of the scale of terrorist violence either political murders or incarceration accompanied by torture, retail terrorism pales into relative insignificance. State terrorism is also much more important than non-state violence because it is rooted in relatively permanent structures that allow terror to be institutionalized, as in the case of Argentina's numerous and well-equipped detention and torture centers. Retail terrorists are frequently transitory, and they are often produced by the very abuses that state terror is designed to protect (a point discussed in the concluding chapter).

If state terrorism *is* designed to protect systems of injustice, to allow them to persist and perhaps even to be extended in scope, this suggests a further aspect of wholesale terror that greatly enhances its potential for evil. A central theme of this book—and one for which substantiating evidence is provided in this chapter—is that the NSS is an instrument of class warfare, organized and designed to permit an elite, local and multinational, to operate without any constraint from democratic processes. This allows the bulk of the population to be treated as a mere cost of production. In NSSs with rapid population growth and rural labor surpluses, as in Brazil, the system is therefore "based directly on bleeding dry the working classes."[1] As one jobless Brazilian father of six children expressed it, "The worst violence of all is total deprivation. Our most basic needs are not being met."[2] Retail terrorists do not deprive large numbers of their subsistence and produce hunger, malnutrition, high infant mortality rates, chronic diseases of poverty and neglect, and illiteracy. This is all done by state terrorists.

A recent account of malnutrition in Central America points out that malnutrition rates are not only very high—on average, one third of all children under five years of age suffered from severe malnutrition in the mid-1970s—they are also rising. It notes further that "The unequal distribution of the productive resources [the top 5% collect 35% of total income], which is compounded by reduced opportunities of the lower income classes, lack of participation in the sociopolitical decisions, and reduced access to services, makes for a very critical situation in the area."[3] In the real terror network that is to be discussed here, it is the *function* of state terrorism to keep popular participation down, to limit services to the lower classes, and to freeze the structures that have generated this "very critical situation." We will see further on in this chapter that the development model put in place by the NSS has succeeded in combining "growth" with continued and sometimes even enlarged mass hunger and systematic neglect of the majority.

This achievement has been grounded in an ideology that rationalizes the collective interest of the military establishment, the local business and landed elite, and the multinational corporation—the joint venture partners who require terror to preserve and enlarge their privileges and the already gross levels of inequality prevalent in the Third World. According to its own ideology, the NSS rests on the primacy of "National Security," which is to be imposed by military force to contain the forces of "Communism" and "Subversion." "National Security," "Communism," and "Subversion" are coordinate terms, all defined in the NSSs with a generous scope that conveniently reaches anything that would threaten elite privilege and power. That the assertion of basic human rights is subversive in the NSS must be taken literally. Thus the adult education programs of Paulo Freire, which stressed literacy, enhancement of feelings of self-worth, and belief in the possibility of improving one's status, were quickly terminated upon the emergence of the NSS of Brazil in 1964—they "politicized" the lower classes and thus constituted a security threat (or, alternatively, were subversive or communistic).[4] Dom Alano Pena, Bishop of Maraba in Brazil, noted that his church in its educational efforts "sought to make the peasant and the worker aware that they have certain basic rights and that they are entitled to exercise those rights. To the military, that is the same thing as subversion."[5]

The NSS emerged in an environment of political upheaval and assertions of claims by the lower classes, and was brought into being by local and expatriate elites to contain the demands of the majority. These stirrings from below threatened to accelerate in the wake of the Cuban revolution, which frightened the U.S. leadership and the Latin American upper classes. James Petras points out that "Rather than a period of Latin American initiative in a revolutionary upsurge following the Cuban Revolution, the years after 1962 were a period of counterrevolution. The United States was on the offensive to forestall revolution, supporting military regimes, organizing counterinsurgency forces and, in the case of the Dominican Republic, carrying out a military occupation."[6] The rapid spread of the NSS ensued, and so did its prime instrumentality, terror—which has followed from the fact that, in the words of Fernando Henrique Cardoso, the NSS "aspires, above all, to produce apathy among the masses."[7] It is therefore easily understandable why it is among this group of states that human torture and "disappearances" have become quantitatively significant and institutionalized as modes of governance. I will discuss briefly below the theory and practical effects of the development model applied in the NSS; why terror fits this model very comfortably; the character of the terror employed as a political ingredient in this model; and the evidence that this system of NSSs is not only approved by, but has developed under the general planning and supervision of the United States.

The Economics of the National Security State

The development model espoused by the leaders of the NSSs (and their external business and intellectual allies) is a free market model which allows for a government role only in creating a favorable investment climate.[8] This may include subsidies and tax concessions to business firms, which increase their willingness to invest, but it excludes any largess to the non-propertied classes, which would worsen the investment climate. For the leaders of NSSs the end sought is not human welfare; in Cardoso's words, "bureaucratic-authoritarianism was not launched to assure the well-being of the people."[9] The explicit aim is "national power," although, no doubt coincidentally, the immediate and only observable beneficiaries are the ruling economic and military elites. According to the NSS development model, the national welfare (= national power) is best served by rapid economic growth.[10] Rapid growth, in turn, requires extreme generosity to entrepreneurs, local and foreign, operating under free labor market and business entry conditions. Free labor markets means an atomized or nonunion condition or unionization under government control and a plentiful "reserve army" of workers. It is assumed that free business entry, which includes that of foreign firms, will stimulate a restructuring of industry and agriculture in accordance with comparative advantage. It will also presumably induce capital to exploit domestic resources fully. GNP growth and national power will thus be maximized.

Among the many problems raised by the development model, as applied in the NSSs, I will address three: (1) its blatant elite bias and political content; (2) its observable regressive impact and failure to meet the basic human needs of the majority; (3) its defective economic rationale.

(1) *Ends served.* The blind-growth, open-economy development model calls for exactly those policies sought by large multinational interests and important local elites. It would be remarkable if what was good for these elites was good for the society at

large. What makes the model doubly suspect is a basic political and economic premise of the NSS—namely, that the majority is not only to be excluded from participation in all policy decisions, it is also to be kept in an atomized and disorganized condition by means of force and the threat of force. Where this is so, the logic of power tells us that the interests of people so excluded will be neglected, and that these unrepresented people will be served only on the calculus of public relations needs or on a balancing of the costs and benefits of concessions versus repression.

Church documents come back to these points time and again—that disenfranchisement means structured neglect of the excluded majority and a corrupt pursuit of self-interest by those who have arrogated exclusive political power to themselves; that decent *ends* are more important than expertise and sophisticated *means*. According to one recent Brazilian church statement,

> What history truly records is the inherent irresponsibility of all despotisms and the almost inevitable corruption of all forms of government that are not subject to the control of the people....

> Political democracy is a form and a prerequisite, whose content and destination is social democracy. Thus, a moral environment and a whole perspective that will orient the choices is more important than techniques for solutions and changes.... Social development has to be attained under certain conditions and it is in pursuit of this objective that economic development must be oriented.[11]

Brazilian social scientists make the same point, for example, with reference to the fearful conditions of urban life in Sao Paulo—the uncontrolled pollution, the power of the land speculators and the business elite to shape public investment, the huge deficiencies in housing, sanitation, and public transport, and the serious malnutrition and high level of industrial accidents. These conditions, they argue, are inherent in the NSS, where the masses are excluded and only elite ends are served by the state:

> As long as the social and political initiatives of the working classes continue to be blocked, it is difficult to imagine Sao Paulo as a truly human city. For it is capital—not labour—which is destroying life in the

city. For capitalists, the city is a source of profit. For workers it is a way of life.[12]

This point is reinforced when control and policy determination within the NSS is exercised or shared by absentee owners, such as foreign governments and multinational corporations with headquarters in the United States, West Germany or Japan. It seems extremely unlikely that, in considering development opportunities in Ecuador or Brazil, these distant and absentee interests will give any thought to the welfare impact of their choices on the Ecuadorean and Brazilian masses. The local elites in the NSSs of Latin America are likely to show hardly greater concern; they have long shared the Somoza view of the majority as "oxen," designed to labor quietly for their superiors. The indigenous roots of these elites withered years ago in a process of integration into western consumerism and by affiliation with multinational companies. They look outward for models and political support.

The military elites, who are the direct rulers of the NSSs, have produced an ideology that puts decisive weight on power and military security and explicitly shunts into the background the well-being of the masses. It rests on an alleged "new dilemma —Welfare or Security—previously pointed out by Goering in less just but highly suggestive terms: 'more guns, less butter.' In fact there is no getting around the necessity of sacrificing Welfare to the benefit of Security when the latter is actually endangered."[13] The reference to the number two Nazi, Goering, in justification for the stress on guns by the Brazilian general quoted here—also for a time president of the Dow branch in Brazil—is an interesting manifestation of the spiritual foundations of the NSS. But the dilemma of welfare-security in Brazil and the other NSSs rests on the special meaning of "security" already discussed, which equates "security threat," "communism," and "subversion" with an *internal* challenge to privilege and elite domination. For Hitler and Goering, who were embarking on a program of external expansion, "security" and "guns" were necessary, and butter clearly had to be sacrificed. In the NSSs there is no external security threat; the "enemy" is the people within the country who are trying to assert basic rights—the "security threat" is that posed by unionism and majority rule. Dealing with internal subversion normally tends to be only moderately expensive, especially when part of the cost has been borne by the United States (see Table 3-4). Military outlays have gone up sharply in the NSSs, but partly because of the institutional bias of the military establishments, which have indulged themselves in expensive irrelevancies and treated themselves generously just because they can[14]—there is no democratic constraint on their choices, and they put little weight on alleviating the misery of the "oxen."

The upper classes in general have not had to suffer any reduction in "butter" under NSS conditions. Absent any populist element in the NSS leadership or ideology (in contrast with German and Italian fascism), a marked feature of NSS economics has been the crass upward shift in income distribution and the great increase in the production and importation of household durables and fashionable luxury goods. The Mercedes Benz has sold extremely well in Pinochet's Chile. The Goering "dilemma" must be modified accordingly—"more guns for internal pacification to allow more butter for the elite; less butter for the majority." The poor must stay poor, or get poorer, because the interests of the joint venture partners require this—but we will call it a stress on "security" in the interest of "growth" and "development"!

The nominal ideology of the NSS, and even more clearly its real purpose, therefore involves a denial of the worth and rights of most human beings and constitutes a throwback to pre-Enlightenment ideas of hierarchy and structured and permanent inequality (including inequality of opportunity). This is a truly reactionary ideology, well designed to rationalize the neglect, spoliation and terrorization of the majority of the population. The development model provides the economic counterpart to this ideological framework.

Not only are the ends and means of the NSS explicitly anti-democratic, its biases are exacerbated by the venality of its rulers. As the local elites are denationalized, lose most of their indigenous attachments and loyalties, and become integrated into a world political economy of "superior" (i.e., more powerful and productive) cultures from which they derive their standards of behavior, they are readily corruptible. Guatemala's Garcia, for example, owns three estates totalling 130,000 acres,[15] modest when compared with Somoza's 8,000 square miles, but Garcia has only been in power for three years. In Argentina, *Latin America Regional Reports* observes ironically that "It is evidence of the economic success of Videla's administration that most of his former aides are now established millionaires."[16] In the Philippines, even *Business Week* remarks that it is "not bad" of Marcos to be able to jump into the ranks of the ten leading taxpayers "on his official salary of $4,500 per year."[17] The most spectacular recent development in NSS corruption, however, has been the rise of military mafias that manage and protect the cocaine and marijuana trade in both Bolivia and Colombia.[18] (The murderous crew in Colombia, which has also been killing and torturing peasants for years under a system of permanent martial law, has logically enough entered into the warmest kind of relationship with the antiterrorist administration in Washington.[19]) I have described elsewhere the fact that an almost uniformly appropriate designation of the Third World client states of the west to whom the development model applies is that of the "shakedown state."[20] From Indonesia, Thailand and the Philippines, through Brazil, Chile, Honduras and Paraguay, to Zaire, the participation of the top military and civil leaders in the heroin trade, in the gambling and prostitution businesses, in payoffs for access to rights to participate in local "development," and in more direct looting, has been chronic and really massive.[21]

With such joint venture partners fixing the goals and terms of development, three things are virtually certain: (1) The time horizon of the dominant business and political-military elites will be short and quick extraction of profits and the buildup of nest eggs in safe havens abroad will be a general characteristic of NSS economies—the operative principle will be grab now as "après nous le déluge." (2) The majority of the population will be regarded essentially as an "overhead" cost, and costs must be kept down for "development." If the convenience of the dominant elites calls for dispossession of large numbers of peasants and Indian tribes who have only traditional (but sometimes legal) rights, machine guns will permit this under NSS conditions; the huge human externalities in the form of millions turned into impoverished and underemployed agricultural laborers and foraging urban slumdwellers are acceptable on NSS economic principles. (3) Other externalities of dependent growth such as work hazards, environmental damage, the weakening of indigenous economic activity and culture, will be disregarded. The NSS can serve as a handy dumping grounds for nuclear power plants unsalable in the developed states and for industries with serious worker hazards or major pollution and waste disposal problems. The dominant elites in the NSS are content to have the indigenous culture eviscerated by the "superior" culture, which has demonstrated its superiority by military prowess, a large GNP, and innovation in style-setting goods that captivate the denationalized affluent.

(2) *Income distribution and human needs impact.* The observed income distribution effects of NSS development are exactly what we would expect from a growth process controlled by small elite minorities who have resorted to machine guns. There has been a major trickle-*up*, and even where GNP growth has been rapid the impoverished majority has in most cases derived marginal benefits at best.[22] Latin America has an exceptional degree of inequality of income distribution, in comparison not only with less developed countries in Europe (both capitalist and socialist), but even in contrast with the LDCs of Africa and Asia.[23] Central America may be the world leader in inequality, with the lower 50% of income receiving units getting only 13% of all income and the upper 5% obtaining a staggering 35% of total income in the mid-1970s.[24]

In the advanced countries there was an increase in inequality during the early stages of modern industrial growth, but inequality diminished in most of them during the twentieth century. In Latin America, growth has not led toward any noticeable trend toward greater equality even over long time periods with high growth rates.[25] There was an interlude of modest reduction in inequality between 1930 and 1950, based on a reduced rate of growth (and a relatively great fall of profits), a spurt of trade union growth and power, and an increase in welfare state benefits. But the post-1945 era of more rapid growth brought with it a sharp turn once again toward increased inequality, a repudiation by experience of the notion that growth and higher per capita income would surely reduce the massive inequalities of the old order. A huge 400% increase in GNP in Latin America between 1950 and 1975 was accompanied by a sharp increase in inequality, and in circumstances where very large numbers were still hungry, malnourished, and suffering from curable illnesses, and where many were experiencing *absolute* reductions in real income. The trickle-down effect in Latin America has been modest at best, even though those at the top, who keep getting the bulk of any gains, are well-off even by U.S. standards, while those at the bottom are in dire straits.[26]

In Brazil, Colombia and Mexico, for example, under recent growth conditions to 1975, "the upper income brackets received the lion's share of the income gains. In Brazil only the top decile increased its share, the 9th decile's share held constant, while those in the remaining 8 deciles fell."[27] Felix's study of Mexico indicates that the substantial growth in 1950-1975 not only saw the lower 60% lose relative share, the lowest 20% lost *absolute* real income.[28] There is some evidence that the income condition of the bottom 40% in Mexico has deteriorated over a century or more;[29] and in Colombia, an agricultural worker may have been better off in the late 18th century than today![30]

The rise of the NSS was surely a factor in preserving these huge inequalities, which probably increased further in the past decade. The Chilean and Argentinian counterrevolutions of the 1970s led quickly to an absolute fall in the real income of the majority, as well as to a shift toward greater relative inequality. Just one year of fascism cost the average *employed* Chilean worker somewhere between 20 and 53% of his real wage;[31] unemployment, of course, soared, and a sharp cutback of social welfare outlays was quickly instituted. The Brazilian counter-revolution of 1964 led to an "economic miracle," as measured by a huge rise in GNP and in the well-being of the upper 10% of income receivers, but it left the bottom 60% not only without significant improvement but with some unknown but probably sizable fraction suffering an absolute decline in real income.[32]

From the standpoint of human welfare, the position of the majorities in the NSSs has worsened during recent decades in a number of important respects. One is a result of the increase in inequality itself. It is a view accepted across a wide spectrum of economists that happiness and a sense of satisfaction and status are dependent on *relative* income position, not absolute income.[33] If an affluent elite enlarges its range of goods consumed while leaving the masses with more or less stable real incomes, but relatively worse off, this should increase their discontent and unhappiness (even ignoring the prior absolute misery levels that they are forced to endure). Table 3-1 shows the great inequalities that prevail in the income distributions of six U.S. client states, where, on average, the top 10% of income receiving units captured a huge 37.5% of total income; the bottom 40% got only 13.7%. It also can be seen on the table that the share of the top 10% exceeds that of the highest 10% in a set of socialist states by 72%; the share received by the lowest 40% in the socialist states is 40% greater than in the U.S. client states. These figures probably understate the real differences because of the greater volume of government provided services, fairly equally distributed, in the socialist states. But whatever the limits of the comparison, it highlights the enormous inequalities in the NSSs, which have been *growing* since World War II. South Korea is one of the exceptions to conditions that are quite widely the rule in the Latin American NSSs. That exception, as with Taiwan also, is based in considerable part on the fact that external forces—war, invasion, the decimation of a traditional landed elite—led to a major and radical land reform.[34] The contrast between the Taiwanese and Korean experience and that in the general run of NSSs, points up the fact that initial conditions of great inequality are likely to be reinforced by growth that is not preceded by serious reform; that an equality and human needs objective has to be sought directly and is not likely to be met as a spinoff of other objectives. In the words of David Morawetz, "it simply may not be possible to 'grow first and redistribute later.' Rather, it may be necessary to tackle asset redistribution as a first priority by whatever means are at hand."[35] With the NSS, however, we are confronted with a system designed to protect and enlarge privileges by force. The result has been an increase in inequality from an already high level.

A second negative welfare effect of the NSS follows from its breaking up and immobilizing the self-help and protective organizations of the majority and its exclusion of the majority from political participation. Atomization and powerlessness

Table 3-1

Income Size, Growth and Distribution for Four Socialist and Six U.S. Client States in the 1970s

	Per Capita Real Income ($, 1979)	Growth in Real Income (annual average % per capita, 1960-1979)	Percentage of Income Going to:		
			Top 10%	Top 20%	Bottom 40%
China	260	2.7	22.5	39.3	18.4
Cuba	1,410	4.4	19.9	35.0	20.3
Roumania	1,900	9.2	NA[1]	NA	NA
Yugoslavia	2,430	5.4	22.9	38.7	18.7
Brazil	1,780	4.8	45.0	61.3	9.3
Chile	1,690	1.2	40.4[2]	51.4	13.4
Guatemala	1,020	2.9	30.0 (top 5%)	58.0	4.8 (bottom 30%)
Indonesia	370	4.7	34.0	49.4	14.4
Philippines	600	2.6	38.8	53.3	14.7
South Korea	1,480	7.1	27.5	45.3	16.9
Average for Socialist States	1,500	5.4	21.8	37.7	19.1
Average of U.S. Clients	1,157	3.9	37.5[3]	53.1[3]	13.7[3]

Sources: Income sizes and growth from World Bank, *World Development Report, 1981.* Income distribution figures as follows: for Yugoslavia (1978), Indonesia (1976), and South Korea (1973), from *World Development Report, 1981*; for China, World Bank, *China: Socialist Economic Development, Main Report*, June 1, 1981, p. 64; for Cuba (1973), Claes Brundenius, "Measuring Income Distribution in Pre- and Post-Revolutionary Cuba," *Cuban Studies*, July 1979, p. 43; for Brazil (1975), *Indicadores Sociais Relatario 1979*, Secretaria de Planejamenta da Presidencia da Republica, Fundacao Instituto Brasileiro de Geografia e Estatistics, p. 207; for the Philippines (1975), *Philippines Yearbook, 1979*, National Economic Development Authority and National Census and Statistics Office, p. 593; for Guatemala, the estimates are those of CEPAL for 1978, provided by private correspondence; Chile, computed from the World Bank's 1968 data, adjusted by a tabulation of the change in consumption expenditures by income size class, 1969-1970 to 1978, in Cristina Hurtado Beca, "Ocupacion, salario y consumo de los trabajadores," in *Chile-America*, Oct.-Dec. 1981, Table 3, p. 41.

[1] While an income distribution breakdown for Roumania is not available, structural similarities suggest that it should be fairly close to that of Yugoslavia. In contrast with the NSSs, also, the distribution trend has been toward greater equality. See World Bank, *Roumania*, 1979, pp. 180-181.

[2] Based on an assumed proportionality between the top 10% and top 20% in 1968 and 1978; probably an underestimate of the 1978 value.

[3] Guatemala is included in the income distribution averages only for the percentage going to the top 20%; comparable figures for the top 10% and the bottom 40% were not available.

bring anxiety and insecurity, a reduction of welfare built into the development model.[36] This political immobilization of the masses serves primarily, of course, to allow for their more efficient spoliation by weakening their bargaining power in private markets and by reducing their leverage in government decision-making processes. I have already mentioned the Sao Paulo study and its findings on the dehumanization of that city under NSS conditions. Peter Hakim and Giorgio Solimano have shown that even in Chile between 1930 and 1970, while under a democratic order, and where a social welfare apparatus was exceptionally well developed for a Third World country, inequalities still widened and the prevalence of malnutrition, affecting principally the poorest 30-40% of the population, did not diminish significantly over 40 years of economic growth.[37] The better organized elements of society were able to capture a disproportionate share of economic gains, because of policy biases toward the politically powerful and a lack of institutional outreach to the bottom 30-40%. Note that this result was obtained in a democratic order, with fairly strong unions and with some modest organizational rights of the rural masses just making their appearance in the 1960s, and before the coming of the counterrevolutionary violence of the NSS. During the brief and troubled three years of Allende rule, when a more dedicated effort was made to reach downward toward the nutritionally deprived, infant mortality rates dropped by 18%, deaths of babies from respiratory diseases fell 30%, and the incidence of malnutrition among children declined by 17%.[38]

The impact of Allende on these basic needs variables encapsulates the great untold and scandalous truth of western priorities and the meaning and significance of the NSS. At the heart of any appraisal of the NSS development model must be recognition of its failure to address seriously the basic needs deficiencies of the majority. In Third World countries the majority have long suffered from chronic malnutrition, high rates of infant mortality, unemployment, and illiteracy, and high incidence of serious diseases like TB, gastroenteritis and malaria that are readily curable with some modest national resource commitment. Alleviation of these deficiencies is a necessary precondition for human happiness and welfare, and any system that leaves large numbers chronically hungry and ill, while increases in national output are drained into more numerous and sophisticated consumer goods for a small elite is a sick system. It is a testimony to the dominance of interest over morals, and in the same moral category as the centuries-long use and toleration of human slavery, that this kind of degeneracy is an integral feature of a system (the National Security State) sponsored and protected by the west.

In the classic words of the head-of-state of Brazil, General Emilio Medici, in 1971, "The economy is doing fine, but the people aren't."[39] "The people" do not do well because they are not *intended* to do well. Kept from effective organization and political participation, the government never manages to get around to "the people" in its tax-expenditure decisions. Thus, in 1980, a decade after General Medici's regretful statement about the economy versus the people, another General-President, visiting the poverty stricken Northeast, suffering widespread hunger in a third year of drought, responded irritably to questions about government plans to do something for that area. It turns out that the government has no plans as yet; that after 16 years of a "miracle" there are still no resources available for this kind of thing. "We have no resources. In 10 or 15 years we might have. Who knows?"[40]

In NSS budgets, military expenditures tend to exceed those for both education and public health, despite the absence in most cases of any *external* security threat and despite the huge deficits in education and health that would press for solution if human needs were given any serious weight. Thus a sample of 10 NSSs in 1978, with the data probably understating military-related expenditures, shows that for seven of the ten states military outlays equalled or exceeded education expenditures; for nine out of ten military expenditures exceeded public health outlays. This is a dismal record even in comparison with the more militarized democracies of the west; and it suffers by contrast with socialist states. In only three of the eight socialist states of Eastern Europe did military outlays equal or exceed educational outlays; and in only in five of the eight did military expenditures exceed public health outlays.[41]

The Third World client states of the west contain vast pools of human misery that persist and even grow in absolute size. The International Labor Office (ILO) estimates that a huge 73 million people, or 27% of the population of Latin America, could be classified as "destitute" in the early 1970s, with destitute defined as having a per capita real income of $90 or under per year. An enormous 118 million Latins (43% of the total) were "seriously poor," meaning with a per capita income of under $180 per year. The ILO also claims that the absolute number of destitute people increased in Latin America during the growth decade 1963-1972.[42] These extremely low incomes for scores of millions are associated with high rates of unemployment (or underemployment), low levels of food intake and high malnutrition rates, poor health care services and high levels of preventable and curable diseases, poor educational facilities and high rates of illiteracy, and high mortality rates.

These abysmal conditions apply to the most advanced and rapidly growing NSSs. A World Bank study of Brazil, for example, cites surveys showing that in 1975, 68% of Brazilians consumed less than an internationally recognized minimum daily caloric requirement for normal physical activity, and that a huge 58% of Brazil's children suffered from malnutrition.[43] The World Bank also points out that health conditions in Brazil are "poor as compared to countries at similar per capita GNP levels."[44] Infant mortality rates actually rose in Sao Paulo for a number of years after the 1964 coup, as a consequence of "the public sector's inability to supply adequate sanitation and medical facilities to the rising number of persons residing in the peripheries of large cities."[45] The Bank notes the post-coup large decline in the "preventive-collective" share of the total health budget and "the progressive marginalization of the Ministry of Health, whose budgetary allocation was lower in real terms in 1970 and 1975 than it was in 1965."[46] In short, a politically "marginalized" majority has been given short shrift by the NSS in the use of public resources. A survey of Indonesian health conditions makes essentially the same point: extremely high child mortality rates from diarrheal and other disorders, 500,000 cases of infectious TB, and many other causes of death associated with poor sanitation and the absence of minimal medical care, could be easily remedied with a modest resource input and some leadership commitment—but these are not present. Public health expenditures per capita in Indonesia were $1.40 in 1977-1978.

> The major causes of death in Java are precisely those for which simple and cost-effective programs exist—or can be readily established: mass vaccinations; nutrition monitoring and early intervention; home treatment of common infections including TB, diarrhea, pneumonia; prenatal care and clean water supply. Unfortunately these programs have not yet been widely enough implemented nor adequately supported to achieve anything like their potential impact.[47]

An interesting contrast is provided by the World Bank itself, which in its *World Development Report 1981*, describes recent Chinese performance trends. The Bank notes that China has given prime weight to a non-elite objective, namely, "elimination of the worst aspects of poverty."[48] To achieve this the Chinese have redistributed property downward and have tried hard to provide and encourage the provision of basic social services. While doing this China did not sacrifice "growth"—from 1957-1979 the per capita real growth rate averaged between 2.5-3.0, and, as the Bank notes, this "is significantly above the average for other low-income developing countries," which was 1.6%. The Bank goes on to say the following:

> Nonetheless, China's most remarkable achievement during the past three decades has been to make low-income groups far better off in terms of basic needs than their counterparts in most other poor countries. They all have work; their food supply is guaranteed through a mixture of state rationing and collective self-insurance; most of their children are not only at school but are also being comparatively well taught; and the great majority have access to basic health care and family planning services. Life expectancy—whose dependence on many other economic variables makes it probably the best single indicator of the extent of real poverty in a country—is (at 64 years) outstandingly high for a country at China's per capita income level...[49]

The same points may be made as regards the Cuban economy after 1959, except that here growth during the first decade of socialism was negligible, for reasons of the exodus of a substantial fraction of the technical and managerial elite, the U.S. sponsored boycott, the secret war, and the inexperience and mismanagement of the socialist leaders. This was offset to an uncertain degree by substantial Soviet economic and military aid, and Cuban growth in the 1970s was respectable.[50] The results in terms of human needs performance even in the troubled 1960s have been striking, and in stark contrast with the treatment of the poor in the Free World. As with China, the focus on the needs of the majority instead of those of the elite resulted in a mortality rate performance that quickly outclassed that of the U.S. clients. One recent authoritative account of Cuba notes that

> Life expectancy at birth for both sexes combined is about 72 years, just two years short of the current level in the United States. Infant mortality—the subject of much attention—was down to 19.4 per 1,000 live births by 1979, compared to 13 in the United States. These values have been attained by few other developing countries and are more favorable than those observed in some of the less advanced European countries.[51]

This occurred because "health facilities and personnel have increased substantially" and health services "have been distributed to provide virtually universal free and low-cost medical coverage across Cuba."[52] The long-standing contrast of rural neglect and urban affluence has been rectified to a great extent by significant investment in rural roadways, schools, health care facilities, water supplies and sanitation facilities. In health, there has been a reorientation "from cure to prevention," strong emphasis has been given to education in public health, and efforts have been made "toward eradicating disease vectors (e.g., mosquitos) and upgrading sanitary standards in previously neglected rural and urban areas."[53] Education has been given high priority and the high illiteracy of the rural areas (35.3% in Oriente in 1953) has been virtually eliminated; 99% of Cuban children between 6-12 were enrolled in schools by 1976. Open unemployment, which in the late Batista years was 10% even in the harvest seasons, 23% in

Table 3-2

Human Needs Performance of Four Socialist and Six U.S. Client States in the 1970s

	1	2	3	4	5	6
	Life Expectancy at Birth (in years, 1979)	Mortality Rate, Infants 0-1 (per 1000 live births, 1978)	Mortality Rate, Children 1-4 (per 1000 in age class, 1979)	Health Outlays/ GNP, %, 1978 govt. (govt. & private)	Adult Literacy Rate (%, 1976)	Education Outlays/ GNP, %, 1978 govt. (govt. & private)
China	64	56	NA[1]	2.6 (NA)[1]	66	6.5(NA)
Cuba	72	25	2	5.1 (NA)	96	10.1 (NA)
Roumania	71	31	1	4.0 (NA)	98	5.9 (NA)
Yugoslavia	70	34	2	4.2 (NA)	85	5.7 (NA)
Brazil	63	92	8	1.7 (NA)	76	3.5 (NA)
Chile	67	55	6	0.8 (NA)	88	1.4 (NA)
Guatemala	59	81	13	0.8 (NA)	47	1.5 (NA)
Indonesia	53	120	14	1.4 (NA)	62	1.7 (NA)
Philippines	62	65	6	0.8 (NA)	88	2.2 (3.5)
South Korea	63	37	5	0.3 (4.7)	93	2.8 (5.6)
Socialist Average	69.3	36.5	1.7	4.0 (NA)	86.3	7.0 (NA)
U.S. Client Average	61.2	75.0	8.7	1.0 (NA)[2]	75.7	2.2 (NA)[2]

Sources: See footnote 56.

[1]NA = not available

[2]Averages not computed where data available for less than half the sample.

[3]Based on the 3-degree Gomez system relating actual to expected body weight; seriously malnourished means falling into the 2nd or 3rd degree class of weight deficiency.

	7		8	9	10	11	12
Unemployment and Underemployment Rates							
7a Open Unemploy't (% actively looking for work)	7b Underemploy't (% who would like more work + % in extremely unproductive work by default)	7c Totals (7a + 7b)	Child Malnutrition: Problem Slight-1 Moderate-2 Severe-3 (% malnourished; % seriously malnourished)[3]	Protein Supply (grams per capita, 1972-1974)	Death Rates TB (per 100,000 deaths, 1975-1978)	Death Rates Gastro-enteritis (per 100,000 deaths, 1975-1978)	Physicians per 100,000 population (1975-1978)
Under 1	NA but low	1 +	2 (NA)	62.8	NA	NA	4.0
2-3	NA but low	2-3 +	1 (NA)	70.4	2.3	6.6	9.0
Under 1	NA but low	1 +	1 (NA)	96.7	3.9	3.0	13.3
Under .5	About 12.5	13	1 (NA)	94.5	7.7	5.9	12.6
6-7	About 25-26	32	3 (58; 21)	63.4	NA	NA	6.1
13.5	12.5 +	26 +	NA	73.9	15.9	17.8	4.5
13	18	31	3 (72; 32)	52.8	10.6	143.5	2.2
2.3	32 +	34.3	3 (37; 17)	42.3	43.1	28.7	0.6
2	18-23	20-25	3 (NA; 31)	46.6	67.2	35.5	3.2
4.1	NA but low	4.1 +	1 or 2 (NA)	73.7	NA	NA	5.0
under 1.2	NA	NA	1.25 (NA)	81.1	4.6	5.2	9.7
6.9	NA	NA	2.6 (56; 25)	58.8	34.2	56.4	3.6

the slack periods, has been greatly reduced by a deliberate policy of full employment. [54] The great reduction of income inequalities and the strict rationing of food has resulted in a virtual elimination of hunger and malnutrition,[55] although choices have been sharply reduced and food conditions are austere.

In short, although it is rarely discussed in the Free Press, the most important fact about the Cuban revolution and its impact on the Cuban people is that the basic needs of a formerly ignored and subjugated majority were quickly met, despite many unfavorable conditions (including, without doubt, internal failures as well as the effects of U.S. hostility and the costs of the revolutionary process itself).

A final and broader comparison is provided in Table 3-2, which places side-by-side data on the human needs performance of four socialist states and six U.S. "authoritarian" clients. These countries cover a fairly wide range of income levels and "special factors" (historic, geographic), but the great superiority in human needs provision in the socialist states is strikingly evident. This is true even if we confine the comparison to China, which has the lowest per capita income of the 10 countries, and Cuba, which is in the mid-range of income levels. Note that the data on life expectancy at birth, which the World Bank calls "the best single indicator of the extent of real poverty," shows China outperforming all of the U.S. clients except Chile (where the effect of the 1973 coup may soon remove it from the "exception" class), and the overall difference between the two sets is very clear. The difference in rates of child mortality and death rates from curable diseases like TB and gastroenteritis is also spectacular. This reflects, in part, the varying level of attention given to the medical needs of the majority, displayed in the supply of physicians (col.12) and health outlays as a percentage of GNP (col.4). The health outlays shown here suffer from the absence of data on private health expenditures, which are relatively important in the U.S. client states. But in the really poor countries, private health care is of negligible importance to the great majority of the population—with the result that in a country like the Philippines, as is pointed out in a World Bank report on that country, "the task of providing health services to the majority has therefore fallen upon the Department of Health."[57] The differences in the national commitment to the health of the majority in China and Cuba, in contrast with the U.S. clients, is evident from this data. The variation in nutritional conditions is also highly significant. Column 9 shows the protein supply per capita adjusted for the export and import of food—adjusting, therefore, for the fact that countries like Brazil and Guatemala export a huge quantity of agribusiness outputs geared to external markets, while large numbers at home are hungry. It can be seen that the protein supply per capita in China exceeds that available in richer countries like Guatemala, Indonesia and the Philippines and equals the level of the much more affluent Brazil (and this does not take into account the greater equality of income and food distribution in China). Column 8 translates the facts on income distribution (Table 3-1), unemployment rates (discussed below) and national priorities into the ugly reality of child malnutrition, which is of serious proportions in four of the six U.S. client states (which in turn contributes to the high child mortality shown in columns 2 and 3).

The unemployment rates shown on column 7 are rough, but probably give reasonable order of magnitude values and differences. There is little debate over open unemployment rates, which are shown here to be significantly higher in the U.S. client states than in the four socialist states. *Under*employment levels are harder to assess, involving judgmental and definitional niceties as to who really wants to work and the adequacy and quality of the work performed by those nominally employed. My own examination of the data (and of the debates as to its interpretation) yields the column 7 estimates, which indicate that the reserve army of underemployed in the U.S. client states is huge—far larger than in the socialist states.[58] There are several reasons why this is the case. First, as we have seen, the welfare of the majority is not an objective of the leadership of the NSSs, and, correspondingly, full employment is not a goal of this leadership (as it quite explicitly is in the socialist states and to a lesser degree in the social democracies of the industrialized west). Everett Martin, writing in the *Wall Street Journal*, mentions in passing that "National unemployment statistics aren't kept" in Brazil,[59] not stopping to reflect on the possible policy significance of a NSS disinterest in this information.[60] Second, the NSS is designed to keep wages low to the advantage of the joint venture partners, and a large reserve army of unemployed serves this interest well. As one protest document from Brazil observes,

> The truth is that in order to concentrate the wealth in a few hands it is not enough to lower wages. It is necessary, beyond this, to maintain a large sector of the population in such conditions that when workers do get a job they will accept it at any price; and when they are jobless they constitute a reserve pool which the employers take advantage of to ensure that the workers fight among themselves for the possibility of a job. Thus there is a large sector of the population in the big cities who will never be employed unless in part-time jobs as odd-jobmen, street peddlers and car-watchers, without any security.[61]

Third, as profit interests call for improved efficiency, in a system where no weight is given to the externalities of technological unemployment, dispossession and landlessness, a great deal of unemployment may be generated through efficiency enhancing processes. In a democratic system, or in a non-democratic system where the interests of the majority were somehow given major weight, labor-intensive technologies would be stressed if there was an unemployment problem, and trade-offs between improved efficiency and the effects of technological change on the peasantry and working class would be evaluated carefully, with any bias leaning toward basic human needs provisions. If the peasants also tend to produce locally consumed foods, whereas the "efficient" agribusiness firms produce for export only, this would be a factor favoring peasant farming. In Brazil and Indonesia, no such calculus of human externalities is made—dispossession is encouraged by positive subsidization of labor-saving machinery and special tax credits are given for exports that displace indigenous food. In Brazil, analysts harp on the "tragic contradiction, in which government economic favors multiply herds of cattle and enlarge plantations, the small laborer sees his family's food supply diminishing."[62] In Java, to give a more specific illustration,

Village makers of bricks, buckets, baskets, rope, soap, shoes and soft drinks have been put out of business by modern factories, many foreign-controlled, that use capital intensive, labor-saving techniques designed to deal with high labor costs in the West...Recently, foreign companies have been competing to sell cultivating machinery to wealthy Javanese farmers and contractors. In the West Javanese village of Tukdana, an agricultural economist named Rudolf Sinaga found five Japanese-built power tillers in operation. Each of them, he calculated, eliminated over 2,000 days of work per year for village laborers, and diverted $2,650 to the owner, dealer and manufacturer. The government subsidizes the machines with easy credit and low import duties...[This same article notes that World Bank loans push Indonesia in the same direction, as most of the money must be spent overseas.] The bank conceded in a recent report that the rules often resulted in an "import bias" against local contractors. In other words, projects that might have used a lot of laborers sometimes use a lot of bulldozers instead.[63]

Cuba and China both prove that, even with a great deal of botching, mass human misery can be alleviated in poor societies, the basic human requirements of subsistence and minimal health care can be met, *where the leaders have some interest in serving the majority.* As we have seen, this interest *conflicts* with the ends of both the NSS and the elites of the west in their dealings with the Third World. This involves the west in hypocrisies and intellectual somersaults of staggering dimension, as it must reconcile its tradition and rhetoric of belief in democracy, individualism and the dignity of each human being with de facto support of a system—the National Security State—which represents the antithesis of each of these values.

(3) *Economic rationale.* That a totalitarian free enterprise system with an economy open to multinational development is likely to yield desirable results in the long run is based on dubious economic premises. It should be noted initially, however, that real world applications of the development model are always compromised by real world facts, like pervasive corruption. In

the description of the model, its spokesmen never discuss the consequences of a situation where, e.g., Indonesian generals and their bureaucratic apparatus might be stealing as much as 30% of the national income,[64] and misinvesting large sums in technological wonders (communications satellites) that meet their military-intelligence biases or that U.S. companies are having trouble selling (nuclear reactors).[65] Nor would the managers of the NSSs, in the ideal model, disregard the human and environmental externalities of agribusiness dispossession of 5 million peasants and the stripping of a hundred million acres of forest cover. The reality of "supply side economics with machine guns," however, is a virtually complete disregard of these externalities—it is "cost-benefit analysis" with zero weight to social costs. The reality adds further weight to the view affirmed here—that the "models" are an ideological cover for local elite and multinational looting of huge and catastrophic dimensions. It also means that the GNP growth figures for the NSSs are fraudulent—that if the external costs being imposed on the politically expropriated were subtracted, as they should be according to orthodox principles, the growth rate of a Brazil would be lower, maybe even negative.

The applied NSS development model also attaches virtually zero value to the preservation of indigenous cultures, traditional modes of work, and community structures and relationships. These may be swept away by business interests whenever large profits beckon. I noted earlier the dishonesty of Kirkpatrick's argument that the NSS preserves traditional ways and modes of work: she transforms the preservation of traditional hierarchical and exploitative relationships, which the NSS surely does preserve, into traditional "ways" in general—but it is precisely the combination of hierarchy imposed by machine guns, plus greater capital mobility, that has allowed the ruthless disruption of the traditional ways of the large numbers who "stand in the way of progress." Agricultural economist Ernest Feder claimed a decade back that this "silent march of the poor," a continuous milling around of poor farm people in search of jobs or land, was already growing by several million per year and constituted "the greatest migratory movement in all history."[66] These rural landless are the *internal* refugees of the NSSs, and they account for a large (and neglected) fraction of world refugee totals. In sum, what the NSS does is allow radical structural transformations and multinational penetration to proceed rapidly and without democratic consent, with appropriate payoffs to the local enforcers to stifle the protests of the victims.

The traditional apologetics for development under Free World auspices, as expounded by W.W. Rostow and assorted other developmentalists of the Chicago School, World Bank, etc., make a number of extremely dubious economic assumptions to arrive at benign conclusions.[67] One is that there is a high degree of competition and capital and labor mobility in Third World countries. If, however, resources do not move easily and monopoly power is widespread, prices do not adjust quickly or at all and many orthodox conclusions do not follow. The opening up of Argentina, Brazil and Chile to a heavy influx of foreign capital decimated small and medium-sized local manufacturing and other businesses.[68] This was partly a result of the marketing prowess, technical resources and better credit access of large foreign firms. These firms also specialize in catering to the expanding elite markets for style goods, whereas many local producers serve a limited and often contracting mass market for indigenous goods. Insofar as the local firms lose out because of differential credit access, or the sophisticated marketing techniques applied by foreign companies, or the contraction of the local market resulting from NSS tight money and trickling-up income distribution policies, denationalization can hardly be said to reflect efficiency factors. Furthermore, when local producers are pushed out of the market, other opportunities do not exist for most of them in the NSS economic environment—nor are there any opportunities for the millions of peasants dispossessed by large soybean and cattle raising firms. A large proportion of the small producers, their employees and the rural dispossessed simply join a growing reserve army of unemployed and marginalized. Argentine industrial employment fell by 30% between 1976 and 1980, while total industrial output was increasing by only 5%. In Chile, employment in the material goods sector fell by 21% from 1970-1978.[69] In Brazil, the number of peasants dispossessed over the past two decades has been estimated by Church sources as in excess of 7 million.[70] The number of landless in the Mexican countryside is estimated to have increased from 1.5 million in

1950 to some 14 million by the mid-1970s. These human resources were not reabsorbed in an "efficient" market economy— GNP, unadjusted for externalities, increased on a smaller human base.

A second assumption of the development model is that the scale, technology and marketing advantages of large foreign firms will gradually be overcome; that they will not constitute a permanent barrier to the development of viable domestic firms and competitive new industries. These foreign advantages presumably will yield to the pressures of competition, domestic shakeouts and growth in firm size, the general accumulation and import of know-how, and technical adaptations to the particular factor and price complex of the Third World. In reality, however, the advantages of large foreign firms have not been overcome. Scale economies keep extending in a technologically dynamic world, and countries without a strong technological base seem to be at a permanent disadvantage. Third World manufacturers suffer from small local markets, kept small by NSS distributive policies, and multinational penetration has further limited the market shares of local firms. With only a few exceptions, the larger foreign markets have not been effectively penetrated by Third World manufacturers for reasons of protection and their continuing scale, marketing and technological disadvantages.[71] Development model rhetoric assumes that with an influx of foreign capital, partly enforced by requirements that goods sold locally be produced locally, there would come an inflow of technological know-how and, eventually, technological autonomy. But not only have foreign companies kept their technological base at home, technology apparently develops only in a system of vertical and horizontal supply linkages that interact with and stimulate one another; linkages which do not easily emerge in a dependent economy.[72] The result is that instead of the balance of payments suffering from large imports of *final* goods from abroad, the balance of payments of Third World countries is kept in troubled condition through another route—greater reliance on imported intermediate goods and technical know-how.[73]

A third assumption of traditional Free World "takeoff" models is that savings rates would be raised during the growth process to levels that would permit the high rates of investment needed for high rates of output growth. This would be supplemented by foreign capital inflows, which would also elevate investment and growth rates. There has been some validation of this assumption, aided by the depressed wages maintained under NSS conditions. But several qualifications have proved to be important: (1) Savings and investment have been kept lower than otherwise by the corruption drain. (2) They have been kept lower by the need for military and other "security" outlays required to keep the populace under control and to meet the interest group demands of the enforcers. (3) Rampant consumerism on the part of NSS elites has limited the growth of saving and has also elicited high levels of infrastructure investment in things like roads and gas stations to service an elite automobile culture, in lieu of productive investment. (4) Offsetting the inflows of foreign capital are outflows of savings and profits in search of safe havens and profitable investment abroad.

Thus in Argentina, Brazil and Chile the gross domestic savings rates *fell* during the NSS years, and in Argentina and Chile the level of gross domestic private investment also fell and stayed below the pre-coup levels. What flourished in Brazil during the miracle years were motor car and consumer durable goods production, government public utilities and public investment projects, and agribusiness. The miracle has worn thin with changed energy and financial market conditions, and Brazil has solved none of its enormous human problems while building up the world's largest foreign debt. In Argentina, export agriculture and finance have been the only growth sectors; while in Chile, financial, marketing and import activities have surged in importance while the material goods sectors have suffered an absolute as well as relative decline. The Argentinian economy is more concentrated, dependent and fragile than it was before the arrival of the NSS. The Chilean economy has similar disabilities, made somewhat more severe by the absolute contraction of the industrial base.[74]

The integration of Third World economies into world markets under NSS conditions has led to a dependent and unbalanced growth process. The NSSs continue to attract investment from abroad, most heavily in mining, agriculture, agribusiness service activities and finance, leaving their economies still vulnerable to fluctuations in raw materials prices and hostage to balance of payments crises and the power of external lenders. The growth of an export agriculture sector, which has generally been subsidized in the NSS, has been associated with a reduction in agricultural production for domestic use, an increased importation of basic good staples, and more widespread hunger.[75] Dependency has persisted with foreign traders and private and public lenders still exercising great power in shaping political structures and social and economic policies. Development has been concentrated heavily in areas still subject to strong international competition and vulnerable to shifts in tastes and technological substitution. And these economies have not developed the internal linkages and balance that make for technological autonomy.

Most important, this dependent growth has been accomplished at enormous human cost, and has been accompanied by an increase in inequalities and the enlargement of human misery and unmet social obligations to a depressed majority.

Terror as an Integral Feature of the National Security State

It cannot be too strongly emphasized that terror is a built-in feature of the NSS, firmly grounded in its ends and in the objective situation with which it was designed to cope. As already indicated, its objectives are those of a small elite minority, who need and use the NSS to implement a system of permanent class warfare. The economic model of Third World development favored by the west does not say "use terror," but the policies that are favored, which would encourage foreign investment and keep wages and welfare outlays under close control, could often not be put into place without it. Privilege cannot be maintained and enlarged from already high levels if "the people" are allowed to organize, vote, and exercise any substantial power. As was pointed out by Martinez de Hoz, the top financial minister of the Argentine military government, in arguing for his 1976-1977 economic plan, "We enjoy the economic stability that the Armed Forces guarantee us. This plan can be fulfilled despite its lack of popular support. It has sufficient political support...that provided by the Armed Forces."[76]

With undeviating regularity, the imposition of a NSS is accompanied by a rapid dismantling, or other mode of neutralization—frequently by killing, imprisoning or exiling the leadership—of working class and peasant organizations, like unions, cooperatives, leagues, and political groupings. The heart of NSS economics is wage control, and the introduction of each NSS has been followed by a sharp fall in real wages and dramatic increase in the rate of unemployment. This is one of those special Freedoms brought by machine guns, which has its own Orwellian-Chicago School designation in the NSS: Thus in explaining the shooting of a trade union leader speaking in favor of a strike, an Argentine army communique of 1977 stated that "the legal forces acted in accordance with orders designed to guarantee freedom of employment."[77] In addition to Freedom of Employment there is also a rapid transformation of the government budget, enlarging "security" expenditures, tax incentives and infrastructure investments that serve the joint venture partners, and a contraction of public outlays for the majority. This could not be accomplished without force and violence.

A primary characteristic of the NSS is, therefore, exceptional numbers, activities, power and rewards of the military and police establishments. The Brazilian military tripled its real budgetary allocations in the decade following the coup of 1964, and the Brazilian generals live well, with butlers, chalets, expense accounts, and substantial returns from their public salaries and private business participations.[78] In Uruguay, the coming of the NSS resulted in a fall in educational outlays from 21% of the national budget in the early 1960s to little more than 13% in 1980. Military expenditures jumped sharply to over half the national budget, and by 1980 one of every 30 citizens of Montevideo was employed in the National Security apparatus.[79]

With the coming into power of forces that explicitly set aside the rule of law in favor of a "state of siege," the potential for serious terror is high. The military-security presence is felt by the population of the NSSs in a pervasive use of informers and by the application of violence that has gone beyond the traditional brutalities of Latin America in both scope and quality. It varies partly in accordance with the level of violence needed for the proper degree of intimidation. But this level is often exceeded by the fanaticism and self-interested bureaucratic desires of the newly dominant "security" forces. In Chile, where class conflict was sharp, and ideological frenzy in the military was deliberately intensified by extreme right factions and the CIA,[80] exceptional violence was unleashed. In Argentina and Uruguay, also, fanaticism and self-interest give NSS violence special momentum. The security forces of the NSSs are given a dirty job, and it frequently grows on them.

In performing their function of returning the majority to a state of apathy, and keeping them there, it is possible that once the leadership of popular organizations is decimated and an environment of fear and hopelessness is created through years of direct violence, that tacit threats alone will suffice. If, however, the very logic of the system is to depress the masses—politically and economically—to allow unconstrained pursuit of elite benefits, to protect an increasing income gap, and to keep costs down in a competitive world, permanent immiseration and permanent repression may be required. This would seem to be implicit in a development model which "creates a revolution that did not previously exist;"[81] that is, which has a special capacity to generate misery and protest which will necessitate repression. Furthermore, where the NSS managers are ideologically conditioned to regard all dissent, protests and lower class (majority) organizational efforts as Communist subversion, a self-perpetuating mechanism of permanent terror is built-in.

I cannot do any justice here to the scope and quality of intimidation under NSS conditions, which quickly overwhelms the reader by the horror of the multitudinous details of pain or the incomprehensibility of the aggregates of numbers tortured, killed and frightened into silence.[82] It is important to understand that the NSS unleashed more sophisticated forms of violence, beyond traditional bloodbaths and intimidation, based on more modern technologies and theories and ideologies of counterinsurgency and Communist omnipresence and total evil, that made for uglier and more ruthless forms of terrorization.

Human torture, for example, only came into widespread and *institutionalized* use as the NSSs emerged and matured in the 1960s and 1970s. By institutionalized I mean employed as standard operating procedure in multiple detention centers (as many as 60 in Argentina, 33 in Colombia), applicable to hundreds of detainees, and used with the approval and intent of the highest authorities. By my calculation, 14 countries in Latin America and the Caribbean, as well as a dozen other countries in the U.S. sphere of influence, were using torture as a mode of governance, on an institutionalized and administrative basis, in the early 1970s.[83] The extent of concentration of this violence in the NSSs of Latin America is evidenced by the fact that 80% of Amnesty International's "urgent cases" of torture by the mid-1970s were coming out of these states.[84] As torture spread through the NSS system a fairly standardized core of electronic and medical technology was used that allowed the victims to be carried to a more severe state of pain and dehumanization just short of death. The fearfulness of the violence imposed on the tortured thousands in the NSSs has been documented extensively, although, as discussed in Chapter 4, this evidence has been muted by the Free Press.

I give here only the following brief summary of processes in Chile and one witness's statement of torture procedures in Argentina. According to AI's *Report on Torture*, in Chile:

> The most common forms of physical torture have been prolonged beating (with truncheons, fists or bags of moist material, electricity to all parts of the body, and burning with cigarettes or acid. Such physical tortures have been accompanied by the deprivation of food, drink and sleep. More primitive and brutal methods have continued to be used. On 19 December one prisoner was found dead, his testicles burned off. He had also been subjected to intensive beating and electricity. One day later another prisoner who died from torture has the marks of severe burns on the genital organs.[85]

A long term resident of Argentina's detention centers gives the following description of his experiences:

> As regards physical torture, we were all treated alike, the only differences being in intensity and duration. Naked, we were bound hand and foot with thick chains or straps to a metal table. Then an earthing cable was attached to one of our toes and torture began.

For the first hour they would apply the "picana" (cattle prod) to us, without asking any questions. The purpose of this was, as they put it, "to soften you up, and so that we'll understand one another." They went on like this for hours. They applied it to the head, armpits, sexual organs, anus, groin, mouth and all the sensitive parts of the body. From time to time they threw water over us or washed us, "to cool your body down so that you'll be sensitive again."

Between sessions of the "picana", they would use the "submarino", (holding our heads under water), hang us up by our feet, hit us on the sexual organs, beat us with chains, put salt on our wounds and use any other method that occurred to them. They would also apply 220-volt direct current to us, and we know that some-times—as in the case of Irma Necich—they used what they called the "piripipi", a type of noise torture.

There was no limit to the torture. It could last for one, two, five or ten days. Everything done under the super-vision of a doctor, who checked our blood-pressure and reflexes: "We're not going to let you die before time." That is exactly how it was, because when we were on the verge of death they would stop and let us be revived. The doctor injected serum and vitamins and when we had more or less recovered they began to torture us again.

Many of the prisoners could not endure this terrible treatment and fell into a coma. When this happened, they either left them to die or else "took them off to the military hospital." We never heard of any of these prisoners again.[86]

The numbers that have been subjected to torture in the NSSs is, of course, impossible to determine with even approximate accuracy, and it varies in severity. Detainees have been subjected to torture ranging from brief and slight to a long and intense use that is continued till death. Frequently torture has been applied automatically to virtually all political prisoners (as in Argentina and Chile immediately after their military coups), but this is not always the case. AI describes it as used in "the majority of interrogations" in post-1964 Brazil;[87] Zelmar Michelini estimated that of 40,000 political prisoners in Uruguay up to 1974, only 5000 were tortured (although he may have meant tortured severely).[88] A more recent witness, Victor LaBorda Baffico, a defecting military officer, reported in 1981 that *everyone* detained in Uruguay regardless of age, sex, or crime is routinely tortured.[89] (Baffico, the fourth such defector-witness from Uruguay in the last year or two, has not yet attracted the attention of the Free Press, for reasons explained in the next chapter.)

The numbers imprisoned for political reasons in the NSSs of Latin America, if we include all who are picked up and taken to police stations for "questioning," probably greatly exceeded a million for the period 1960-1980. In Sao Paulo, Brazil, 28,000 were picked up for questioning as possible subversives in the year 1977 alone.[90] Over 100,000 were detained for political reasons in Chile during the post-coup period of 1973-1976. Of these, a large fraction were killed (over 20,000), and a still larger fraction were subjected to torture.[91] Given the high rates of torture of political prisoners in the larger states like Brazil, Argentina and Chile, the numbers tortured in the NSSs, 1960-1980, run into the hundreds of thousands.

This is terrorism in a form that retail terrorists cannot duplicate.[92] Applicable as a mode of governance in more than a dozen NSSs, it is an important part of a *real* terror network that the Free Press pretends does not exist.

The "death squad" has been an equally noteworthy aspect of NSS terror, complementing the seizure, torture and killing activities by the regular police, army and security forces. As can be seen on Table 3-3, death squads came into existence in ten separate states of Latin America during the past two decades. Usually they are composed of regular military, police and intelligence personnel working in "off-duty" functions. According to AI, in Argentina:

> Each sector of the armed forces has established a small operational force for this specific purpose [the eradication of "subversion"]. To carry out the kidnappings, they use stolen vehicles; to evade detection they have false identity papers; and although they can act with

Table 3-3

The Origin and Spread of the Death Squad in Latin America*

Country	Death Squad Organization	U.S. Role in Introduction of Responsible Government	U.S. Police Training	Numbers of U.S.-Trained Military Personnel 1950-1980	U.S. Military Aid 1946-1979 ($ million)
Argentina	1973[1]	Acquiescent	Extensive	4,017	263.6
Bolivia	Late 1970's	"	"	4,896	80.7
Brazil	1964	Major	"	8,659	640.0
Chile	1973	"	"	6,883	217.0
Dominican Republic	1965	"	"	4,269	43.0
El Salvador	1963-66[2]	Acquiescent[3]	"	2,097	5.0
Guatemala	1966-67	Major	"	3,334	41.5
Mexico	Early 1970's	Not applicable (government of long standing)	"	1,003	0.1
Nicaragua	Early 1970's	Major	"	5,673	32.4
Uruguay	1968-70	Acquiescent	"	2,806	89.2

*This table is confined to countries in which semi-official death squads are well established—in still others there are unexplained political murders and disappearances of dissenters, and systematic torture. Sources for this compilation are: Amnesty International, *Report on Torture* (1974), *'Disappearances'* (1980), *Testimony on Secret Detention Camps in Argentina* (1980); *Guatemala, A Government Program of Political Murder* (1981), and other AI country reports on the relevant states; the books by Black, Langguth and Lernoux cited in the text and footnotes; Norman Gall "Slaughter in Guatemala" and "Santo Domingo: The Politics of Terror," *New York Review of Books*, May 20, 1971 and July 22, 1971; Argentine Information Service Committee, *Argentina Today, A Dossier on Repression and the Violation of Human Rights* (1976); Nacla, *El Salvador* (2 parts, March-April and July-August 1980); on Mexico, see releases of the Council on Hemispheric Affairs on Human Rights dated February 3, 1979 and June 8, 1981; AID, *Congressional Presentation, Fiscal Year 1982*, Annex III (3), Latin America and the Caribbean; Nacla, "The Pentagon's Proteges, U.S. Training Programs for Foreign Military Personnel," (Jan, 1976); Michael T. Klare and Cynthia Arnson, *Supplying Repression*, Institute for Policy Studies, 1981, p. 5.

[1]Death squads and systematic torture originated in the Eva Peron era of declining constitutional government—they increased sharply in importance after the military coup of March 1976.

[2]Orden, a para-military network of spies, informers and enforcers was founded by General Medano in the mid-1960s to combat "subversion." One of its functions is to "handle 'disappearances' of community leaders." Lernoux, *Cry of the People*, p. 72.

[3]On the Kennedy administration's support of the military government of Col. Rivera, and the 1972 U.S. support of massive election fraud and a still more repressive military regime (helped along by Nicaragua and Guatemala), see Nacla, "El Salvador—Why Revolution?," *Report on the Americas*, March-April 1980, pp. 13-17.

autonomy, they have to make daily reports to their superiors about the prisoners they have taken. At times these groups indulge, for personal gain, in kidnappings for ransom.[93]

In other NSSs, while the death squads are often official personnel working secretly, sometimes they are made up of former police or military personnel; or they may be mainly civilian paramilitary rightwing groups who kill people the NSS wants, or doesn't mind being, killed. In almost all cases the activities of death squads are under the direct supervision of the authorities in their political kidnapping and murder activities. In Central America, paramilitary groups of the extreme right are more common than in South America, but even here they are often organized by the official forces (as with Orden in El Salvador) and, "Despite protests to the contrary by the governments concerned, they operate with impunity, outside the law but fully integrated into the regular security network."[94]

The idea that the "death squads" are "out of control" is, of course, part of the NSS apologetics and part of the reason for the very existence of the death squad. Its separation from the regular forces allows systematic murder to be carried out for which the state may wish to deny knowledge and responsibility. A corollary is that its allies abroad who like the NSS, and their mass media parrots, will also be able to use "plausible denial" as a defense. It is not very plausible, but Jeane Kirkpatrick waxes indignant at the outrageous notion that the governments of the NSSs condone the nasty doings of the death squads![95]

The NSSs exterminate a great many dissident guerillas; i.e., a left "out of control." That rightwing killers out of control could not be similarly exterminated if they were felt detrimental seems unlikely. That they have emerged "out of control" so regularly is also remarkable. That they are composed of people who, either right now or in the past were "under control," that they kill the same kind of people as the official forces of the NSSs, that they operate in broad daylight and are never apprehended—all suggest a simpler hypothesis—that the death squads are under good control and do what the leaders of the NSSs want done. As indicated above, there is a great deal of evidence that they are usually quite definite parts of the organized military forces; where they are not, they are usually still under official control.

Death squad murders in Latin America have been a daily occurrence now for several decades. In the Dominican Republic, where the La Banda death squad was "openly tolerated and supported by the National Police" in the early 1970s, there was an average of one disappearance per day.[96] In Argentina, after the 1976 coup the daily average of disappearances was five or more for an extended period.[97] In Guatemala death squad murders averaged almost ten a day through the first half of the 1970s.[98] The total numbers kidnapped and murdered by NSS death squads over the past two decades is not known, and is somewhat ambiguous as the distinction between regular force / death squad abductions and murders is vague, possibly untenable. A sizable fraction of the "disappeared" have been victims of death squads, but many death squad victims have not disappeared. The estimate of numbers of disappeared in Latin America given at the First Congress of Relatives of the Disappeared, 90,000, is nevertheless a rough order of magnitude figure for death squad victims, comparable to estimates that can be built up from individual country values.

Important characteristics of death squad activities in Latin America, which bear on the nature and purposes of the NSS, have been their sadism and their tie-in with ordinary illegal activities like theft, kidnappings for ransom and the drug trade. They are serviced by thugs. In Argentina, Brazil, Chile, El Salvador and Guatemala death squads rarely just kill; they rape, torture and mutilate. AI mentions the fact that the security operations of Paraguay are "carried out by teams whose members include the mentally deficient and the sexually disturbed."[99] And fanaticism and pathology are evident throughout the NSS system in the cigarette burnings, amputations, and sexual violence and mutilations. AI notes, for example, that "It is invariably reported in the Guatemalan press that [death squad victims] show signs of having been tortured and mutilated before death."[100] Raids by death squads, and for that matter regular security forces, are very often looting expeditions in the NSSs, and there have been numerous cases of kidnappings quite plainly for pure ransom. Lernoux quotes the head of a large U.S. subsidiary in Buenos Aires, acquainted with a jeweler whose daughter was abducted while the "security forces" ransacked his apartment for money and jewels, who told Penny Lernoux that "stealing is officially approved as a means of encouraging these thugs."[101]

The thugs have a role to play in the NSS—they eliminate "subversives" and intimidate and create anxiety in the rest of the population, all potential subversives.

U.S. Sponsorship and Support of the System of National Security States

The establishment analysts of terrorism have strained hard to find ties and surrogates that would link the assorted retail terrorists of the left to the Soviet Union. Their job would have been so much easier if they had looked at the acres of terrorist diamonds in their own backyards! The linkages between the United States and the NSSs are clear and powerful—one can show interest and purpose on the part of the superpower, ideological harmony, and a flow of training and material aid that is both massive and purposeful. It is, once again, a testimonial to the power and patriotism of the Free Press that, not only is the terrorism of the NSSs underrated, but the role of the United States as the sponsor—the Godfather—of this real terror network is hidden from view. As I will show in Chapter 4, the United States is portrayed as an innocent bystander, occasionally making mistakes in its anxiety to protect the citizens of Latin America from the evils of Communism, but regretful of any excesses that may sometimes occur there. This amazing pretense is carried through despite the historical record of an openly announced role of Godfather dating back at least to 1823 (the Monroe Doctrine), the more or less steady interventionism since then, the remarkable degree of homogeneity within the NSSs, and the recent record of our role in sponsoring and managing the terror network.

In this section I will show that U.S. links to this terror network are not only very extensive but that this network is also in significant measure a product of U.S. interest, intent, initiatives, and material and moral support.

(1) *U.S. interest in the NSS.* It was shown earlier that while the Soviet Union had a strategic interest in alliance with some retail terrorists, its interest in many of them was unclear or implausible. There is no such ambiguity in U.S. interest in the NSS, although there are those who claim that any benefits rest on

a short view. In the short-run, however, nationalist-reformist-socialist movements in the Third World have long been perceived by the business political-military elite as "threatening."[102] Pressures from the lower classes in traditional inegalitarian societies in this era of nationalism, and with the spread of both democratic and socialist ideas, mean higher wages, higher business taxes, reduced access and privilege, and even more dire possibilities. It is clear why businessmen would so readily see merit in rightwing repression that would contain these threats. The U.S. military and political establishment also prefers highly reliable allies who escape the local tides of nationalism and reformism and look abroad for ideals and material support. These are the "friends," like Somoza and Stroessner, who are dependents precisely because they are denationalized looters.

As noted earlier, the real growth period of the NSS followed the triumph of Fidel Castro, which produced a huge, well-organized, well-financed counterrevolutionary effort by the United States that focused heavily on building up the Latin American military as a political counterweight to popular forces and "educating" it on its Free World responsibilities. One reliable form of evidence for U.S. interest in the NSS is the encouragement given, and the effusive warmth with which the U.S. elites (business, military and political) have greeted the establishment of virtually every NSS, and the national policy support which has quickly followed these shifts even when they have involved the overthrow of constitutional governments. David Rockefeller waxed positively ecstatic over the new Armed Forces regime of Argentina, which, in his view, really "understands the private enterprise system."[103] Lincoln Gordon's enthusiasm for the "totally democratic" military coup in Brazil in 1964, which he characterized as "the single most decisive victory for freedom in the mid-twentieth century,"[104] expressed well the attitude of U.S. business and officialdom to the emergence of another key NSS. An equally classic remark of business approval that greeted Marcos' establishment of "stability" in the Philippines in 1972 also throws light on U.S. interest in the NSS: "According to one U.S. oilman, Marcos says, 'We'll pass laws you need—just tell us what you want'."[105] With such leaders in place it is clear that important U.S. interests will be well served.

Another measure of U.S. interest in the NSS is the economic stake of U.S. business, which is large and has been growing by leaps and bounds over the past decade. U.S. merchandise exports to Latin America amounted to $38.8 billion in 1980, imports $37.5 billion—both totals larger than the comparable trade volumes with Japan. U.S. direct investment in Latin America grew from $12.2 billion in 1970 to $38.3 billion in 1980, with earnings from these direct investments rising from $1 billion to $4.6 billion. These investments have been highly profitable, with nominal rates of return in recent years averaging between 15 and 20 percent,[106] but with higher real rates, obscured by transfer pricing inflation (which allows profits to be hidden in the prices of the intermediate goods supplied to foreign subsidiaries by their parent firms).[107] The most notable recent development in the growing U.S. stake in the NSS has been the enormous rise in multinational bank lending and profitability, a response to the oil price increases, to the development strategies of the NSSs, and to banker perceptions of their "creditworthiness." Total U.S. cross-border bank claims on Latin American countries reached a staggering $77.3 billion in June 1981, a figure which does not include so-called "local currency" loans, where the funds lent out are obtained as deposits within the borrowing country.[108] Adding these in would push the U.S. bank loan total in Latin America to somewhere in the vicinity of $100 billion. And loan rates have been high. Under the tight money and overvalued currency conditions that have prevailed in the NSSs, banking has been a bonanza business, and the U.S. majors with a large presence in Latin America have made very large profits. Citibank, with 1979 assets in Brazil of $4.2 billion, is reputed to have been making more money in Brazil than in the United States in recent years. The special enthusiasm of the bankers for the NSS is understandable.

(2) *U.S. intent and the emergence of the NSS.* While the NSS meets the criterion of satisfying primary U.S. interests, it is conceivable that the United States still did nothing to bring the NSS into existence, but merely failed to oppose it. This is implausible given the tremendous relative power of the United States in the western hemisphere and its long record of willingness to intervene there to serve its perceived interests.[109] But positive

U.S. intent to foster the NSS can be shown more directly by both actions and words. There are two kinds of actions that are relevant. One is those of direct encouragement and participation in the establishment of NSSs, and supporting and protecting them once they are in place. The other comprises acts which are likely to lead eventually to the emergence of the NSS, such as deliberate strategies to build up the strength of military factions in the Third World and "educating" them on their political obligations to combat subversion—to be found in all popular movements. The *words* suggesting intent are those that explain why all these strategies and developments are desirable.

Concerning deeds, the wide-ranging U.S. complicity in the Brazilian coup of 1964 and the Chilean coup of 1973 were of outstanding importance. In both cases, U.S. efforts at subversion were of long duration, multidimensional, extensive at each level, and brazen. They included economic and political destabilization efforts, propaganda, and large scale funding of and conspiracy with Brazilian and Chilean politicians, journalists and editors, military and security personnel, intellectuals and labor leaders. The military establishments of both countries were encouraged to carry out the coups and the outcomes were greeted with great warmth and protectiveness by Washington. In the immediate wake of both the Brazilian and Chilean coups, U.S. personnel actually helped in the writing of White Papers justifying and explaining these constructive developments.[110]

These are key states and the intent of U.S. authorities to produce the resultant NSSs is extremely clear. In later sections of this chapter it will be shown that intervention has been not only extensive but unidirectional in its efforts to undermine any groupings or parties that threaten serious reform and to strengthen organized groups (including the military and police) that will protect the status quo. There are exceptions to this pattern, but they are of minor importance.[111] U.S. intervention has tended either to bring NSSs into existence directly, as in Brazil, Chile or Guatemala, or to create a balance of forces that made the NSS probable. When NSSs emerge without direct U.S. connivance, they are always acceptable, although in a minority of cases, where conservatively dominated constitutional governments have been overthrown in an especially clumsy manner, and/or the NSS leadership is notoriously venal or violent, under liberal administrations there may be a brief period of chastisement and curtailment of aid (often coupled with offsetting increases from international institutions and private banks). But as the NSS leaders have ties to the U.S. military-intelligence apparatus, rely on foreign capital, and are prepared to carry out NSS functions, acceptance and supportive relations gradually emerge. Stroessner, Somoza and Pinochet demonstrate that with the proper degree of deference and accommodation to foreign economic interests *there is no level of corruption or violence that would bring about rejection of a NSS by Washington.* Total withdrawals of support and participation in the overthrow of governments by violence have been confined almost exclusively to constitutional-reformist or radical governments.

The other set of *deeds* that reveal a U.S. intent to create the NSS is the greatly enlarged training and supply of the military and police establishments of U.S. clients and the deliberate attempt to cultivate personal relationships with them and to make them dependents. This was done with many accompanying statements that stressed the usefulness—the wisdom in our own interest—of an investment in building up, winning over, and "educating" these police and military forces. They were viewed as already conservative and anticommunist, and capable of being reinforced in the needed ideology and tied to us by training, personal linkages and arms. They would then serve as a force for "stability" and "nation-building" in ways consistent with our interests.

Following the triumph of Castro, and then increasingly during the Vietnam war buildup and escalation, the idea of preventive counterinsurgency took hold in U.S. political and military circles, and still greater stress was placed on the role of the police and military as agents of "internal stability." In appeals to Congress for money for military aid and training, U.S. leaders regularly put forward the claims that building up the Latin American military and police: (1) enhance the power of "a very strongly anticommunist force" in these societies;[112] (2) tightens personal as well as professional bonds between foreign police and military personnel and our own; (3) establishes a dependency relationship "for the equipment, training services and economic support they are unable to provide themselves," and which are important, therefore, "in terms of their continuing ties with the United States" and as an "important instrument of United States foreign policy."[113]

The explicit purpose of U.S. military training and supply programs was to provide what General Robert Porter called "a very modest insurance policy protecting our vast private investment in an area of tremendous trade and strategic value to our country."[114] The training programs were "aimed less at military expertise than...at the cultivation of internal political attitudes favorable to the United States."[115] They focused heavily on the menace of Castro, the evils and omnipresence of communism and subversion, methods of counterinsurgency, and the beauties of foreign private investment for development. These perspectives were addressed especially to the Latin officer corps—with enlisted personnel much more emphasis was placed on purely technical matters.[116]

Robert McNamara argued in 1962 that U.S. training of the Latin military would be a "democratizing" force. The 18 military coups in Latin America between 1960 and 1968 suggest the enormity of McNamara's misperception of reality (or deception of Congress). There is a large body of evidence showing that U.S. training has given not the slightest nod toward either democratic values or human rights; instead, *it has provided all the essentials of NSS ideology*, plus the encouragement, means and support to put the NSS in place. The intent and effect of the U.S. training programs was to elevate the status, self-esteem and confidence of the Latin military and to politicize it in conservative directions. Frederick Nunn has stated that "subject to United States military influence on anticommunism the professional army officer became hostile to any sort of populism."[117] The fundamentals of National Security ideology as regards the omnipresence of the subversive (communist) threat, total war between the forces of good and evil, and the importance of the military-security forces as protectors of Christianity, Democracy and the Free World is extremely close to the substance of thought of the U.S. military-security complex.[118] This makes it more comprehensible that the NSS ideology blossomed in Latin America in parallel with U.S. training inputs and that relations between the U.S. military establishment and its counterparts in Latin America have been close and warm.

The "tools the military leaders [of Brazil] found compelled to use against a lethargic Congress and wholly corrupted and communist-infiltrated system...[were] necessary to reform the Brazilian houses of Congress.... Brazil was extremely fortunate to have a far-sighted man of General Branco's [sic] calibre wielding this kind of power." "The first order of business for Branco [sic] was to oust or restrict those individuals who proved the greatest threat or impedence [sic] to his energetic and idealistic program." "Communism is relentlessly waging warfare against established societies in Latin America as well as our own country. Their battleground is across the whole spectrum of national life and activity."[119] These are statements of the supposedly "democratizing" U.S. military establishment, and hundreds could be cited, with apologetics for totalitarianism and with explanations of the primacy and inherent ferocity of the struggle against the omnipresent forces of communism, that are quite indistinguishable from the ideology of official Latin ideologues of the NSS.

The U.S. training programs of recent decades also put great weight on developing personal relationships that would create bonds of friendship and trust and make for ready communication and continuing influence. This has been pursued deliberately and by plan.[120] The training programs have been heavily larded with vacation excursions, entertainment and guided tours designed to impress Third World officers with U.S. success and power. The individual trainees have been assigned to individual counterparts for cultivation, and followup contacts have been maintained via huge U.S. military missions, arms supply and accompanying advice and further training, and continued individual contacts.

It is no coincidence, then, that the Sorbonne group of the Brazilian military, closest to the United States in personal affiliations and training, was the most aggressive in overturning constitutional government in 1964.[121] Some 80% of the core group of generals participating in the 1964 coup were U.S.-trained, whereas 22% of the non-participants were U.S.-trained.[122] According to Edwin Lieuwen, "Most of the Latin American military leaders who conducted the nine coups between 1962 and 1966 had been recipients of U.S. training."[123]

The NSS was an intended outcome of U.S. efforts to contain popular forces and preserve a favorable investment climate. This conclusion follows from the open design to build up the Latin American military as a *political force*, the nature of the training which tended to make already conservative military personnel into reactionaries and zealots, and the general approval and support of the NSSs that emerged from that process. This conclusion is in no way qualified by the limited slaps on the wrist applied at one time or another to some of the most grotesque fascist excesses.

(3) *U.S. aid and training and their relationship to NSS terrorism.* As has been noted, the Soviet terror network theorists assume as a matter of course that supply and training by the Soviet Union or one of its alleged surrogates *means* something in terms of Soviet policy choices. If something nasty ensues, it is presumed that this was intended and based on Soviet purpose, and that the Soviets should be held accountable. A review of Sterling's *Terror Network* in the London *Economist* (Sept. 19, 1981), after noting Sterling's own concession that direct links to the Kremlin are often not there, concludes: "The Soviet Union, as it were, merely puts the gun on the table and leaves others to wage a global war by proxy." It simply never occurs to the *Economist* or the U.S. mass media to evaluate the guns which the United States "puts on the table" in similar terms, even though the gun volume is the world's largest and the *design* for use by client state terrorists is clear. I have shown that the results conform to short-run U.S. corporate interest and policy intent. It has been shown that U.S. training and supply were *intended* to increase U.S. influence, and that that influence was directed toward encouraging military activism with a conservative-reactionary bent. I will show now that the volume of these arms and training flows has been of staggering dimension over an extended time period, which strengthens the case for domination or substantial influence by the United States. I will also show that U.S. training and supply have tended to encourage human torture and that, correspondingly, there are significant positive relationships between U.S. flows of aid and *negative* human rights developments (the rise of torture, death squads and the overturn of constitutional governments). This is a result, not of any U.S. elite

attraction to human torture, but rather of the demands of the higher priorities (favorable investment climate, worker and peasant atomization) that regrettably necessitate the support of torturers.

The United States has towered above all other countries in arms supply and the training of military and police personnel abroad. Military aid programs of the United States between 1950 and 1979 transferred a huge $107.3 billion in equipment and services to friendly powers, in addition to some $121 billion in arms sales.[124] During Claire Sterling's Fright Decade, the United States sold a vast $93.7 billion worth of arms and ammunition to its various clients. Since 1950 the United States has trained over 500,000 military personnel from some 85 countries at the U.S. Army School of the Americas in Panama and several hundred other military schools and bases within the United States and abroad.[125] Under police training programs that began in 1954, and up to the termination of the Public Safety Program in 1975, over 7,500 police officers had received training in U.S. schools and over a million regular policemen had been given training abroad. Huge sums in arms and equipment were also dispensed to foreign police departments.[126]

As in Vietnam, much U.S. effort went into improving police information systems, communications networks and response capabilities. Computerization, the use of radio and TV equipment, and coordination of police in various parts of the country and with friendly police forces in other countries, was stressed. I have described the cross-border murder program named Operation Condor as a proud result of these efforts. The CIA also helped along these efforts in various ways, like providing information on Latin American and foreign religious personnel to a network of NSSs to enable them better to follow this important base of subversion.[127] The U.S. training programs for the police of Latin America have been strongly oriented toward counter-insurgency and social-control efforts "ranging from demonstrations, disorders, riots through small-scale guerilla operations."[128] Training was provided in the design and manufacture of home-made bombs and assassination devices, and such learning appears to have been put to use by police-intelligence forces in countries like Uruguay.[129] Even more important was training in methods of interrogation, both in the United States and by field personnel of the Office of Public Safety. I return to this below.

The rise of police and military training and material aid by the United States in the 1950s and 1960s parallels a rise in physical torture by the use of similar technologies over a wide geographic area extending from South Vietnam to the Philippines to Brazil, Argentina and Uruguay. Table 3-4 provides more details on the relationship between U.S. material support and training and the presence of systematic torture. The table shows that 14 U.S. client states, each of whom used torture on an administrative basis in the early or mid-1970s, received military training under U.S. auspices, with the number of trainees averaging over 4000 per country. Half of them received police aid under the one specific program included in this table and *all* of them received police training in some police training program provided by the United States. All of them received military assistance and bilateral economic aid of substantial volume. There were 12 other countries in the U.S. sphere of influence that received significant U.S. aid and training that also used torture on an administrative basis.

Is there a cause and effect relationship in this pattern? Even if there is none demonstrable, or none in fact, this table shows massive support provided to people who practice terror in one of its most horrible forms. The U.S. government has, at a minimum, "voted with its guns and money." It has also been shown, moreover, that U.S. aid to the Third World is *positively related* to terror and human rights violations. A quantitative analysis of this relationship by Lars Schoultz disclosed that the correlations between "United States aid to Latin American countries and human rights violations...are uniformly positive."[130] This confirms an earlier finding of my own, which also established that this positive relationship was itself linked to factors that measure "favorable investment climate."[131] A plausible causal relationship is thus to be found in the primacy of investment climate and the service of the NSS—and torture—to this higher purpose.

A causal relationship is also suggested by the specific training programs offered to Third World countries. Much official palaver has been given to the "humane" methods of handling various internal security problems our training would bring.

Table 3-4

U.S. Military, Police and Economic Aid to Countries Using Torture on an Administrative Basis in the 1970s[1]
(Figures in Millions of Dollars)

	Military Assistance[2] (1946-1979)	Commercial Arms Exports[3] (1950-1980)	No. of Military Personnel Trained by U.S.[4] (1950-1980)	Police Aid[5] (1973-1981)	Bilateral U.S. Economic Aid[6] (1946-1979)	International Aid[7] (1946-1980)
Argentina*	263.6	90.4	4,017	.45	199.1	2,946.7
Bolivia	80.7	4.28	4,896	15.78	801.8	1,027.2
Brazil	640.0	83.31	8,659	.77	2,424.1	9,080.6
Chile	217.0	8.76	6,883	.14	1,163.1	1,046.6
Colombia	240.9	19.40	8,349	34.17	1,340.7	4,095.6
Dominican Republic	43.0	2.59	4,269	—	589.4	733.9
Guatemala	41.5	5.09	3,334	—	417.4	703.5
Haiti	5.9	1.87	643	—	251.8	305.0
Mexico	.1	12.97	1,003	95.1	2,691.9	5,807.3
Nicaragua	32.4	4.24	5,673	—	298.9	537.1
Peru	239.7	25.63	8,160	8.4	609.3	1,434.1
Paraguay	30.3	2.45	2,018	.09	177.8	629.1
Uruguay	89.2	1.67	2,806	—	159.5	632.3
Venezuela*	152.3	60.33	5,540	—	201.1	657.0

[1]For the concept and criteria of torture on an administrative basis, see Chomsky and Herman, *The Washington Connection and Third World Fascism*, frontispiece and explanatory footnotes.

[2]Agency for International Development, *Congressional Presentation, Fiscal Year 1982*, Annex III (3), Latin America and the Caribbean.

[3]U.S. Department of Defense, Congressional Presentation, Security Assistance Programs, Fiscal Year 1982.

[4]Ibid.

[5]Michael Klare and Cynthia Arnson, *Supplying Repression*, IPS, 1981, p. 3. This column refers to police aid provided for a brief period under the International Narcotics Control Program. The much larger Public Safety Program supplied $324 million of arms and training to Third World police between 1961 and 1973 (*ibid.*, p. 21).

[6]See footnote 2.

[7]Ibid.

*The data source for both Argentina and Venezuela, for military assistance, bilateral, and international economic aid categories was: US A.I.D., US Overseas Loans and Grants...July 1, 1945-Sept. 30, 1979.

Thus in the 1974 final study of the Public Safety Program in Guatemala, the OPS concluded that "Riot control training and related phases of coping with civil disturbances in a *humane* [sic] and effective manner became institutionalized in the National Police within the past three years."[132] The evidence on the impact of U.S. training on Guatemala is on the record. There is also a large body of evidence that U.S. training and aid programs directly and indirectly encouraged and promoted death squads and torture. First, there is the stress on the great desirability of foreign investment, and therefore of a favorable investment climate for economic growth. Second, there is the focus on subversion, counterinsurgency, and a holy war against an insidious Communist enemy who comes in many guises, and who actually hates our beloved protector, the Godfather! This provided the spiritual backup to torture. Third, there is a great deal of evidence of U.S. provision of torture technology and training, which have been diffused among a great variety of client states. Electronic methods of torture, used extensively in the field and in the Provincial Interrogation Centers in South Vietnam, have spread throughout the system of U.S. clients. A.J. Langguth claims that the CIA advised Brazilian torturers using field telephones as to the permissible limits that would avoid premature death.[133] Klare and Arnson show that U.S. firms and agencies are providing CN and CS gas grenades, anti-riot gear, fingerprint computers, thumbscrews, leg-irons and electronic "Shok-Batons" among a huge flow of "equipment, training, and technical support to the police and paramilitary forces *most directly involved in the torture, assassination, and abuse of civilian dissidents.*"[134] Langguth also notes that one of the pioneer death squads in Brazil, Operacao Bandierantes (OBAN) was financed through the auspices of a local business man widely thought to be a CIA agent, with encouragement given to U.S. local corporate funding by the U.S. consulate. And one of the most notorious Brazilian torturers and death squad organizers, Sergio Fleury, was introduced to the Uruguayan police through CIA contacts.[135]

As the United States has supported torture directly via training programs and the implements of torture, and indirectly by means of its sponsorship of the NSS, it is natural that it also protects the torturers by apologetics and silence. This being official U.S. policy, the mass media have done the same. In Paraguay, for example, AI points out that although "Stroessner has said that he considers the American Ambassador to be an ex officio member of his Cabinet, the U.S. has never officially acknowledged or taken steps to prevent the use of torture by a government which appears to be very much within its sphere of influence."[136] In Greece, to take another interesting case, torture on an administrative basis was introduced in 1967 with the takeover by the U.S.-trained, supplied and supported colonels. AI noted in its 1974 *Report on Torture* that "In terms of power and influence the U.S. government plays the predominant role in Greece." AI also points out, however, that U.S. criteria of acceptability and serviceability seem to be confined to strategic interests and a "congenial environment of political stability." Since the Greek torture regime met these criteria, other matters were of little account, and U.S. policy on Greek torture "as expressed in official statements and official testimony has been to deny it where possible and minimize it, where denial was not possible. This policy flowed naturally from general support for the military regime."[137]

AI has pointed out "a seeming paradox" in the fact that "never has there been a stronger or more universal consensus on the total inadmissability of the practice of torture: at the same time the practice of torture has reached epidemic proportions."[138] This paradox is resolved by the fact that the greatest superpower on earth finds regimes that torture useful, and thus torture thrives and the Free World has learned to look the other way (toward the problems of Solidarity, for example).

Table 3-3 above shows that the United States has also "voted" with its guns and money for the death squad. It can be seen in this table that all ten countries in which death squads made their appearance, or were active in the 1970s, were recipients of extensive training by U.S. military and police experts, and that except for Mexico (whose death squads have been the least conspicuous of the ten) all have been heavily subsidized militarily. Perhaps when McNamara spoke of our "democratizing" impact he was referring to the democratization of death. We may note also that in the four cases where the U.S. played a leading role in the introduction of the responsible government, death squads appeared very quickly and were of major importance in the repressive operations of the newly established NSSs. Again, the U.S. role, at a minimum, was support of the states using death squads, and thus indirect responsibility for the death squads themselves. But U.S. responsibility runs deeper when we recognize the extent of overall domination exercised by the United States over this region (considered further in the next section). On one of the principles employed to justify U.S. assistance—that it would allow greater "influence" by the supplier— we must conclude that the death squad is a manifestation of U.S. influence. Torture and the death squad are as U.S.-related-American as apple pie.

The U.S. Natural Right to Subvert

As the superpower traditionally dominant in the western hemisphere the United States has long taken the position that it has the right to "protect" the countries in the region from intervention from outside the hemisphere. Who will protect these countries from the *United States* is a question of importance in Latin America, but it does not arise in the United States itself on the patriotic assumptions that we wouldn't intervene, or, alternatively, if we did, it would no doubt be in the best interest of the locals. This is the claim of any great power, and the United States has so much power that self-righteous apologetics not only reach awesome levels at home, they are diffused throughout the west according to degree of subservience of the lesser powers (in the early 1980s, more subservience from Great Britain, Canada and France; less from West Germany, Sweden and the Netherlands). Thus, open U.S. intervention in El Salvador in favor of a regime of complete inhumanity, with SS quality mass murders of more than 20,000 civilians in a single year (many raped and mutilated in addition), with the *planned* rape-murder of four U.S. nuns[139] (and numerous other killings of religious leaders and workers), justified by a patently fraudulent White Paper proving *somebody else's* external intrusion—this is treated *respectfully* in the west. Only France and Mexico have been bold enough to recognize the insurgents as having some legitimacy, and this acknowledgement, extended quietly and without fanfare, elicited considerable abuse from other members of the Free World. As in the case of the Vietnam war, no government in the west is able to denounce the

United States as the true underpinning of the official death machines in El Salvador (and in Guatemala)—the only serious intruder from outside and the clear source of power and sustenance of Duarte and Garcia. The same respectful treatment applies to the entire network of torturers and death squads described above.

The western underlings to the superpower, in short, must accept its natural right, as top dog, to intervene freely when it sees fit. Efforts to subvert by the superpower are rarely described as subversion—there is a sort of implicit Zhdanov doctrine applicable, using euphemisms appropriate to the west. Thus, instead of protecting the "people," or "the revolution" against "imperialist aggression," the west "contains" "Communism" and "subversion," the latter usually by a people unappreciative of the gift brought by a Martinez de Hoz and his Armed Forces enforcers.

If one strips off the patriotic blinders and looks at U.S. intervention as one might look at that of the Soviet Union or Cuba, it is quickly obvious that the relevant intervention levels in Latin America and the Caribbean have been of exceptional scope and scale. This is the result of the disproportionate power of the United States, the huge spread of its interest, the previously mentioned spectacular sense of virtue, and the tacit subservience of its western allies, satellites and mass media. Thus the enormous provision of military and police aid and training shown on Table 3-4, which, as I have indicated, was part of a definite strategy of altering the balance of power within Latin American states by building up, educating in the appropriate counterrevolutionary ideology, and politicizing a military elite tied to ourselves, was itself a gigantic effort at subversion—and it succeeded, leaving a continent full of National Security States.

Let us consider, however, some of the more conventional criteria of subversion like invading or sponsoring invasions, military occupation, encouraging and participating in coups, or bribing powerful citizens (politicians, military and intelligence personnel, journalists, labor leaders) to provide information, to serve as a propaganda conduit, or to carry out other purposes of a foreign power. Table 3-5 shows 12 classes of direct subversion, with a cross-tabulation of pluses and minuses indicative of applicability to U.S. intervention in eight neighboring countries

Table 3-5

Forms of Subversion Engaged in by the United States
in Eight Countries in Latin America and the Caribbean, 1950-1980
(+ means evidence of use, − means no evidence of use)

Forms of Subversion	Brazil	Chile	Cuba	Dominican Republic	Ecuador	El Salvador	Guatemala	Uruguay
Direct invasion or sponsorship of invasion	−	−	+	+	−	−	+	−
Participation in coups (directing, encouraging, lending support to)	+	+	−	+	+	−	−	−
Assassination or attempted assassination of leaders	−	+	+	+	−	−	−	−
Sabotage (property destruction)	−	−	+	−	−	−	−	−
Destabilization (economic or financial)	+	+	+	+	−	−	+	−
Buying politicians and other officials (including military and security)	+	+	+	+	+	+	+	+
Buying media and media personnel	+	+	−	−	+	−	−	+
Buying intellectuals	+	+	−	−	+	−	−	+
Buying labor leaders	+	+	+	+	+	+	+	+
Black propaganda (lies and rumors dispensed without attribution)	+	+	+	−	+	−	−	+
Subsidizing student, youth, women's organizations	+	+	−	−	+	−	−	+
Providing military forces for occupation or counterinsurgency operations	−	−	−	+	−	−	+	−

Sources: (Principal).

General: Penny Lernoux, *Cry of the People*, Doubleday, 1980; Ronald Radosh, *American Labor and United States Foreign Policy*, Random House, 1969; Philip Agee, *Inside the Company: CIA Diary*, Bantam, 1975; Victor Marchetti and John D. Marks, *The CIA and the Cult of Intelligence*, Dell, 1974; Miles Wolpin, *Military Aid and Counterrevolution in the Third World*, Lexington, 1972; *Alleged Assassination Plots Involving Foreign Leaders*, Senate Select Committee on Intelligence, Rep. No. 94-465, 94th Cong., 1st sess. (1975).

Brazil: Jan K. Black, *United States Penetration of Brazil*, University of Pennsylvania, 1977.

Chile: *Covert Action in Chile 1963-1965*, Staff Report of Senate Select Committee on Intelligence, 1975; James Petras and Morris Morley, *How Allende Fell*, Spokesmen, 1974; Saul Landau, *They Educated the Crows*, IPS, 1978; Fred Landis, *Psychological Warfare and Media Operations in Chile: 1970-1973*, Ph.D. dissertation, University of Illinois, 1975.

Cuba: Warren Hinckle and William Turner, *The Fish Is Red*, Harper and Row, 1981; William Schaap, "New Spate of Terrorism: Key Leaders Unleashed," *Covert Action Information Bulletin*, Dec. 1980.

Dominican Republic: NACLA, *Smouldering Conflict: Dominican Republic 1965-1975*; Carlos Maria Gutierrez, *The Dominican Republic: Rebellion and Repression*, Monthly Review Press, 1972; Norman Gall, "How Trujillo Died," *New Republic*, April 13, 1963.

Ecuador: Agee, *Inside the Company*.

El Salvador: NACLA, *Guatemala*, 1974; Stephen Kinzer and Stephen Schlesinger, *Bitter Fruit*, Doubleday, 1981; Blanche Wiesen Cook, *The Declassified Eisenhower*, Doubleday, 1981.

Uruguay: Agee, *Inside the Company*; A.J. Langguth, *Hidden Terrors*, Pantheon, 1978.

between 1950 and 1980. This table represents a preliminary summary of a larger study still in progress attempting to assess the scope of U.S. intervention in Latin America and the Caribbean. The states included here are ones for which information is relatively plentiful as a result of excellent and detailed studies. There may be a bias as between these and other countries in that the countries studied most are the ones where U.S. intervention may have been greatest; but this is not certain.[140] In any case, the scope of intervention in the eight states displayed in the table is important in itself, and extensive, and there is no reason to believe that more knowledge would not lead to a filling in of some of the few remaining gaps for these countries.

What is more, this simple enumeration really just brushes the surface of each dimension of intervention. The reality of U.S. intervention frequently defies belief without concrete details that often show U.S. officials and intelligence personnel treating our Latin clients as colonial underlings or purchasable as a matter of course. The details of the individual cases are remarkable in showing the scope and brazenness of U.S. subversion. Philip Agee's account of his stay in Ecuador in 1960-1963 is notable for its demonstration of the many dimensions of our interventionary processes and the large number of private citizens and officials of Ecuador who could be induced to serve undercover on the payroll of a foreign power. Agee shows that at one point the second and third highest officials in the Ecuadorian government were on the CIA payroll (including the Vice President, a retired army officer who had been trained at Fort Riley and Fort Leavenworth in the United States). The nephew and personal physician of the head of state, the Minister of Labor, the head of personnel of the National Police, and other high police officials, were CIA agents. High officers of two political parties were on the CIA payroll, two other conservative parties were funded by the CIA, and the political campaign of a rightwing ex-army officer was underwritten by the CIA. Candidates in student and labor union voting contests were financed by the CIA. A major liberal journalist served as a CIA news conduit, and huge volumes of anticommunist propaganda, much of it known to be fraudulent, were funneled through unions, rightwing patriotic organizations sponsored and funded by the CIA, and friendly journalists. The CIA in Ecuador planted forged documents (usually to show *Cuban* subversion!) and funded demonstrations and groups whose explicit role was violence (breaking up demonstrations and bombings). Most importantly, the CIA tried hard and effectively through a steady stream of planted propaganda, and through innumerable secret paid agents, to discredit and split the political left and labor movement by constantly harping on the communist menace as the criterion of evaluation and policy. In short, the scope of U.S. subversive operations in Ecuador in the early 1960s was almost limitless—the CIA was a state within a state, and as Agee noted in his Diary, "we aren't running the country but we are certainly helping to shape events in the direction and form we want."[141]

Brazil is even more important than Ecuador as an illustration of U.S. subversion, as the record shows that even in this largest state in Latin America, U.S. power was so great that massive intervention was institutionalized and taken as a part of nature. In the pre-coup period, the presidents of Brazil felt it necessary to clear things with the U.S. ambassador, and Washington had no compunction in telling the leaders of Brazil what they had better do in order to avoid our disfavor. And when a Brazilian government was seriously displeasing to U.S. business, representatives of the latter indicated that the Brazilian government was "not acceptable" and had to go—as if the determination of who rules in Brazil was in their hands.[142] This was in fact the case—Goulart and his (constitutional) government being unacceptable, out they went.

In the early 1960s Brazil was effectively *occupied* by the U.S. economic, military and political establishments, and actions which, if taken by the Soviet Union, Cuba, or even France, would be regarded as outrageous infringements of sovereignty, were part of normal reality. That U.S. economic interests should be able to buy up a large chunk of the Brazilian mass media, and dominate the advertising industry (and thus indirectly influence the content of the media) is a kind of penetration that defines satellite status. That the U.S. should train, arm and service a large fraction of the higher military, police and intelligence services, and deliberately attach these strategic forces to their U.S. correlates, is a major form of subversive penetration. The United States went well beyond this, subsidizing publishing houses and research-propaganda institutes, buying newspaper editorial space and journalists, disseminating propaganda, introducing labor leader training and financing programs designed to influence the political orientation and power of Brazilian labor, subsidizing literally *hundreds* of Brazilian politicians, dispensing foreign aid money in a highly political way to reward friendly state politicians and to penalize national leaders deemed hostile—and, in the end, conspiring with military and business leaders to overthrow the legally elected government.[143] In Chile the subsidization of politicians, conspiracies with military personnel, and the subsidization and manipulation of the Chilean news media assumed even larger dimensions.[144]

These extensive subversive efforts in Brazil, Chile and Ecuador, and in the other countries listed in Table 3-5, add strength to the contention here that the NSS in Latin America, and all of its ugly terroristic and exploitative qualities, came into existence in accord with U.S. desires and plans. This is a region of preeminent U.S. influence, and it has gone to great lengths to assure that political economies are in place that suit its desires. There can be little doubt that, while U.S. efforts have not been uniformly successful, the main drift has been in accord with U.S. preferences.

FOUR

Contemporary Terrorism (3): The Role of the Mass Media

Introduction

The mass media of the United States are a part of the national power structure and they therefore reflect its biases and mobilize popular opinion to serve its interests. This is not accomplished by any conspiratorial plotting or explicit censorship—it is built into the structure of the system, and flows naturally and easily from the assorted ownership, sponsor, governmental and other interest group pressures that set limits within which media personnel can operate, and from the nature of the sources on which the media depend for their steady flow of news. As we have seen, these interest groups find the National Security State (NSS) good, and this preference underlies U.S. sponsorship and support of this terror network. We would therefore expect the mass media to treat the NSS kindly and deflect attention from its abuses. Any other route would be very surprising as the "national interest" itself has long been defined by the very forces that cause the country to support the NSS.

If we examine the larger patterns of selection by the mass media, one of its most notable characteristics is stress on "enemy" misbehavior and problems and a corresponding deemphasis of misbehavior and problems of "friends." Terror abroad can be classified roughly but usefully as *constructive, benign* and *nefarious.* Constructive terror is defined as that which positively serves important domestic interests; benign terror is that which is of little direct interest to the U.S. elite but may sometimes serve the interests of a friendly client; and nefarious terror is that committed by enemy states (or by bearers of hostile ideologies).

.   Constructive terror would include the holocaust in Indonesia in 1965-1966 and the large scale political murders in Chile in 1973-1974, where the terror in both instances decimated a political opposition deemed threatening to U.S. and western interests, and was quickly followed by an opening of the door to relatively free western economic penetration. In such cases, where business and government *like* the political outcome, and in fact make notable contributions to the origination and implementation of the terror,[1] the mass media play down the violence irrespective of its level. Reports on the scope and character of the terror are few and antiseptic, details of the human suffering involved are sparse, indignation and rage at the human agony are rare, and no sustained campaign of daily information or appeals for intervention is mounted. Government attitudes range from mild expressions of regret at the alleged excesses, interspersed with a hard-headed recognition of the (implicitly) just grievances that led to the violence, (communist provocations and threats), to even more explicit apologetics. Thus, Robert McNamara, the U.S. Secretary of Defense at the time of the 1965-1966 Indonesian coup and massacre of an estimated 500,000-1,000,000 people, described these events as a "dividend" showing that our military aid and training there "was well justified."[2] James Reston of the *New York Times* wrote of "A Gleam of Light" rising in Indonesia as a result of "developments" in process there.[3] It is worth noting and reflecting on the fact that the numbers slaughtered in cold blood in Indonesia in 1965-1966 exceed by a substantial factor any official U.S. or scholarly estimate of numbers *deliberately killed* in Cambodia by the Khmer Rouge.[4] As regards the Chilean massacres of 1973-1974, probably in excess of 20,000, William Colby, then CIA head and formerly manager of a national system of death squads in South Vietnam, explained to a Congressional committee in late 1973 that the ongoing mass murder by the

Chilean junta was a "good" thing, as it was "rooting out Marxist influence" and reducing the possibility of a civil war which might otherwise have taken place.[5]

Benign terror is well exemplified by the Indonesian invasion and occupation of East Timor from 1975 up to the present time. As Indonesia is a friendly client, its aggression in East Timor aroused negligible interest in the west (with the exception of neighboring Australia), because the health and welfare of the Indonesian NSS was important to western interests (notably those of the United States and Japan), whereas East Timor was otherwise of little concern. The Indonesian invasion was a blatant act of aggression that resulted in the deaths of somewhere between 100,000 and 200,000 victims. U.S. arms were extensively employed in this invasion and occupation, in violation of U.S. law, but U.S. officials, including Presidents Ford and Carter, Vice President Mondale, and Secretary of State Kissinger, colluded with the Indonesian generals in playing down the aggression, its illegalities and its savagery. In fact, during the Carter years 1977-1978 arms flows to Indonesia were sharply increased, facilitating the huge massacres of that period. It has been shown in detail elsewhere that, given western support of the Indonesian NSS, and thus the "benign" character of the terror brought to East Timor by the Indonesian military, *this* quite brutal and illegal state terrorism was off-the-agenda for the western mass media.[6] And just as the media played down this terror, similarly, any explanations and questions about the selective suppression were also duly suppressed!

In sharp, even startling, contrast with western media silence on the events in East Timor was the attention given to Cambodia. There undoubtedly was a holocaust in Cambodia during the same period in which Indonesia was invading and attempting to subjugate East Timor, with many thousands executed and a great many more dying of disease and starvation. A question that western patriots hate to confront, however, is: why the immense attention to the Cambodian violence and the virtually total suppression of discussion of the Indonesian violence in East Timor? It should be noted that the indignation over Cambodia had no practical significance for the victims, as events in that country were beyond western influence after April 1975, and no useful suggestions for alleviating Cambodian misery were even put forward; whereas, in contrast, East Timorese deaths were being carried out in the U.S. sphere of influence, with U.S. weapons, and therefore under circumstances where western indignation and pressure might have had an impact. (It may also be asked, similarly, how we reconcile the outpouring of compassion and indignation over Cambodia and the placidity and apologetics about *dividends* and the *gleam of new light* in reference to the even larger massacre in Indonesia in 1965-1966?) Patriots react negatively to a focus on this *selectivity* of concern because it obviously compromises the idea that western benevolence is pure—or perhaps even real—and suggests essentially political definitions of worthy victims, and a large measure of hypocrisy. Precisely. This is not to imply that many individuals concerned about Cambodian violence were not sincere and honorable. What happens, however, is that the more powerful forces in the system succeed in mobilizing human decency in a highly selective and politically skewed manner. Sometimes decent things are done for those selected as *worthy* victims. But victims of benign terror (East Timorese) or constructive terror (500,000 or more Indonesians, 20,000 or more Chileans, many millions of dispossessed and abused peasants in Brazil, Chile, Paraguay, Indonesia and the Philippines) are frozen out of this system of channeled benevolence.

Returning to the contrast between devoted mass media attention to Cambodia and neglect of the East Timor massacres, it will not do to pretend that this can be explained by the level of violence, or by our "sense of responsibility" to the Cambodians, or by our "ignorance" about East Timor. The numbers killed by deliberate acts, as opposed to deaths by the war-related ravages of disease and starvation, which were of predominant importance in Cambodia, do not appear to be of different orders of magnitude.[7] Furthermore, the western sense of concern toward Cambodians was not evident during the huge B-52 bombing campaign of 1973, when 240,000 short tons of bombs were dropped on rice fields, water buffaloes and villages over a 160 day period, killing large numbers of Cambodians and setting the stage for the later and *further* terrible events, especially the massive starvation. Why did the west feel "responsible" for the death of Cambodians only after the Khmer Rouge took power, not during the Lon Nol regime when the deaths were the United States' direct responsibility?[8]

Western "ignorance" about East Timor can hardly be advanced as a serious explanation of non-concern—this differential knowledgeability is precisely what has to be explained. Cambodia is a very remote and small country, and U.S. citizens could have been allowed to remain in ignorance of the sequel of events there (as they have about events in, say, Burma, or Thailand since 1975). What is more, media attention to East Timor was not negligible in 1974-1975, during the period of Portuguese withdrawal, when the fate of Timor was of some interest to the west. East Timor became "remote" *after* the Indonesian invasion, and western media coverage was inversely related to the extent of the Indonesian massacre![9]

It is clear, then, that if the *Readers Digest*, *Time*, the *New York Times*, the U.S. government, or important businessmen in the United States had concluded that the Indonesian invasion of East Timor was detrimental to U.S. interests, or that political capital could be extracted from focusing on its victims, the U.S. public would have become quickly "knowledgeable." But the important power interests in the United States, including multinational investors and the military-security complex, were closely tied to the Indonesian invaders, and there was certainly no political advantage to be gained from focusing on the abuses of a NSS. U.S. policy, in fact, was supportive of the invasion and the massacre, both in the U.N. and via arms transfers (provided in violation of U.S. and international law). The mass media saw things in the same light, and decided to "lay off." This was helped along by the fact that primary government sources also clammed up, provided no news, and were obviously interested in a coverup—which ensued.

This spectrum of power interests had no reason to "lay off" Cambodia. This was *nefarious* terror, the form which serves primary system propaganda needs, and which, according to my hypothesis, the mass media will rush to exploit at the slightest opportunity. Circumstances in Cambodia were especially favorable for a propaganda campaign. There was not only a substantial bloodbath of vengeance killings, ruthless and murderous treatment of the former urban elite, but there was also a vast residual toll of disease and starvation that was already foreseen and predicted by U.S. and other experts even before the Khmer Rouge took power. There were large numbers of refugees in

Thailand and elsewhere whose stories (many no doubt quite accurate) could be selected, embellished, processed and retailed to produce a desired line and effect.[10] In a sustained mass media campaign that might be a propaganda model of its kind, the extreme violence of the earlier conflict, and the U.S. bombings and sponsored invasion—very important contributors to postwar events—were quickly set aside; Pol Pot murder totals were inflated, as standards of evidence were suspended for this special case; and, in the end, the western propaganda machine succeeded in attributing every Cambodian victim of disease, starvation and retaliatory killing to Pol Pot and/or the inherent qualities of "Communism."

My purpose here is not to debate the facts about Cambodia or East Timor, but to use them to illustrate the hypothesis that mass media attention is a function not of terror per se but of the relation of terror to larger "national interests." The point is also strikingly evident in the case of "martial law" in Poland, which dominated the headlines and aroused the mass media and political leadership to a state of frenzy in the United States in 1981 and early 1982. In contrast, martial law imposed in Turkey in 1980-1981, accompanied by mass arrests, torture and executions (which threatened to engulf a good part of the trade union leadership by early 1982), aroused little attention and no indignation. "Frightful abuse" in the enemy sphere equals a "return to stability" in the client state.

In short, what the general public knows and is interested in is *managed*. A small elite sets the agenda for discussion, and while there are limits on its ability to make people think in a certain way, through the mass media it is "stunningly successful in telling [the public]...what to think *about*."[11] The U.S. people knew about and were interested in Cambodian atrocities because the mass media latched on to Cambodian violence and made it familiar ground (although the level of distortion was extraordinarily high). They are able to prove the evils of Communism by focusing attention on negative events in Poland, and by simultaneously "blacking out" the facts on the literal murder of hundreds of trade union leaders and permanent martial law of varying levels of intensity in more than a score of western client states. This is a system of self-fulfilling "news interest management" in which constructive and benign terror are *never allowed* to become the subject of intense scrutiny and concern.

As the NSS has come into being and is protected and supported by the economic and political elite that defines the national interest, its ugly proclivities produce "dividends" and are "constructive." As was the case with the huge bloodbath in Indonesia, therefore, the mass media of the United States will not characterize its organizers as madmen, mass murderers and terrorists. By one route or other the Suhartos, Pinochets, Stroessners and their NSS colleagues and operatives will be protected. I will consider first the forces that drive the media into this apologetic function. Then I will examine the devices used that allow the media to combine massive bias with the outer garments of objectivity.

The Mass Media as Protectors of the Real Terror Network

Bias is built-in by a number of basic structural facts. One is the close relationship and literal overlap between the leaders of the mass media and the businessmen and officials who like the NSS. The dozen or so top level mass media enterprises that have real clout[12] are all large, profit-seeking businesses, with boards of directors that interlock with the rest of the business community. Most of them have diversified out of single media operations, some of them out of exclusive media activity, so that they are generally business conglomerates. Some of them are in the defense business (most notably, RCA, the parent of NBC), and a number have substantial foreign interests that make them dependent on the goodwill of host governments. The second tier of mass media enterprises includes even more diversified, defense-oriented and multinational enterprises—most significantly Westinghouse, General Electric, Avco and Kaiser Industries. This commonality of corporate purpose, structure of interlocks, and geographic and product diversification make it likely that the mass media leaders will have the same values and the same vision of the national interest as the general community of large corporations. Eric Barnouw goes farther in his survey of TV, the most powerful of all media forms.

> The symbiotic growth of American television and global enterprise has made them so interrelated that they cannot be thought of as separate. They are essentially the same phenomenon. Preceded far and

wide by military advisers, lobbyists, equipment salesmen, advertising specialists, merchandising experts,
and telefilm salesmen as advance agents, the enterprise
penetrates much of the non-socialist world. Television
is simply its most visible portion.[13]

A second structural fact is the importance of the sponsor.
The mass media depend heavily on advertising, which produces
well over 50% of their gross revenue. Advertisers are mainly
business firms, although the NSS governments also advertise
fairly heavily with large ads and supplements in newspapers like
the *New York Times* and *Wall Street Journal* and business-
oriented publications like *Business Week*. The general interest
and even the specific interests of these advertisers are likely to
have an impact on mass media selection processes. Thus, during
ITTs time of troubles in the early 1970s, sponsorship of its Big
Blue Marble program on TV led to a significant dropoff in
mention of ITT on TV news programs.[14] Far more important,
however, is the general effect of sponsorship as the prime source
of TV revenue—the need to produce programs that will not
seriously offend sponsors, and the mutual interest of network
and sponsor in providing an environment congenial to selling
advertised goods. CBS president Frank Stanton explained in
1960 that "Since we are advertiser-supported we must take into
account the general objectives and desires of advertisers as a
whole."[15] Barnouw gives persuasive evidence that the sponsor
exercises a huge influence on TV programming.

> Their influence over it is spearheaded by "commer-
> cials"—the "focal point of creative effort"; protected by
> "entertainment" designed to fit sponsor needs; bordered
> by a fringe of successfully neutralized "public service"
> elements; and by a buffer zone of approved "culture."[16]

Barnouw uses as an illustration of sponsor impact the long-time
suppression by the TV networks of any negative or minimally
objective analysis of the implications of nuclear power. Until the
end of the 1960s, "nothing seen or heard on television could lead
viewers to think that atomic energy involved risks of any serious
kind. Documentaries and public service messages had come over-
whelmingly, perhaps exclusively, from those who had a stake in

promoting the industry;" and, "As in the early stages of the Vietnam war, the medium had served largely as a transmission belt for official and corporate promotion, closely coordinated."[17]

On foreign news and conditions in the NSSs, the situation tends to be even worse than in the handling of domestic issues like nuclear power, as negative impacts on distant peasants have no political consequences in the home country. As *Time, Readers Digest* and dozens of U.S. multinational banks and non-financial corporations have extensive interests in Brazil, built up under the auspices of the hospitable generals ruling that NSS, these important members of the mass media and powerful advertisers have an important vested interest in the NSS status quo. The mass media may occasionally bite the hands that feed them, but not very hard or long, and they more than make up for these small falls from grace. They do not focus on dispossessed Brazilian peasants.

The ideological range of the top media leadership extends from enlightened cold war and corporate liberalism to militant conservative or reactionary. For the latter, in large circulation publications like *Readers Digest, TV-Guide* and within the Hearst and Luce empires, news and opinion bias is blatant and oriented to conservative ideological mobilization. In these publications, the death squads of Latin America, the systematic torture, the looting, and the condition and treatment of the lower 80% of the population, are for all practical purposes completely suppressed. Retail terror and Communist abuses are given enormous and highly emotional play. The *Readers Digest*, for example, over the decade 1971-1980, had more articles on Castro's Cuba than it did on all 26 U.S. client states that were using torture on an administrative basis in the early and mid-1970s.[18]

This large and blatant brainwashing by the right has no counterpart on the left in the United States—the "left" in the mass media is cold-war liberalism, strongly pro-free enterprise and devoted to the national interest as it would be defined by the progressive managements of large multinational corporations such as IBM or Bank of America. Not exactly a real left in the sense of a critical opposition. Therefore, in the mainstream respectable mass media, abuses in the NSSs are mentioned, and on rare occasion are even highlighted, but always episodically, never in a sustained manner that would build up public indignation and bring political consequences. Relatively miniscule abuses in the Soviet Union can produce day-in-day-out coverage in the mass media; huge and sustained abuses in the NSSs cannot.[19] That the NSS abuses were a result of U.S. intervention, as in Guatemala, where the CIA-sponsored coup, military aid and training, and the huge U.S.-managed counterinsurgency operations of 1966-1968 were absolutely decisive factors in maintaining 27 years of rightwing terror, is rarely noted and never given its proper weight.

A third structural constraint is the nature of mass media sources. Analysts of the mass media point out that they need steady and reliable sources to meet their day-by-day demands for news, and that the only sources that can produce large volumes with some minimal credibility are very powerful and rich entities—like governments and, secondarily, business firms. Thus, 46.5% of the information sources for stories appearing in the *New York Times* and *Washington Post* between 1949 and 1969 were U.S. government officials and agencies, and the trend toward reliance on government sources during that period was upward.[20] The business community is the next most important information source. *Foreign* news is even more thoroughly dominated by a small and powerful group with vested interests in the NSS—U.S. government officials, the three western news services (A.P., U.P.I. and Reuters), businesses operating abroad and foreign governments. The big news services rely heavily on the local governments for news about events in the NSSs, as do the small contingent of western reporters located there. The news services depend on these governments not only for news, but they also sell news *to* these governments, who are frequently owners of large media units. The news services are also sold to private NSS media. Any sustained focus by the media on torture, or on the parlous state of the NSS peasantry, would jeopardize relationships with primary and efficient news sources (and, for the wire services, buyers of news services). The U.S. government and businesses operating in the NSSs are the other leading news sources—the former is the Godfather; the latter are the Godfather's progeny obtaining the benefits of the immiserating economic growth in the NSS's.

The lower echelons of the mass media are given a fair amount of freedom of action by the top managements. The top managements themselves, or at least some of them, accept an ideology of staff freedom to do things based on news value, postulated as an objective standard. Is it not possible that this ideology allows reporters, writers, editors, analysts, researchers and broadcasters to disseminate a broad range of views, some hostile to establishment interests? There is some truth in this, and I have noted that NSS abuses can be aired—it is a question of how frequently and in what terms relative to the newsworthiness and human values involved. The terror that has engulfed Guatemala under the Garcia regime (to go back no farther in time) has involved *thousands* of deaths, unimaginable violence against ordinary civilians—in a region of predominant U.S. influence and frequent intervention. Trade union leaders have been murdered by the hundreds, peasants have been killed, robbed and pushed off their lands by the thousands with Nazi-like ruthlessness; the *center* parties have been decimated by scores of murders. By any standard of human values and responsibility Guatemala deserves more indignation than Poland. I have offered the simple and obvious explanation of the lack of attention and indignation in the U.S. mass media: these terrible events and large social processes of abuse in states like Guatemala are serviceable to important domestic economic interests. The abused do not advertise, vote, threaten or complain in ways that can be heard; Bank of America, Dow, GM, Westinghouse, the U.S. Chamber of Commerce and the U.S. government *can* be heard, often and with compelling force. In the face of this complex of interests, well intentioned individuals in the mass media, while they can occasionally help lift the lid a little, can have only marginal impact; they cannot alter the overall drift of mass media priorities, which rests on basic structural facts and constraints.

Media staff are also predominantly middle class people who tend to share the values of the corporate leadership, and they are affected by the fact that approval, advancement and even job survival depend on acceptance of certain priorities. The biases at the top are filtered down by long term penalties and rewards. The mass media top leadership puts into key positions individuals who reflect their values: "I surround myself with people who generally see the way I do...," says Otis Chandler, publisher of the *Los Angeles Times*.[21] Bias is also a consequence of the nature of mass media news sources and the subtle impact of depending on and entering into relationships with them. In the NSSs primary news sources are government officials and local and multinational businessmen, not peasants or disaffected intellectuals. Newspeople who actively sought out abused people would run into difficulties: (1) They would weaken their links to primary sources in these states. (2) This might result not only in loss of availability of ready information but possibly also complaints to the head office, ouster and even physical damage. (3) They would have to work harder, in contrast with the case of reliance on official sources. (4) Their stories might well be rejected at the top as (a) too controversial; (b) lacking in adequate source confirmation; or (c) not of general interest. Reports seriously critical of the NSSs would elicit flak from the powerful friends of the NSS, including enforcers like Accuracy in Media, Freedom House, the U.S. government, the governments of the NSSs, businesses and banks operating there, and advertising firms and their customers who have relationships with the NSSs. In consequence, the sources for stories describing abuses must be extra authoritative. But most dissident sources are inherently unauthoritative and will be contradicted by official sources. The Latin Church is, of course, an exception—a credible source of abuses—which is why it is feared and persecuted by the NSSs, and why it is under increasing attack by current U.S. leaders now aggressively protecting NSS terrorism. It takes a combination of extreme abuse, exceptional reporters and receptive home office people in the media agency for such news to surface. Since this kind of news does not surface that often, it tends to be unfamiliar and is therefore not of "general interest." Thus we have a full circle, in which NSS abuses are suppressed by a built-in process.

My conclusions then, are first, that most members of the mass media avoid a focus on NSS terror for ideological reasons; terror that is "constructive" from the standpoint of important U.S. interests is seen as a regrettable necessity serving the "national interests." And although some of the leaders and a still larger number of the lower echelons of the mass media find the reality of terror reprehensible and push for some coverage, since terror is a regrettable necessity, the *primary* route taken is looking the other way. Second, this ideological bias is strongly reinforced by the fact that primary sources of information on which the mass media depend are either pro-NSS or have ties of interest and reciprocity that compromise any ability to focus on serious abuses. Third, as the generation and production of information on abuses would involve extra costs in search, and assured negative repercussions from the vocal supporters of the NSS, even episodic treatment of NSS abuses is further constrained, and tends to be handled with a balance and a degree of understatement that is not required of enemy terror. Fourth, this system of watered-down and episodic treatment of terror, in the larger context of mass media protectiveness of the NSS, may actually serve the interests of the real terror network. The muted treatment of friendly terror gives the mass media more credibility as purveyors of "all the news that's fit to print" than would total suppression. The dispensing of small doses of the uglier aspects of the NSSs makes the central apologetic and diversionary role of the mass media less obvious. This allows the more liberal western elites to deceive themselves into thinking that the United States has been a neutral bystander, not an active sponsor of these unfortunate NSS "abuses," which are discussed and debated so openly here at home. We may even be too harsh in criticizing human rights violations which seem to arise so naturally in these backward cultures.

Principles of Apologetics for the National Security State

I turn now to an examination of the methods used by the mass media to cover up and divert public attention from the abuses of the NSS. I will use this format, first, as a means of further documenting the fact that there *is* massive bias and a de facto coverup. My second aim is to alert readers to the variety of tricks employed and to sensitize them to the forms that bias takes. For these purposes I have organized the treatment around ten "principles," to dramatize the many varieties of bias. This list is hardly exhaustive, and the categories also overlap. I have "stripping of context" as one principle and the "United States as disinterested party" as another, but a common form of stripping of context is pretending that the United States is not an active, interested and responsible party to ongoing terror. I do not include "lying" as a separate category as it appears directly or indirectly in most of the others, in "objectively" transmitting lies of the government, or suppressing available information that would call into question a government lie or half-truth. Most of the principles enumerated below are really subcategories of the first—"averting the eyes," or plain suppression. There can be direct suppression of important facts or evidence, which is what I encompass in that principle, or there can be eye aversion by a variety of deceptions, misrepresentations and diversionary ploys. If 20 human beings on a given day are murdered and mutilated in El Salvador, averting the eyes includes not merely failing to give these major crimes front page and detailed attention, it also includes choosing something in their place as fitter news to print—such as shortages and arrests in Poland, Andrei Sakharov's hunger strike or house arrest, or State Department handouts on the Cuban threat.

It is extremely difficult for readers and observers of the U.S. mass media to get outside of the media's premises, to look at their priorities and tricks from any critical perspective. The mass media are so powerful that their choices seem natural and the enormous everyday bias becomes a background norm like the rising and the setting of the sun. Thus when they deign to lift the veil a bit and write up in some detail events in Guatemala, such as the murder of the 76 Christian Democratic leaders in 1980, the question "where was the reportage, detail and indignation for each one of these murders?" is rarely raised.

A useful device for getting a feel for the dimension of the normal massive bias is to substitute the facts of NSS violence into a Soviet context, and try to imagine western mass media responses. I refer the reader back to the Preface where a translation is made between Lech Walesa and Brazilian labor leader da Silva, who somehow doesn't qualify for U.S. media attention, and the labor leaders in Guatemala, murdered 30 at a crack without eliciting a word from the mass media or Lane Kirkland. Or the reader might experiment with the language of Edward Schumacher's warm accolade in the *New York Times* for General Robert Viola, one of the principal organizers of Argentine torture and murder since 1976, analysed below under Principle 6

("With the NSS let us look at the bright side"). Test out how Schumacher's wording sounds when applied to other statesmen-hangmen—say, that "gruff Georgian with a warm but sly smile and walrus mustache, Joseph Stalin," or the stern gauleiter Reinhard Heydrich, a "quintessential German," beneath whose tough exterior beat a heart that had a warm spot for the music of Mozart.

1. The principle of averting of the eyes from NSS terror.

The primary method of protecting Pinochet, Viola and Marcos is averting the eyes, or, in less metaphorical language, suppression. Most of the other principles examined below are more or less refined modes of achieving the same broad end, but the rudimentary and basic route is simply non-reporting or under-reporting. I described in the last chapter the extensiveness of terror in the NSSs, the use there of the most horrendous forms of dehumanization, and the fact that this terror serves the terrible end of keeping millions of people in a deprived and miserable state. Important mass media publications engage in complete or close to complete suppression of facts about the real terror network—the *Readers Digest*, for example, had a grand total of three articles describing abuses and direct violence in the NSSs through the entire decade 1971-1980. The more news-oriented and quality mass media present a much more complex picture, but suppression is still the most important single ingredient of the package they offer as news and commentary on countries like Brazil, Indonesia and Guatemala. There is total suppression of thousands of details of specific events and larger sequences of abuse that would be newsworthy if they occurred in an enemy state. I referred in the Preface to the First Congress of Relatives of the Disappeared, held in Costa Rica in January 1981, an exceedingly dramatic occasion with all the ingredients of news-worthiness, except for that one key variable—the murderers are our allies, and their murders are therefore "constructive" or "benign," as I defined these terms earlier. The murdered Christian Democratic politicians in Guatemala fall into the same category. When the numbers murdered reached 76, and with the internal conflict and slaughter in that country attaining high levels of ferocity, the victims became newsworthy, as an aggregate; but the public's eyes were averted from the individual murders. Even larger massacres are suppressed by the U.S. mass media, one of the most notable being that carried out on May 14, 1980 on the banks of the Rio Sumpul river by the El Salvadoran National Guard, where,

> On that day, fourteen National Guard trucks arrive around 7:00 A.M. in the villages of San Jacinto and La Arada. All the inhabitants, men, women and children, are gathered by the river that partially follows the border. The massacre lasted ten hours. In total, more than 600 people murdered, houses looted and destroyed, corn fields burned with gasoline; a policy of "total scorched earth". Corpses were either left lying to be eaten by predators or thrown in the Rio Sumpul. Honduran peasants caught in a fresh-water fishing net the bullet-riddled bodies of five children. Area inhabitants affirm that Honduran soldiers were posted up on the hills and watched the massacre without intervening. How could they have intervened without starting an armed conflict with unforseeable consequences? But, about ten days beforehand, Salvadorian and Honduran officers met at El Poy, a border town. On the eve of the massacre, over 150 Honduran troops had arrived in the area, forbidding the population to move.[22]

This huge crime was unmentioned in the U.S. mass media at the time, and has been mentioned only briefly and rarely since, although it was newsworthy in Latin America and Western Europe. This was constructive terror, and occurred shortly after new Carter administration moves to step up military assistance to the El Salvadoran military regime, as well as to Honduras. At the Rio Sumpul massacre, as with Operation Condor murders, we can see U.S. efforts at training, aid and inter-NSS coordination coming to fruition, bearing "dividends." Armstrong and Wheaton point out that during the day-long slaughter "[U.S. made] trucks, jeeps, communications equipment and helicopters were used by the Honduran forces—who maintained ongoing communication with Salvadoran armed forces via U.S.-made walkie-talkies."[23]

In Guatemala, Church and other sources have collected and eagerly offer innumerable well-documented and detailed accounts of army and paramilitary murders, rapes and thefts that occur on a daily basis against the Indian and peasant populations. These are almost entirely ignored by the western media, but show up occasionally as dry statistics—matter-of-fact notings that 30 or 40 bodies were found on Guatemalan roadsides today. When these daily murders are spelled out and humanized, they can make an impression. Thus in an article entitled "Violence Batters The Church In Guatemala," June Carolyn Erlick writes,

> Father Carlos Galvez was on his way to baptize a child in a Guatemalan rural community on May 14. Suddenly shots rang out. He, like seven priests in Guatemala before him, was murdered in cold blood.
>
> "There were only horrified neighbors who could do nothing to keep his life from spilling out onto the stones of the street," wrote a nun who works in Guatemala. "When his body was removed the parishioners circled the pool of blood with rocks and filled the circle with flowers. But soon no blood was visible. It had been reverently gathered up with the dust of the road and carried home by grieving townspeople in much the same way that the early Christians gathered the blood of their martyrs as relics of their witness to their faith on the sand of the coliseum."
>
> The funeral in Tecpan, where Father Carlos worked, was massive. Three bishops and over 30 priests concelebrated the Mass, even though they knew they were risking their lives to do so.
>
> "But the greatest tribute to Father Galvez, the sixth priest to be killed since May 1980, was the enormous crowd of townspeople at the Mass," writes the nun. "Shoulder to shoulder...stood wealthy and poor, young and old, men and women, Indians and mestizos."[24]

Multiply this story by 2,000 or more a year for Guatemala alone, adding in the frequent pre-killing violence of rape and torture, the subsequent mutilations, the widespread thievery, and we see a picture of the human but de-humanized Guatemala—but we also see why it is important that the U.S. public be spared such details.

Indonesia is another country almost completely "blacked out" by the mass media of the United States. This is in perfect accord with a hypothesis proposed here: namely, that a friendly NSS which allows easy penetration by western economic interests can engage in virtually unlimited abuse of its own citizens without attracting substantial attention or expressions of concern, let alone denunciations, by the U.S. mass media. Really sensational events can occur; people of the same high quality and nobility as Sakharov can be harassed, arrested, tried, imprisoned and killed in Indonesia, *and the U.S. public will never know about it*. I will give two illustrations. One is the arrest and trial in 1979 of Heri Akhmadi, general chairman of the Students' Council of the Bandung Institute of Technology. This episode directly followed widespread student protests at Suharto's unopposed election for President in 1978. In retaliation, and to help return the students to the proper state of fear and quiescence, the army invaded dozens of college campuses in January 1978 and arrested scores of student leaders. This was followed by an even more violent invasion of the campuses in February 1979, when many students were injured, hundreds more were arrested, and the army units confiscated and took off "evidence." (At his trial, Akhmadi asked: "Does the law actually provide for such a method of confiscation?", but he never received a reply.) The protesting students, largely middle-class, were objecting to a comic opera election by generals without legitimate authority, who had chosen (in Akhmadi's words) "the easiest and laziest way" of growing, namely, attracting as much foreign investment as possible without regard to domestic impact, and who had been looting on their own without restraint, in a system of managed privilege,[25] while doing very little to alleviate truly massive poverty and distress.

The trial of the most prominent student leader in Indonesia had three features that one would have thought would make it newsworthy. First, it was a trial of someone protesting political tyranny, which is supposedly a western value of importance. Second, Akhmadi was being tried for allegedly "insulting" the head of state, Suharto, again presumably a basis of arrest and trial contrary to western ideals. And, third, Akhmadi put up a bold and eloquent defense, of sufficient interest and quality that the Cornell Modern Indonesian Project published a translation in 1981 under the title "Breaking The Chains of Oppression of the Indonesian People, Defense Statement at His Trial on Charges of Insulting the Head of State." If Akhmadi had been a communist, allegedly conspiring against the state, perhaps his trial would have been newsworthy; but as he was a strongly anticommunist nationalist, who presented a serious indictment of the Suharto regime for looting and selling out the national patrimony to foreign interests, his dramatic statement and his victimization failed to make the grade in the western media. Once again, the reader is urged to translate to a hypothetical "Moscow equivalent" student leader, and trace out the probabilities of equivalent media suppression.

Another illustration concerns the distinguished Indonesian novelist Pramoedya Anata Toer, a nominee for the Nobel prize in literature, referred to in the *Far Eastern Economic Review* as Indonesia's "best living novelist," who, "from the beginning of his literary career...has been functioning behind bars."[26] His first major works were written in a Dutch jail in 1949. Between 1965 and 1979 he was imprisoned by the Indonesian generals without charges or trial (along with tens of thousands of others). During this 14 year imprisonment, Pramoedya wrote, among other things, four historical novels. Two of them, *World of Man* and *A Child of All Nations*, were secretly published in 1980 and widely distributed, even though quickly banned by the authorities. Pramoedya was subject to multiple interrogations and harrassment following a lecture in September 1980 at the University of Indonesia, and four students who arranged the talk as well as his publisher were arrested. The publisher was held incommunicado and had not been released by year-end 1981. Ten thousand copies of Pramoedya's two novels were burned by order of the Attorney-General of Indonesia in October 1981.

Keith Foulcher, commenting in the *Times Literary Supplement* of August 7, 1981, wrote on the ban on Pramoedya's two novels:

> His situation, just eighteen months after his release, may again be precarious. For the rest of the world, the ban serves as an indication that Indonesia's one major novelist to date still awaits the basic freedom to practise his art, let alone official recognition of it.

Once again, the dramatic event of the arrests, the nobility and prestige of the victim, an official book-burning, would seem to define a newsworthy violation of human rights. Benedict Anderson of the Cornell Modern Indonesian Project even received a call from the *New York Times* to get his confirmation (which he gave) of the fact of the book-burning. The *Manchester Guardian*, in England, carried a letter of protest against the treatment of Pramoedya with distinguished signatories from 16 different countries (October 23, 1981). But nothing materialized through 1981 in the *New York Times* or elsewhere in the mass media of the United States. Pramoedya chose the wrong country in which to suffer repression, and his condition is what we may call "structurally unnewsworthy."

I will give one final illustration, of averting the eyes by underreporting, a case that is of interest because it combines partial suppression with hypocrisy. In October 1979 a political refugee from Paraguay living in Brooklyn recognized there Americo Pena-Irala, a police inspector general from Asuncion and a member of a team that tortured and murdered assorted opponents of General Stroessner. Pena had been accused by the father of one victim, a 17-year old boy named Joelito Filartiga, of kidnapping, torturing and murdering him. The *New York Times*, in a small back page article of April 5, 1979, noted that

> A confidential report prepared by the Inter-American Commission on Human Rights of the Organization of American States, contended that Mr. Pena and three other policemen kidnapped the Filartiga youth on March 19, 1976, with the intent of forcing him to incriminate his father falsely in sedition charges. The report, obtained by the New York Times, asserted that the boy had died of a heart attack after being beaten and receiving high-voltage electric shocks.

The boy's father, a physician and painter of renown, started an international campaign to bring charges against Pena, and the case was investigated by Amnesty International as well as by the OAS. Pena was under such pressure that he decided to leave Paraguay temporarily, and the kindly U.S. consulate in Asuncion gave him a visa to enter the United States. Following the sighting noted above, Pena was eventually taken into custody by the U.S. Immigration and Naturalization Service, which held him on bond pending deportation hearings. The father of the murder victim brought a suit for damages against Pena in a U.S. court to prevent his deportation to the safety of Paraguay and, hopefully, to try to obtain justice by law in this country. This effort failed as the suit was lost on appeal to the Supreme Court and Pena was allowed to leave the country.

Several points are worthy of special note here. First, this case involved facts of huge dramatic potential, human interest, and state terror in its most terrible form. A young boy tortured to death in a police state, with photos available of slashes, whip wounds, an erect penis from unremoved wires still in the dead body. The father pursuing justice and catching up with the torturer-murderer, who, according to the Council on Hemispheric Affairs, was not only one of the most detested and feared police killers in Paraguay but also a drug dealer and pimp, very possibly bringing into New York City unsuspecting Paraguayan teen-age girls for sale as prostitutes.

Point two, however, is that this remarkable story was not found very newsworthy in the United States. The *New York Times* gave it an aggregate of four small back-page items of coverage and failed to interview Dr. Joel Filartiga, the father, and get his views on these events, despite his distinction, the nobility and justice of his effort, and his presence in New York City. This conforms to an earlier pattern noted by Richard Arens in his *Genocide in Paraguay*: namely, that the U.S. press in general, the *New York Times* among them, "shamefully buried" stories about the destruction of the Aché Indians that were found newsworthy in Great Britain, West Germany, Switzerland and elsewhere.[27] It also conforms to the hypothesis advanced here, that the leading mass media enterprises have a strong propensity to suppress or play down terror in U.S. client states. From the media's viewpoint, Dr. Filartiga chose the "wrong country" in which to have his son tortured to death.

A third point concerns the protective cover given this client state terrorist by the United States government. Pena was initially provided with an entry permit on the basis of a fraudulent claim. When he was discovered in Brooklyn, it took months, and the impetus of aroused congressional interest, before the Immigration and Naturalization Service took Pena into custody. The government then tried as hard as it could to get Pena deported back to the safety of Paraguay, and fought the attempts by the father of the torture-murder victim to keep Pena in the United States to stand trial.

This brings us, finally, to the matter of hypocrisy. On August 20, 1980, the *New York Times* had an editorial entitled "Foreign Torture, American Justice," dealing in large part with the Pena-Filartiga case. It describes briefly the background and legal process, but focuses on a decision by Judge Irving Kaufman in the Court of Appeals, that allowed Pena to be sued as a violator of international law if justice is unobtainable in the home country of victim and victimizer. The hypocrisy rests in the fact that at the time Pena was in the United States, when a trial against him would have been meaningful, and when extensive news coverage and editorial indignation would have been of practical significance, the *New York Times* was exceedingly quiet. Its editorial on the case features U.S. judicial nobility in the cause of justice, whereas U.S. *practice*—sustained by the *New York Times*— features the glossing over and protecting of friendly terror, no matter how outlandish.

2. The principle of reliance on government as the source of the relevant and the true.

This is a principle with obvious exceptions, but the exceptions do not vitiate its importance as a powerful basis of brainwashing under freedom. The *main* exception is the government of enemy states, whose pronouncements are normally neither sought out nor taken at face value. In reporting on Vietnam and Cambodia, U.S. reporters and western wire services almost never communicate with and convey the explanations and rationales of the leaders of those governments on internal economic problems or sources of violence. There, refugees and western official sources have sufficed. Whereas, on economic problems and violence in the NSSs of Indonesia, Thailand and Chile, the views of the NSS officials are important, both directly and via wire service reports. This was applicable, for example, in the case of the South

African incursions into Angola in mid-1981, where, as I described earlier, the press gave dominant coverage not to the Angolan victims, the damage sustained by Angola, or Angola's
accounts or explanations of events, but rather to South Africa's
views. There was heavy front page play to the South African
capture of "Soviet advisers" and attention was given to the
"spoils" captured by the apartheid regime in its invasion. As in
the case of East Timor, there was a minimum of indignation.

The U.S. government, as sponsor of the NSS, provides it
with a protective propaganda cover. And it succeeds because of
its power as a preeminent news source, its special relations with
the mass media, and their patriotic refusal to challenge patriotic
lies. When they do raise questions about really egregious lies,
they do it in so muted a fashion—while continuing to allow the
government unlimited space for reiteration—that the public is
still hardly aware of the fact that the government is lying. There is
an important difference in this regard even as between the western European and U.S. media, with the former tending to look
more closely at U.S. government claims, the latter more likely to
do very little independent search and more inclined to transmit
the official line. A comparative study by Moraes and Lawton of
European and U.S. press coverage of the 1973 Chilean coup, for
example, shows clearly that the major U.S. papers followed a
"line" that stressed Allende mismanagement as the root of the
coup, deemphasized internal and external opposition and destabilization efforts as factors contributing to Allende's difficulties,
and, following the coup, underplayed the torture and murder and
stressed the "return to normality," precisely in conformity with
"one of the major themes appearing throughout the junta's own
propaganda."[28] Moraes and Lawton show that the European
press used a wider range of sources and disputed this State
Department-Pinochet party line disseminated by the U.S. press.

When the U.S. government wants to establish some policy-
justifying "truth"—e.g., that the problem in South Vietnam in
1961-1962 or 1964-1965 was North Vietnamese aggression, or
that the rebels in El Salvador are "extreme leftists" under the
"discipline" of World Communism—the U.S. mass media cooperate and the patriotic truths are established. This is accomplished
by the sheer volume of government claims and handouts and

their uncritical transmission by the media that count. A study by Gusmao and Benjamin of the *New York Time's* 1980 coverage of El Salvador, for example, found that 60% of the attributed sources represented the official government viewpoint, and that although the majority of the victims of violence in El Salvador have been peasants, the *New York Times* quoted only two peasants in 75 articles on that country.[29] With this dependence on official sources, the mass media can be "used" to convey a propaganda line. When the State Department wanted to show that the Nicaraguans were helping the El Salvadoran guerilLas, a beach landing of "well-armed guerilLas" and a huge battle was reported by Christopher Dickey in the *Washington Post* of January 14, 1980, based on telephone calls from his hotel room in San Salvador to U.S. officials. On January 19 Dickey reversed himself, still claiming an engagement of troops, "But where they came from and who they were has not been established and U.S. officials here now are saying that White 'overemphasized' the supposed invasion and no longer thinks the evidence about it as 'compelling' as the day he spoke." This is "news" in a Pickwickian sense, depending on the fluctuating emphases desired by various U.S. officials. Maslow and Arana, in their examination of the media's gullibility on El Salvador, conclude that "Dickey, it seems, had been used by intelligence agencies to spread the evidence of Nicaraguan intervention and thus bolster the case for renewing military aid to the junta."[30] Former CIA employee Ralph McGehee noted that,

> Although the reported battle between the invading guerilLas [allegedly 100 or more men] and the Salvadoran security forces lasted all day, the Government troops failed to kill any guerilLas, capture any prisoners, or recover any weapons. A second sea raid was reported on January 22—again without casualties or prisoners. This was considered sufficient evidence, and on January 24, the United States signed a $65 million aid package with the Salvadoran Government. On January 29, two Salvadoran government officials resigned, charging that the two "invasions" were staged in order to justify the sending in of American troops.[31]

According to a "Dissent Paper on El Salvador and Central America," put out by individuals in the State Department at odds with official policy, there has been a deliberate effort by the authorities to "misrepresent the situation in El Salvador," and, with the help of "liason and public relations" efforts, "media coverage of El Salvador has been responsive to official government policies." This is clearly evident in the media's handling of the El Salvador White Paper. The government issues White Papers that offer alleged proofs of its claims in a charged atmosphere that produces enormous headlines. There may have been "leaks" to favored reporters and columnists in prior weeks. The mass media uniformly feature these claims as hot news irrespective of their plausibility or validity. In the lesser media (from the standpoint of circulation) the government's charges are often contested and are sometimes shown to be the inverse of the truth. Thus the Johnson adminstration's White Paper of 1964 was utterly devastated by I.F. Stone and by the editors of the *New Republic* (among others), but the charge of North Vietnamese aggression was nevertheless institutionalized. The El Salvador White Paper of 1981 has been similarly taken apart and shown to be crude even by traditional White Paper standards by James Petras, John Dinges and Philip Agee. Somewhat later the *Wall Street Journal* itself featured a long news article that pointed up the careless packaging of this propaganda piece.[32] The Reagan administration apparently understands that fact and consistency are irrelevant, and can be overridden by the mass media's deferential role playing as conduit for whatever claims the authorities wish to disseminate. Thus once again, as with earlier White Papers and the Red Scares of 1919-1920 and 1949-1955, the mass media of the United States failed to examine the foundations of a party line that was not true.

The government White Paper claims of a large-scale outside Communist arms flow into El Salvador are based on alleged captured documents. The secret of U.S. mass media apologetics is to pass on official claims and interpretations of documents immediately as truth, without even examining the documents, without independent checking of the claims, and without any context. The *Baltimore Sun* carried a front page article headlined "Haig Describes Salvador Insurgency As Soviet Attempt To

Overthrow Junta," and Roger Mudd conduited the State Department view on NBC: "The [State] Department said weapons are being supplied by the Soviet Union, Vietnam and East Germany among others, and that the whole operation is being coordinated by Cuba." Juan de Onis of the *New York Times*, also "objectively" conveyed the message that the Soviet bloc nations had pledged arms to the Salvadoran rebels according to captured documents which "are considered authentic by U.S. intelligence agencies."[33] This last point is not knowable by de Onis—it would be more "objective" to say that the documents are *alleged* to be considered authentic by these agencies, as a de Onis knows that such agencies may occasionally leak fabrications to people like himself.

Both John Dinges and James Petras have shown that even taking the documents at face value, all they demonstrate is an effort to mobilize support abroad by the rebels; an effort not confined to the Communist powers, and one that met with only modest success.[34] The Soviet Union is mentioned in the documents only in a report of El Salvadoran Communist Party chief Handal's tour of the Communist states, in which he expresses disappointment at a refusal of a high official of the Soviet Union to meet with him and in "the non-resolution of the request for help." Nothing in these documents anywhere suggests that the Soviets have made more than token moves to aid, or that either the Soviet or Cubans initiated or coordinated anything. In short, the Haig claims of a Soviet attempt to "overthrow the junta" is demagogic lying of the most egregious sort.

The White Paper's evidence for a large and rapidly growing Communist arms flow to the rebels is extremely muddled and obscure, but it took an outsider, Christopher Wren of *The Times* of London, to look at the facts on the scene. He went to the head of the Salvadoran National Guard, which had allegedly captured the documents, and he looked over the captured weapons themselves— which he found to be in small quantity, many home-made, and including a British Lewis machine gun of First World War vintage.[35] The White Paper charges that some 800 tons of arms were promised to the rebels and 200 delivered, but the *documents* give evidence of perhaps 10 tons having crossed over the borders. Those who have looked closely at the arms flow to the rebels find the distinctly small flows to be coming from Costa Rica, Panama,

Florida, and, in general, mainly from a flourishing international black market in which the rebels appear to be buying. The White Paper focus on Cuba and Nicaragua as major sources of arms is unsupported by the allegedly supporting documents and is contrary to independent evidence on the arms flows.[36]

The White Paper is a throw-back to 1965, when the U.S. Indochina assault was preluded by similar claims of an enormous flow from North Vietnam, also not sustained by the accompanying "documents." I.F. Stone went to the trouble of actually inspecting the documents, which the mass media did not do—and still do not do—and was able to compute that approximately 2½% of the captured weapons of the previous 18 months were of Communist origin, 80% were captured from the United States or one of its proxies.[37] With only rare exception, it is outsiders who investigate and contest major government claims that prepare the ground for foreign intervention; the mainstream reporters, publications and stations are part of a national institutional apparatus whose function in such cases is the institutionalization of patriotic truths. The main qualifications to this normally cooperative relationship occur when the government is threatening encroachments on mass media prerogatives, or in those very special cases where the government is operating in a manner deemed threatening by important domestic power groups. Ordinarily foreign policy rests on an elite consensus, and a symbiotic relationship between government and the mass media follows. The threat of sharply escalated intervention in El Salvador in 1981 and early 1982 led to heightened public attention, some elite reservations and suggested caution, and an opening up of publicity on details of the junta's anti-civilian violence. At the same time, U.S. government claims were allowed full head, and its misrepresentations of the nature of the junta, the rebels and the threat of "foreign intervention" were the dominant factors shaping general public understanding of the issues and allowing continued U.S. support of state terrorism in its ugliest form.

3. Stripping away of context

Facts have meaning only in context. Mindless reporting of Haig claims that X-tons of arms are flowing into El Salvador from the Communist powers is not "objective," even apart from veracity—it allows a propaganda source to define which facts are important and which are to be ignored. As a propagandist, Haig's aim is to push into the background the U.S. role in El Salvador, past and present, to create a context in which whatever we may be doing or have done we have a right to do; whereas Cuban and Soviet intrusions are a priori illegitimate. As in Guatemala, however, the El Salvadoran "security forces" that have been killing peasants by the thousands and ravaging the countryside for quite a few years are products of an exclusively U.S. investment in military training and arms, which became especially heavy and intense in the "counterinsurgency 60's." Security assistance was only $16.9 million between 1950 and 1979, but over 2,000 El Salvadoran officers were U.S.-trained and the paramilitary security force, Orden, was encouraged in the 1960s as part of post-Castro counterrevolutionary strategy. There was a cutback in military assistance to El Salvador during the early Carter years, but it was never terminated, and the slack was taken up by U.S. "surrogates" like Israel and Brazil. U.S. military aid to the El Salvador junta in 1980 totalled only $5.9 million, but economic aid amounted to a substantial $72.5 million and additional multilateral aid brought the grand total to $183.9 million.[38] It is elementary that a dollar provided to a general pool releases a dollar to acquire "lethal" weapons.

The U.S. mass media pretend that third party supply by our clients and surrogates is not a worthy subject for discussion. An arms shipment from Nicaragua to the rebels is newsworthy and somehow sinister—arms transferred from Honduras or Brazil to the El Salvador junta is not news. Rebels and governments opposed by the United States, such as the Arbenz government of Guatemala in 1954, are subject to serious military threats by generous U.S. supply and training of rightwing forces and by U.S. encouragement of neighboring clients to invade or threaten groups or states on our hit list. The latter will have to seek arms to survive. Boycotted by the U.S. and its clients, the rebels will reach out to any friendly powers for arms and other assistance. But arms coming from Czechoslovakia in 1954, and trickling in in the early 1980s from Nicaragua, Cuba and more distant Communist powers show the international Communist conspiracy at work trying to undermine Free Societies. This parody is close to the workings of the propaganda machine. Since the mass media will allow a Dulles, a Rusk and a Haig to get away with identifying any trickle of arms from the Communist world as sinister and proof of some dangerous Red plot, even if defensive and provoked by gross U.S. and U.S.-client intervention and threats, the system will always work to create a propaganda rationale for anything the United States chooses to do.

In short, if arms to El Salvador were discussed in a full context, it would be seen that the United States has been the only serious supplier of arms to that country over the past several decades, that the murderous central regime of El Salvador is a product of long and extensive U.S. training, supply and political manipulation, and that the only long-term conspiracy to dominate from the outside is quite clearly located in Washington, D.C.

The stripping away of context has long been a feature of U.S. mass media reporting on Indochina. As indicated earlier, deaths under the Khmer Rouge regime were ultimately attributed to Communism and Pol Pot—period. Antecedent factors involving the west, such as the murderous warfare prior to April 1975, the devastation of the land, and the already endemic starvation conditions were set aside to allow a focus on the desired locus of terror. A superb recent example was provided by Henry Kamm in his article in the *New York Times* of November 8, 1981, "In Mosaic of Southeast Asia, Capitalist Lands Are Thriving." Kamm finds, "sadly," that conditions of life in Vietnam, Cambodia and Laos are bad, in contrast with the rising living standards and a "state of peace in the countries of the region that reject Communism." I think we must concede that 10 million tons of bombs, supplemented by a boycott of the victims of the bombs, is less serviceable to per capita income growth than no bombs and positive external aid. But Kamm does not even mention that the countries which failed to "reject Communism" were invaded by a distant great power and subjected to a bombing onslaught unparalleled in human history. He even states with great matter-of-factness, as if part of a long and undisturbed historical process, that in the countryside of Indochina, "even working animals are rare, and men, women and children do the work done elsewhere by machines or beasts of burden." That the vast proportion of these beasts of burden were killed quite recently, during more than a decade of warfare—a large fraction by U.S. bombs—is unmentioned, as is the fact of a post-1975 U.S. boycott and deliberate effort to impede the replacement of beasts of burden by other states.[39] This, I believe, carries "stripping of context" to the limit of its theoretical potential.

Kamm also provides some observations on changes in the level and distribution of income in Southeast Asia that are worthy of note. He tells us that a first-time visitor to Manila or Jakarta will be impressed by the prevalence of luxury motor cars in the midst of penury; but longer term observers (i.e., Henry Kamm) can see that "the floor has risen for the many." What is the proof? Motorbikes owned by the "average man" clogging the streets, people better dressed, and cassette recorders and cameras more prevalent. In the villages, bicycles and frequent sewing machines "tell of a gradual, if uneven, amelioration in the standard of life." This evidence leaves something to be desired on matters of representativeness, rigor and consistency with more detailed studies. Motorbikes observed on the main streets of cities with millions of inhabitants, even if measured closely rather than by casual impression, hardly tell us much about the human condition of the 99% of unobserved cases, possibly living in the huge shantytowns that have grown on the periphery of NSS big cities. There is no indication in Kamm's reporting that he ever gets off the main streets. One wonders, also, how many of the thousands of villages in rural Indonesia and the Philippines Henry Kamm has visited, and how many households he checked out concerning the number of sewing machines. If he visited as many as one tenth of 1% of the villages, and checked as many as 20 households, I would be surprised.

The World Bank 1980 report on Indonesia, which goes as far as one can go in looking at the bright side without doing gross violence to the facts, gives a quite different picture from Kamm. In contrast with Kamm's "gradual amelioration" up and down the line, the World Bank says that "the overall impression one gets [from studying data on the wages paid by business firms and governmental bodies] is that real wages of unskilled workers in these firms have at best stagnated." The "at best" is generous as virtually all sectors, including the government, "show a decline in real wages [between 1973 and 1977] ranging from 3% in government administration to over 50% in a large hotel."[40] The Bank also concludes that improvements which have occurred "still amount to only a tiny diminution in the problem of poverty in Indonesia...[with] 50.1 million people altogether existing on less than US $0.25 per day."[41] The situation in the Philippines has been worse, with virtually nobody claiming any improvement in the condition of the huge numbers of destitute, and with that total itself increasing. Szal shows that urban real wages fell for both skilled and unskilled workers during the 1970s, and he cites Philippine evidence (incorporated into Table 3-2) of serious levels of malnutrition.[42]

On the question of the distribution of income between rich and poor, Henry Kamm puts the matter this way: "there is ample proof [not anywhere cited by Kamm] that the floor has risen for the many, while the ceiling has gone higher for the few." He thereby carefully sidesteps the question of differences in the *degree* of benefits between classes, although every serious observer of the facts (including the World Bank) is very clear that in both Indonesia and the Philippines the "few" have significantly increased their proportion of the total.[43] And Kamm gives no figures on the actual distribution of income, although data are readily available.

The NSSs in Kamm's beat have also been characterized by elite looting and conspicuous consumption of really notable proportions,[44] but Henry Kamm has long steered clear of any close look at the details. Ingrid Palmer suggests a phenomenal 30% of national income corruption drain in Indonesia, where the generals have a long established record of venality,[45] and the lavish life style and large scale corruption of Marcos and his cronies is also well known. In the Kamm article, there is an antiseptic statement about luxury motor cars and "economic injustice evidenced by this conspicuous consumption in the midst of penury"—but this exhausts his discussion, and it is surrounded by the claims of an alleged rise in the bottom, the average man's motor bike in Jakarta, and a statement on income distribution that suppresses evidence of a redistribution upward. No statements on magnitudes, or suggestions of venality, or details regarding housing conditions, servants, forms of elite consumption and outlays for entertainment, size of Swiss bank accounts, or other matters that would give any substance or life to NSS inequality and other abuses.

It is not that Henry Kamm never gets indignant over unequal life styles—e.g., on March 3, 1980 Kamm had an article on "Pol Pot Living in Jungle Luxury in Midst of Deprived Cambodia," in which he is quite sarcastic about the plush conditions of the Khmer Rouge leadership, with "smiling waiters" in a camp that is "the latest in jungle luxury," the visitors received in a room with "a handsome vaulted roof of dried leaves over a table at which coffee was served to refresh the visitors." Each of four guest bungalows had four beds made of wood and bamboo, with homemade mattresses, blankets and pillows. And bamboo vases contained flowers "that must have been brought from Thailand." Thus Kamm is capable of providing details of luxurious living, but he selects according to the principles that I have already spelled out. Even in the article I am focussing on here on Capitalist Lands Thriving, while Kamm provides no detail on the elites of the NSSs, he does get a bit angry at the high living of the bureaucrats of the Communist states, juxtaposing a remark on the badly fed condition of the people with the assertion that "motorized transport [is] reserved for high Government and Communist Party officials."

It is fitting that Henry Kamm should close out his 12 year stint in Southeast Asia with an article covering up the structured deprivation and injustice of the NSSs, and discoursing at length on the performance differentials between the Indochinese states and the U.S. clients without once mentioning any possible relevance of the 10 million tons of bombs dropped on the former!

4. The principle of balance

The classic modes of expressing balance to protect NSS violence are to pretend either that there is an equivalence of state and "left" violence, or that the government stands in the middle between a left and right that is independent of the government and which the government is trying to control. As I described earlier in the case of Sterling, this can be done with a further apologetic twist in which leftist terror comes first, then the military reluctantly enters to rectify matters. Why the military keeps on killing, as in Uruguay, long after the extermination of the leftists, is not discussed. In treating Brazil, where state terrorism produced a responsive left terror that had not existed previously at all, Sterling suppresses the causal sequence and then attributes the *further* abuses of the military regime to the (quickly exterminated) leftists!

The principle of balance invariably involves lying, as the balance usually does not equate, or the matters put in the balance are not comparable. Thus, Warren Hoge suggests that Guatemala is "in the grip of an escalating balance of terror" between incompetent terrorists and an "inept" army.[46] This balance is false, first, because official killings have exceeded the killings by the "left" (which actually includes the middle) by an enormous factor; surely better than 25 to 1. Between 1966 and 1976 some 20,000 people were killed by government forces, initially in a huge counterinsurgency campaign which eliminated a guerilla force estimated at a peak level of 450, plus thousands of "others." More recently, just since Garcia came to power in 1978, his program of political murder has resulted in over 7,000 deaths. "The bodies of the victims have been found piled up in ravines, dumped at roadsides or buried in mass graves. Thousands bore the scars of torture, and death had come to most by strangling with a garrotte, by being suffocated in rubber hoods or by being shot in the head."[47] These are victims of rightwing-state terror. Even the Guatemalan government does not pretend that these are victims of leftists—its claim is that they are the results of the actions of autonomous rightwing death squads.

The second deception of the "balance" line in its application to Guatemala is its failure to recognize that the guerillas have come into existence once again under the most extreme provocations—most notably, pacification by deliberate and extensive murder. Many of the thousands of murders have been indiscriminate, carried out sometimes on whim or on the basis of rumor or alleged associations. This is especially true of people of low status, who have constituted "the vast majority" of victims of official violence. As noted by AI,

> The precarious balance for the poor in Guatemala between life and death at the hands of the security services is illustrated by the testimonies in this report. The former soldier describes house-to-house searches

in which the discovery of certain "paper"—leaflets or circulars—was sufficient reason to wipe out an entire family. The prisoner [who described his ordeals to AI], who was brutally tortured and escaped only the day before he was due to be executed at Huehuetenango army base, believes that a neighbor denounced him as "subversive" because of a dispute over the village basketball court—a good enough reason, as far as officers of the Guatemalan army were concerned, for him to be tortured and put to death.[48]

But official violence in Guatemala is not entirely random. According to AI,

By far the majority of victims were chosen after they had become associated—or were thought to be associated—with social, religious, community or labor organizations, or after they had been in contact with organizers of national political parties. In other words, Amnesty International's evidence is that the targets for extreme governmental violence tend to be selected from grass roots organizations outside official control.[49]

This system of anticipatory pacification by systematic murder has been carried out under conditions of appalling exploitation and oppression of the Indian and peasant population. The remarkable inequality of income distribution in Guatemala and the horrendous conditions of the majority as measured by unemployment, malnutrition, child mortality, life expectancy, illiteracy and curable disease rates were described in the previous chapter (see Table 3-2). This is a NSS at its most violent, rapacious and cruel, with large scale expropriations of peasant and Indian lands by force (as in Brazil and Paraguay), extensive and uncontrolled use of pesticides like DDT and Endrin on open fields in which Indian men, women and children are working, and regular murder of any elements of the lower orders that raise their voices or attempt any self-defence. No independent political activity has been possible in Guatemala since the U.S.-sponsored rightwing coup of 1954. As noted, even the modestly liberal Christian Democratic Party had virtually its entire body of officials murdered by the Garcia government, and it has closed down its office in Guatemala City. In this environment "guerillas" have emerged, have killed a few score members of the "security forces" and their supporters and sponsors, and thus we have a state of offsetting terrorism of the left and right!

Warren Hoge quotes an unnamed scientist who suggests that the Indians of Guatemala will be hard for the "guerillas" to mobilize as "they are real good at stepping aside and getting out of the way." No suggestion of the possibility that the *guerillas* may be Indians, although Church and other independent sources in Guatemala say that the escalating abuses—both forcible expropriations plus continuous search and destroy missions involving arbitrary killing and regular thievery—are literally forcing them into self-defense, and that many Indians have already joined the guerillas.[50] Although Hoge gives a few rather antiseptic figures on the concentration of wealth and the imperfections of the electoral process and human rights situation, there is nothing on the quality of treatment of the Indians, the forms of exploitation, or the extensiveness, character and role of political murders in Guatemala. He does cite an expatriate who had worked for a social action group: "The head of one such group who has just left the country because his life was threatened said the overreaction to ordinary organizations occurred after the Sandinista victory in Nicaragua and civil war in El Salvador. 'Suddenly, everything that had been normal became suspicious to the army,' he said." Notice how the cause of the violence in Guatemala is shifted to the outside; the death squads are just "overreacting" to what is, by implication, a legitimate external threat. The overreacting implies that the prior behavior of Garcia and company was perhaps reasonable. So does the quoted phrase about what had been "normal" in the past. This is classic apologetics. And, having quoted the "opposition" (or misquoted it, or paraphrased it to apologetic purpose), Hoge can close out this article with two paragraphs on the views of the Reagan administration.

Flora Lewis, an old hand at apologetics for U.S. intervention in Guatemala,[51] provides a genuine classic in the use of "balance" in her article on "The Danger of Absolutes," in the *New York Times* of October 16, 1981. This article is, in fact, an absolute gold mine of clichés. A delightful one of ancient vintage takes this form: "The left, with considerable historical support, attacks America [sic: she means the United States] for supporting dictators. The right complains we don't support them enough." Her fair-mindedness is demonstrated by the concession that there is "considerable" historical support for the left contention of U.S. aid to dictators; but, as the right claims a deficiency of U.S. support, does this not suggest to a reasonable person that actual policy, condemned by both extremes, is not far off the mark? (Try this one out on, say, Botha's policies: criticized by those on the left, who muster "considerable historical support" for the view that blacks have not been well treated in South Africa; but also criticized on the right by some who say that Botha is moving too fast, etc. Ergo.)

In her balancing act on Guatemala, Flora Lewis writes,

> Jacobo Arbenz, the Guatemalan President overthrown in 1954, turned up later in Prague and openly discussed his ties to the Soviet bloc. But the fact that the C.I.A. arranged the coup to oust him has converted his memory to one of mild liberalism for many who are now shocked by Guatemala's ruthless right-wing regime. The habit of absolutes makes people imagine that if one side is bad, its adversaries must be all good.

Observe, first, that while pretending to be interested in contesting the tendency of people (unnamed) to take absolutist-opposite positions (if the United States was bad, Arbenz must be good), she herself uses relativism as a means of blatant apologetics. If Arbenz was also bad, maybe the United States is not so bad after all. This little trick allows her to bypass the questions of just *how bad* the U.S.-sponsored terror regimes have been, and, even if Arbenz was proved bad (which she does not do), why the United States chose to organize and support the thoroughly vicious system of gradually escalating terror that developed after 1954. Notice how the United States is only implicated in the *coup*; the "ruthless right-wing regime" is placed a bit apart, as something that emerged perhaps inadvertently and not as a planned result of the coup and definite U.S. follow-up policies. This is dishonesty by omission. The United States did not just organize the coup and *leave*. It shaped the course of terror in crucial ways, and, instead of constraining counterrevolutionary terror, U.S. leaders displayed obvious distress only at the unwillingness of the newly chosen managers to kill with sufficeint energy. Thus, U.S. Ambassador to Guatemala, John Peurifoy, presented to interim post-coup president Colonel Carlos Enrique Diaz a long list of "Communists" to be killed within 24 hours. Diaz' refusal and his expressed intention to proclaim a general amnesty were the "last straw" for Peurifoy, and Diaz was quickly ousted.[52] Even Castillo Armas, carefully selected by the U.S. authorities, and generally following orders in detail, offended Dulles by his unwillingness to seize the 700 or so Arbenz followers who had taken refuge in foreign embassies after the coup. Kinzer and Schlesinger point out that

> Dulles advanced a new doctrine: communists should be automatically denied the right of asylum because they were connected with an international conspiracy...In the end Castillo Armas disregarded Dulles' advisories. He himself was a product of widespread belief in Latin America that embassy asylum and safe exits were a fair resolution to political conflicts.[53]

But Dulles and Peurifoy felt that Armas had "betrayed them." In short, book burnings, the murder of numerous trade union leaders, the termination of political freedom, elicited not a word of complaint from U.S. authorities in 1954. Only restraint in seeking vengeance bothered them.

The first durable state terrorist, Castillo Armas, was directly chosen by the United States. But the United States also arranged a further coup in 1963 when, in the words of Kinzer and Schlesinger, "Kennedy gave his approval to dissident Guatemalan army officers to overthrow Ydigoras" in order to prevent an election campaign by the popular former president Arévalo. The U.S.-chosen successor to Ydigoras was "an officer decidedly more reactionary than Ydigoras," under whose auspices "the Guatemalan dictatorship took on new zeal," and "murdered hundreds of anti-government activists..."[54] In 1966 U.S. intervention intensified, Green Berets were introduced, military aid was stepped up, familiar anti-guerilla warfare tactics were used on a large scale, "but a new weapon was also introduced: political assassinations on a mass scale." "Thousands of people suddenly met death at the hands of unseen gunmen" as the new campaign began to reach "anybody tinged with liberalism."[55] In brief, the *progress* of Guatemalan terror from 1954 onward was a result of steady U.S. intervention, carried out by U.S. trainees, with U.S. arms; and at each major political turn—1954, 1963 and 1966— the United States played a decisive role in consolidating the power of forces that carried terror to greater heights. The U.S. choices and the "absolute" level of exploitation and murder are of enormous importance and relevance; the bringing in of Arbenz is a classic use of "relativism" combined with a red herring.

Returning to Flora Lewis' equation, how does she prove that Arbenz was bad? The answer is that she does not—rather, she uses a McCarthyite trick that does not withstand the most superficial inspection. Her language is an interesting exercise in deceptive ambiguity: Arbenz "turned up later in Prague and openly discussed his ties to the Soviet bloc." From this she implies that he was a Soviet puppet while in power at an earlier time in Guatemala, though she avoids saying this directly. Notice her failure to spell out just what Arbenz *said* in Prague. Did he say more than that he was happy to be in a country with which Guatemala under his regime had had friendly and sympathetic relations? Observe the phrase "openly discussed his ties," with the sinister connotation that "ties" (unstipulated)—which of course the United has in great number with the Soviets (trade, loans, exchanges both political and cultural)—must have been sub rosa and illicit. The historical context of Arbenz in Prague is also ignored —Arbenz was a refugee, ousted from his legal position in Guatemala by completely illegal U.S. subversion, which suggests several further questions: What weight do we give his statements as a refugee-dependent? (I repeat, though, that Lewis' evasions suggest that Arbenz said nothing incriminating anyway.) Had he become embittered as a result of his experiences? If so, were his views as a refugee and victim of U.S. intervention the same as those he held in Guatemala some years earlier?

Flora Lewis also carefully avoids discussing the evidence regarding Arbenz in Guatemala. She makes no mention of the fact that he was elected democratically and received 65% of the vote in the last free election seen in that country. Nor does she discuss the fact that Arbenz was doing a great deal of very decent things for the long-repressed majority, who were allowed to unionize, to vote, and given land in a land reform that conformed rather closely to that urged at the time by the World Bank. The rabid hostility of United Fruit to these policies was far more important than any alleged Communist ties in determining U.S. hostility, and all of these reforms were quickly and savagely undone in the counterrevolution that followed under U.S. command. I mentioned earlier that the propaganda line pursued by the PR counsel for United Fruit and its government allies, with careful calculation, was to play down the land reform and union threats, which were the substantive issues of real concern to United Fruit, and to stress the "international Communist conspiracy." Even the CIA-sponsored study by Ronald Schneider made no claim of Soviet control or significant influence over Arbenz,[56] and the recent study by Kinzer and Schlesinger shows more directly that the alleged control was a propaganda fraud unsupported by any evidence.[57] The latter authors do establish the fact of a very important set of ties underlying the early sequence of events in Guatemala—they point out that "almost every one of the significant figures [in the United States] behind the Guatemalan coup was intimately acquainted with high United Fruit executives," leading them to conclude: "The takeover of United Fruit land was probably the decisive factor pushing the Americans into action."[58] But Flora Lewis operates on the selection principles described earlier in this chapter—she is interested only in enemy terror, and as the Guatemala story indicates, if she cannot find it in the real world she will construct it out of the whole cloth.

Another irresistible classic is provided in Edward Schumacher's reporting on El Salvador, where "balance" is regularly achieved through two routes: by offsetting nasty facts with propaganda claims of the authorities (not "apples versus oranges"— "apples versus wisps of hot air"), and by a highly selective culling of alleged facts to achieve the preconceived result. Only once, to my knowledge, did Schumacher ever actually refer to direct evidence from a peasant. On that occasion, the woman stated that regular soldiers brutalized and murdered her 67 year old husband, and beat her, for no reason. Before even concluding his first-ever first-hand report paragraph, Schumacher remarks with even-handed balance that this peasant woman's testimony demonstrates "what high Government and military officials say is their frustration in trying to control their own troops without destroying morale."[59] Note that Schumacher repeats this government claim as truth, never raising the possibility that it could be a propaganda ploy. Nor does he raise the deeper question—if this is the way government troops behave in fact, killing the innocent without discrimination, does this not constitute a criminal operation whatever its pretended goals?

Having inserted uncritically a government propaganda claim, Schumacher then quickly adds further balance to the empirical fact of an indiscriminate murder. He presents an account of an interview with Archbishop Arturo Rivera Y Damas, who he designates as "a critic of the government." Without quotations he claims that the Archbishop said that "while killing by Marxist guerillas appeared to be increasing, killing by government forces was decreasing. He attributed the decline to the government's efforts to curb the security forces." Examining Schumacher's use of the Archbishop more closely, some questions arise. Why no direct quotations? The phrase "Marxist guerillas" is used by the State Department and Duarte, but does the Archbishop use it? What else did he say? The line which Schumacher attributes to the Bishop, without quotation marks, is an exact replica of the one that the U.S. government and the El Salvador junta were trying to peddle at that time. If Schumacher were lying or stripping context, the Archbishop could not easily reply because he is in a highly vulnerable situation. Critics of the government in El Salvador are often murdered, including Archbishop Damas' predecessor. This threat of murder might be mentioned in a honest news account. So would the fact that Archbishop Damas was "under instructions" by the Vatican to work for the unity of the Church,[60] and that he has taken a centrist line in a desperate effort to use a nominal even-handedness to preserve his credibility and bargaining power with the right and the United States. According to a Catholic church official in the United States who met with the Archbishop shortly after Schumacher's article, "Rivera's public indecision (he's much clearer in private) is designed to enable him to function within the dialog process." [61] Is it not a bit unscrupulous on the part of a news reporter to use this compromised political position to extract "facts" that can be put forward as by a "critic of the government." Instead of asking somebody on the left, or somebody in the Church's Legal Office who follows political murders closely—and asking them off the record—Schumacher sticks to the very decent but politically confined Damas to give a critic's position.

We may note also that in Schumacher's paraphrasing of the Archbishop, no numbers are given, only an alleged direction of movement. It would be consistent with the Archbishop's alleged statement if government murders had declined from 500 to 480 whereas rebel killings had increased from 6 to 10. The implication in Schumacher is that the Archbishop is attributing the bulk of the killings to the rebels, not the government. As both the Archbishop and the Church Legal Office keep saying the opposite, Schumacher is lying by omission as well as by implication.

Another reason why Schumacher carefully avoids citing the Church's Legal Office is that it not only attributes the vast bulk of civilian killings to the military junta, it keeps suggesting quite openly that the *United States* is at the root of the murders, that this is a "prolonged, cruel and bloody *North American* military intervention," and that it is "military regimes educated, financed, advised and armed by the United States who are the ones who have generated the violence."[63] Clearly this will not do. Such a view, although as obvious as the sun at noon on a clear summer day, has no place in a Schumacherized version of murder in El Salvador. Neither do AI's outcries, which have also stressed the blind indiscriminateness of the official killings in El Salvador— of a death machine run amok. In a letter to Alexander Haig in June 1981, AI points to the large scale killings of people who have no connection with guerillas—of conclusive evidence of "a consistent pattern of killing by the security forces of peasants, young people and other victims who had no part in guerilla activity." This is "constructive" terror, however, supported by the United States, and Edward Schumacher suppresses accordingly.

5. The principle that the NSS is led by moderates standing between two poles of extremists.

This classic ploy is used even for Guatemala. The former press secretary of the Ministry of the Interior, Elias Barahona Y Barahona, claimed that one of his prime concerns while in that office was to get the media to swallow the notion that there were left extremists and right extremists *independent of the government.* He told AI that this ploy was based on a direct lie; that the names to be used for death squad murders were prepared from the records of Military Intelligence and National Police, and the blank letter-head stationary of the leading death squads were stored in the office of the Minister of the Interior, who was in charge of internal security.[63] Nevertheless, Associated Press reports from Guatemala continue to say that "The violence appeared part of the terrorist war that has been raging for years between leftist and rightist groups."[64]

This technique has also been used heavily in reference to Argentina and Brazil, where the extremists were long alleged to be a left and *segments* of the military—who do the killing, regrettably out of control of the "moderates" who otherwise exercise supreme power. This propaganda device allows a distribution of functions between government torturers and killers, the bad guys, on the one hand, and the struggling moderates, on the other. We may sympathize with the latter group, and align ourselves with the government, without implicating ourselves in the torture or compromising our well-known dedication to the rights of each and every individual. More important, we can convey this distributed function picture to the rest of the world, along with our support for the struggling moderates, which makes *us* moderates.

The difficulty has always been that the distinction between rightwing terror and government terror, and the alleged struggle between the forces that kill and the moderates, are both largely fraudulent. As I discussed earlier in connection with the death squads of Latin America, many of them are regular military cadres, and all of them—regular and irregular—are under the general direction of their respective governments. And while there has been infighting at the top of these military gravy trains, there is no evidence whatsoever suggesting that death squad and detention center torture and murder have not been under top level general control and direction.

The "moderate center" gambit reached its propaganda zenith in the Carter-Reagan effort to apply it to the murderous thugs ruling El Salvador. The State Department Dissent Paper stressed that a "moderate and reformist image of the current regime" was one of the deliberate misrepresentations that the government has foisted, with the aid of the media. The U.S. government propaganda line is that the violence and killing by the military and paramilitary forces are not actions of the "government," but of a "right" that is either separate from government forces or regrettably "out of control" (there has been some confusion on which line to take, but the media have not pressed the point). According to William Bowdler of the Carter State Department, "we have vigorously supported the Junta and opposed a repressive or non-reformist solution for El Salvador... the former [sic] association of elements of the security forces with the extreme right has left suspicions that undermine the moral authority of the new regime."[65] This separation has never been accepted by any serious investigator or respected foreign journalist—Orden and other paramilitary forces work in tandem with the regulars, are supplied by the government, and there is no reported case of incarceration or other serious action taken against any member of these rightwing groups for murder. AI is explicit that they are under the direction of the top military command. Even the apologists usually don't pretend with Bowdler that there has been a separation—as shown in discussing Schumacher's "balance," his contention and that of El Salvadoran authorities is that indiscriminate murders by regular and irregular forces are being *brought under control*, not that these irregulars have been disbanded or pushed out of the orbit of government authority. The truth is, however, that in the last two or three years, rightwing—that is to say, government sponsored and controlled—murders of civilians have escalated greatly. The Salvadoran Church's press bulletin, *Solidaridad*, estimated that the rate of political assassination of civilians rose from 144 in 1978, to 768 during the first nine months of 1979. After the ouster of Romero in September 1979 and the takeover of the U.S.-sponsored "moderate center" the murder rate rose to 1,800 in

1980, then to 1,200 *a month* in 1981 (an annual rate of 14,500). According to *Solidaridad*, "In the first nine months of 1981, 10,714 defenseless people were executed" by government forces, with 4,000 more killed by "unidentifiable paramilitary bands."[66]

Despite the almost uniform opinion of close observers that paramilitary murders are government murders, the U.S. mass media have usually followed the Bowdler-official propaganda line, although inconsistently stumbling a la Schumacher between an independent paramilitary and a government arm under tightening discipline. The content analysis of the *New York Times* by Guzmao and Benjamin reveals that just as the U.S. government and Duarte junta "displaced the responsibility for the violence onto nongovernmental sources," so did the *Times*' news reports, attributing the killings to government forces in only about one-third of its news articles whereas El Salvador church sources attributed over 80% of the violence to those forces.[67]

A second facet of government and mass media misrepresentation of the centrism of the junta is in their analysis of junta composition and power. The coup of October 1979 led to the formation of a relatively moderate junta, which included several reform-minded civilians and a diversified group of military personnel. That junta was decimated by resignations only three months later, in January 1980, based on the inability of the reformers to stem the increasing tide of official murders or to institute any reforms. The subsequent ouster of the only military moderate, Majano, would seem to have left the rightwing military in even firmer control. The belated arrival of Duarte, in the midst of an intensifying war and in the wake of the departure of all known moderates, would suggest that Duarte is a figleaf for a victorious rightwing military elite. This point is reinforced by the fact that Duarte, although the President, is not Commander-in-Chief of the armed forces; that post is held explicitly by army Colonel Gutierrez. Gutierrez was one of the two rightwing generals, the other Garcia, both affiliated with U.S. business firms operating in El Salvador, who were pressed by U.S. officials upon the original organizers of the reforming junta in October 1979, a highly significant U.S. intervention that effectively cancelled out the power of the military and civilian moderates.[68] Thus, if a "center" ever had any potential to influence the course of events in El Salvador, this was precluded from the beginning by the direction of U.S. influence.

Complementing the treatment of the "centrist" government has been the media's regular characterization of the Democratic Front as "Marxists" or "extreme left." When several moderate civilians joined the junta in October 1979, this was used as evidence of its broad-based and centrist character. When these civilians resigned and joined the FDR, by some miracle this did not reduce the centrism of the junta or broaden the base of the Front. The Front also included representatives of 49 unions and a large array of peasant, student, health, teaching and other professional organizations, as well as other political groupings. It even included 80% of the splintered Christian Democratic Party. The European and Mexican press featured the breadth of the Front and the integration of the far left and the moderate democratic oppositon. This did not happen in the United States, where much attention is given to the fact that the Communist Party is a part of the whole (without discussion of its weight, which is small), and words like "leftist" and "marxist" have generally been used as descriptive adjectives. The Front's composition, program and support base is distorted or suppressed, and the savageries being carried out against its leaders and mass constituency are being downplayed.

The analogy with U.S. intervention in South Vietnam is fairly close. There also moderate reformers or unduly independent nationalists were eventually squeezed out in favor of murderous thugs (Ky, Thieu) willing to pursue a savage anti-people's war against their own rural population. In Vietnam there was also a "land reform" foisted from Washington D.C., that was a complement to the primary program—counterinsurgency warfare. In El Salvador the land reform program was enacted in March 1980 simultaneously with the army's primacy being enacted by law and the army carrying out the occupation of the large plantations to be reformed, and the whole national territory. John Bushnell of the State Department stressed to Congress the linkage between security assistance and "our support of reform" in El Salvador, both of which give us "unique opportunities to change the political balance in our favor." The "protection and security provided by the Salvadorean army" is an integral part of reform in the U.S.-arranged package, and it was this central role of the military arm and its assured primacy that won rightwing support in El Salvador, while the "reform" aspect immobilized liberals in congress. Armstrong and Wheaton note that "It is instructive to recall that this is precisely the form and sequence of the U.S. model of rural pacification used in Vietnam and the Philippines: Reform with Repression. In the case of the Phoenix program in Vietnam, at least 35,000 Vietnamese peasants were systematically murdered."[69]

The special feature of the El Salvador political scene, in contrast with Vietnam, is the up-front man Duarte. But the official position of Gutierrez as Commander-in-Chief, the predominance of the military in the El Salvador political environment of intense warfare and a State of Siege, and the departure of all independents from the junta point up the fact that only a propaganda system could maintain the fiction of a centrist government ruling that country. What remains in El Salvador in 1982 is a highly militarized right, representing under 10% of the population, and a left-oriented coalition that represents a large majority. And as in Vietnam and Nicaragua, the only important external force—the only thing keeping the rightwing death machine functioning—is the United States.

6. With the NSS let us look at the bright side

As a focus on the many unpleasant aspects of the NSS would offend important people, and thus the "national interest," the mass media tend to accentuate the positive. There are exceptions to this principle, but the exercise of the power of positive thinking about the NSS is impressive. This has three main variants—a focus on personalities and pleasantries, alleged "improvements," and a look at the details of economic progress. A good illustration of the first is Edward Schumacher's October 1980 article in the *New York Times* describing Roberto Eduardo Viola, the "newly named" President of Argentina.[70] He is portrayed there by Schumacher as a warm human being, a "quintessential" Argentinian, with immigrant Italian parents, a "populist," a "compromiser," a peace-maker in the conflict with Chile, a man of the people, loving the "working class" passions of soccer and pasta. Schumacher neglects mentioning that this man of the people owns a 10,000 acre estate on the pampas, and that this man with "working class" passions led the army in the liquidation of hundreds of working class leaders, the serious weakening of working class power, and a large decline in working class real income and employment. Schumacher also fails to note that Viola, as Army Chief of Staff, was in charge of the counterinsurgency war of torture and disappearances. He does mention that there was a dirty war, but he carefully avoids linking Viola, as he should be linked, to its precise quality of dirtiness. Viola, as Penny Lernoux observes, "was a pillar of the institutionalized terror as army Commander-in-Chief," and he still "adamantly refuses to discuss the fate of the thousands of disappeared Argentines kidnapped and murdered by the security forces."[71]

Schumacher does say that Viola, while a compromiser, "can be tough." This is as close as he gets to suggesting that he may have been an organizer of mass torture and murder. The word "tough" is one the Nazis liked to apply to themselves: in contrast with words like murderer, killer, or madman, the word tough implies the ability to do things that are unpleasant but necessary. As Himmler noted, executions have been "necessary and in many cases will continue to be necessary...Most of you will know what it means to see 100 corpses piled up, or 500, or 1,000. To have gone through this and...to have remained decent, that has made us tough."[72] Apropos of the Nazis, in one of his speeches Viola remarked that "There wouldn't have been a Nuremberg trial if the Reich armies had won the war...Nobody investigates a victorious army." The Buenos Aires *Herald* pointed out in response that "Viola...is supposed to be a moderate, and if moderates think that the only thing the Nazis did wrong was to lose, the normal mind would find it hard to imagine what the view of the hard-liners must be."[73] This is a reflection that escapes Schumacher and the U.S. mass media in general.

Viola is quoted by the kindly Schumacher as favoring "a stable, and modern democracy, authentically representative," etc., but he is against "demagogic populism." Although Viola was a leader of a carefully planned coup that eliminated democracy and unleashed a reign of terror, his muddy vacuities are given full head by Schumacher, without comment. There is even a nice touch of apologetics for the coup, which Schumacher says had "great popular support," but which has since then "dwindled." Viola would say the same, and perhaps this is Schumacher's source for these findings.

Schumacher also suppresses the fact, widely disseminated in Latin America, but ignored in the United States, that Viola was a major figure at a secret conference of Latin American intelligence services held in Bogota in November 1979. Out of the conference came a "Viola plan" for extending the National Security Doctrine and curbing any further democratic threats in the region, a plan which had its first material impact in the Argentina-sponsored coup in Bolivia in July 1980 (discussed in chapter two). Colombia's Conservative Party ex-Foreign Minister Alfredo Vasquez Carrizosa told *Latinamerica Press* that

> The moment has arrived to give warning that Colombia figures in the "fascist international" in Latin America. For General Viola to think and do as he wants in his own country is another matter. We Colombians need some explanation about his coming to Bogota and outlining models to which the intelligence services of countries of the region must be coordinated under the direction of the military junta of Buenos Aires...[74]

Clearly this kind of information also has no place in an article that could have come out of the public relations arm of the Argentine National Security State.

Another good illustration of looking at the bright side is provided by Juan de Onis' article "Chile's Regime Sees New Economic Hope," published in the *New York Times* of February 28, 1980. It is a fairly representative sample of the more sophisticated type of mass media apologetics for the development model in application, and I will use it to show how bias is implemented. The article is characteristic de Onis[75] in that the view of Pinochet and the NSS leadership is paramount—the frame is *their* problem and the reader is asked to identify with Pinochet, recognize his legitimacy, and accept his alleged concern for the Chilean people. De Onis mentions that "the armed forces took power six years ago"—very neutral, with no mention here or elsewhere in the article of extensive torture and murder, or that the taking of power involved the overthrow of a democratic and legally elected government—and this neutral phrase is preceded by the claim that "prospects look brighter" for Pinochet and company, enveloping the fact of an illegal seizure of power with a warm and optimistic glow.

The article starts out in an even more positive vein, remarking that there had been a riot in an overcrowded jail in Santiago, embarrassing Pinochet, but that he "ordered the immediate construction of a new prison, the first since 1893." This act was encouraged by an alleged new "sensitivity" of the regime to criticism "and a new ability to pay for public investments." De Onis goes on in the same warm tone, telling us that "President Pinochet feels that he is in a position now to convince a majority of Chile's 11 million people that the free market capitalism being practiced here offers solutions to basic problems like jobs, housing, health and social security." Sustained growth and a better distribution of wealth "are now being promised." And although "no elections are foreseen" under military rule, "public support" is contingent on fulfillment of economic promises.

Perhaps the most notable thing about this article is de Onis' willingness to cite at length somebody's "promises," "feelings," and "sensitivity" on his own say so. That de Onis does this for the leader of a police state noted for its cruel violence speaks volumes about his own (and Free Press) principles. De Onis points out that the U.S. Embassy in Santiago had just issued a "highly favorable" report on the NSS program that "accepts uncritically" Pinochet's estimates of prospective investment, income redistribution, etc. This, of course, places de Onis in the middle between the "extremes" of harsh critics and the uncritical Embassy, although Sherlock Holmes would be hard pressed to detect the critical elements in this news report. What the Embassy accolade *really* shows is not de Onis' moderation but the root of his apologetics—namely, that he is a reporter for a newspaper in a country whose dominant economic-political-military leaders are extremely well satisfied with fascist Chile.

A second notable feature of de Onis' article is that it contains a political contradiction which he leaves unresolved. He cites Pinochet's claims of a commitment to jobs, social justice, etc., and the necessity of meeting these promises in the interest of obtaining "public support." But no elections are foreseen. Why not? If Pinochet is serious about the new promises, why fear elections? If elections are not to be allowed, why any need to worry about "public support"? De Onis goes on to say that elections and union autonomy are ruled out because "the success of the program depends on stability and investor confidence." But if these criteria still rule, why will they now be compatible with improving the distribution of wealth, health and social security, and jobs? De Onis doesn't attempt to reconcile these two irreconcilable strands—which of course suggests that he is allowing himself to be used to create a propaganda aura for the Chilean NSS.

While he cites Pinochet's promises of "improvements" de Onis carefully avoids discussing *what has happened* in Chile that might make improvements needed. The one spot where de Onis injects a critical fact about Chilean developments reads as follows:

> Critics of the present economic "model" generally agree that the situation today is an improvement over the breakdown in 1973, but they emphasize persistent unemployment, which is about 15 percent of the labor force, and indications that wealth is increasingly concentrated in an elite, with wage earners and peasants making less than before.

Observe that the single critical fact, about the rate of unemployment, is preceded by a "positive" claim that critics all say that the situation is improved from the "breakdown" of 1973. The choice of base of comparison is a marvel of NSS apologetics—not only does de Onis select a completely abnormal point in time, he neglects mentioning that the "breakdown" was engineered by the same forces that introduced the NSS.[76] Quite a few critics claim that the Chilean NSS performance has been a human catastrophe and a failure even on NSS principles—but de Onis does not cite one of them. Note also the terseness of de Onis' reference to persistent unemployment of 15%—a figure at the low end of credible estimates, and with no comparative data for reader context—and the lack of any detail on income redistribution or its human consequences. Unemployment, which averaged under 6% between 1960-1973, was somewhere between 15 and 30% in 1980 depending on how one handles disguised unemployment and the significant numbers hired under the Program of Minimum Employment (PEM), which pays nominal wages (and no social security or related benefits) for arduous jobs in the public and private sector, and which accounted for about 7% of the workforce in 1980. Unemployment among farmworkers was about 35% in mid-1980 and underemployment was even more widespread.[77]

As noted, although de Onis says that "economic prospects look brighter" for Pinochet and "Chile" he gives no details that would support the brightening, except for the fact that copper prices were rising and might allow Chile "to cover the higher cost of petroleum imports." This provides the basis for his statement about a "new ability to pay for public investment." Again he makes no mention of what *actually happened* to public investments after the coup. The public sector was sharply reduced by the NSS in a massive sell-off of public enterprises, often at bargain prices. A huge readjustment in the shrunken public sector saw all social service outlays fall (health by 22% and housing-sanitation-community services by 60% of the reduced total)—while defense expenditures increased by 100%. The social security system is in the process of being dismantled and turned over to the private sector.

A few other points that de Onis neglects to mention give a different picture of NSS developments and prospects. First, it took the Pinochet NSS until 1980 to get Chilean domestic output per capita back to the 1970 level of the Frei regime. And, despite the terror, the drastic fall in real wages, and the large upward redistribution of income, in 1980 domestic saving and investment were both below their late 1960s levels. It should be recalled that supply side economics with machine guns is supposed to stimulate saving and investment. Second, the real value of imports was up by 38%. Most of this import increase was in the form of luxury consumer goods—motor cars, household durables, sumptuary goods, beverages, and clothing—with capital goods imports that would bear on "development" increasing negligibly. Between 1970 and 1978 capital goods imports fell from 20 to 13% of total imports; luxury goods imports increased by 276%. The shifts in the composition of Chilean output reveal growth largely in financial, service and trading activities, with the goods producing sectors of the economy showing absolute declines. Between 1972 and 1979 employment in industry in Chile fell from 24.6% of total employment to only 16.5% while employment in commerce and services together expanded from 38% to 52.3% of total employment.[78] There has been a surge in foreign credit, and transnational credit has been the motor for whatever feeble growth has taken place, but a large portion has been used to finance the import of high-priced consumer goods, luxury housing, takeovers of local firms and speculation. An internal tight money policy, and relatively easy credit from abroad available to large interests and transnational corporations, have combined to decimate local small and medium sized businesses—NSS economics in Chile has led to the most concentrated market system in Latin America.

Third, foreign debt has risen enormously, equalling 2.3 times export receipts in 1980; and in that year the Chilean ratios of debt-service charges to exports and debt to GNP were the highest in Latin America. The current account deficit was 8 percent of gross domestic product in 1978 and rising rapidly. Between 1977 and 1980 Chile's gross foreign debt doubled in size. This debt is indexed to the exchange rate, and the junta has therefore kept the peso overvalued, which has stimulated imports, increased the pressure on exporters, raised the unemployment rate, and reduced the rate of inflation. But the size of Chile's debt and debt service requirements are so great that at present new debt is needed to service old debt—a situation referred to as "Ponzi financing," and widely regarded as a perilously speculative and hazardous condition. The economist David Felix contends that "The choice now is essentially how Chile wants the crisis to come."[79]

The negative human impact of the Chilean counter-revolution has been enormous. The union and peasant movements have been crushed, thousands of their leaders tortured and killed, and peasant cooperatives and union membership decimated (the number of unionized farmworkers fell from 65 percent of the total in 1972 to 10% in 1980). NSS economics has produced a huge reserve army of unemployed, which, along with the pacification of the labor movement, has caused the real wages of the employed to fall sharply (as noted earlier, estimates range from 20 to over 50%). The upward redistribution of income from labor to property has been of major proportions, although estimates are necessarily tentative (Table 3-1 above) given both the authoritarian conditions of research in Chile and the natural reluctance of the leadership to divulge the impact of direct class warfare. But it clearly manifests itself in the sharp rise in imports of advanced consumer goods, which has taken place even while the Chilean economy stagnates and approaches a debt crisis. Chicago School economist Arnold Harberger, in fact, points to the enhanced availability of elite boutiques and stylish goods as proof of the success of the Chilean NSS:

> Santiago has never looked better. Consumer goods from all over the world are readily available at cheap prices. All the things you get from Japan—Sony tape recorders, televisions, Honda cars—are readily available.[80]

This language should, I think, take its place alongside of Vittorio Mussolini's description of the impact of a western bomb unfolding like the petals of a rose among Ethiopian natives.

As described earlier, the NSS systematically ignores the needs of the majority, but in a case like Chile the function of state terror was to *reverse* a welfare state tradition and reduce the well-being of the majority absolutely and substantially. There is evidence that all human needs trends in Chile have been adverse. No word about this from Juan de Onis. He tells us that prospects for improvement are bright, which flies in the face of the economic realities of the debt-ridden economy with its "low investment rate and flabby productive structure that lies beneath the glittering facade of ostentatious import-intensive consumerism and financial wheeling and dealing."[81] He tells us that Pinochet intends to solve basic problems, but he makes no effort to reconcile this with the Pinochet policies on the record or with the model and economic strategies pursued. He suppresses almost every relevant fact about the impact of NSS economics on the majority, and the gains accruing to the joint venture partners.

The small touches of scepticism and distorted references to critics do not add balance, but, on the contrary, strengthen the force of the apologetics.

7. With the NSS the relevant world is that seen by the elites

This principle, closely related to looking at the bright side, also follows from the fact that the dominant forces in the United States are allied with these elites. Since things are going pretty well for the military leaders who have seized power, and the businessmen with whom they are aligned, they find the NSS good. A steady stream of such articles by Everett Martin in the *Wall Street Journal* stick to this perspective almost exclusively; to such a degree that Martin frequently forgets that there are any "people" beyond the tiny business elite with whom he is preoccupied. Thus in Argentina, under inflationary conditions "They [i.e. the Argentine people] also started playing the stock market with a vengeance. It looked like a reasonable gamble."[82] Frequently the NSSs are personified, with "Argentina," "Brazil" and "Chile" transformed into entities that are then identified with the business leadership or the ruling generals and their policies— "Brazil Raises Exports of High Technology To Pace Third World;"[83] "Brazil's Liberalization Survives a Scare;"[84] or "Brazil Stresses Farming and Enrolls Its 'Miracle' Worker."[85] A great deal of attention is devoted to business success stories—Daniel Ludwig, chicken and orange juice export developments, the coming of McDonalds to Brazil— and to the trials and tribulations of the elite in combatting traffic conditions and crowded beaches.

The perspective of the majority within the NSSs is not often on display in the western mass media. Consider the almost totally neglected phenomenon of street urchins—uncared for vagrant young children, whose numbers in the big cities of Latin America are estimated to reach into the millions. In Colombia, for example, "thousands of street children, so-called gamins, struggle to survive with little or no support from the traditional institutions of family, church, school, or state."[86] Or in Brazil, where the huge numbers of abandoned children are treated as cases for the police. Lernoux states that

Abandoned children are officially considered eyesores to be removed from downtown streets, usually by police trucks which round up the unlucky youths and transport them to another state, where they are left with warning never to return. Brazil's 3.5 million abandoned children are not seen as a social ill but as statistics to be eliminated. These roundups are normal procedure, explained Police Investigator William do Amaral, after one such operation came to light in Sao Paulo.[87]

As another example of the different world of the majority, unattended by the western mass media, we read in *Latinamerica Press*, about "Civil War in Rio De Janeiro,"[88] with more than a million citizens in that city robbed in 1979-1980 and its 60,000 soldiers and police unable to stem the tide, which comes from the NSS conditions of staggering inequality and massive dispossession and poverty. The armed forces still try. "*Veja* reported that last year 2,006 bodies were 'planted' by parapolice bands along thoroughfares in the *Baixada Fluminense,* all with signs of savage torture and abuse. However, this terrible, massive, disguised government repression was not enough to halt the increase in crime." Two million live in the slums of Rio and another 3 million live in "bedroom cities," like Nova Iguazu, where 1.5 million people make do with 290,000 houses, only 30 percent with running water, 8% connected to a sewer system, and with minimal health and educational facilities. This article concludes that

Fear is so great that some inhabitants have asked for the region to be occupied by army troops. The commandant of the First Army Corps, Gen. Gentil Marcondes Filho, categorically turned down that possibility because it would be admitting that the country is in a state of civil war. 'I cannot use guns against marginalized people or patrol Cinelandia (a downtown section of Rio) with war tanks,' he said. This is Brazil today.

This is Brazil of the majority of urban Brazilians, not the Brazil of the U.S. mass media.

8. The United States as a disinterested party

This is a principle applied only when convenient. Thus, in the case of El Salvador, it means that the United States is not to be allocated any responsibility for the evolution of the terrorist government that preceded the October 1979 coup, or Orden; and any arms and training that flow to the El Salvadoran army and death squads directly or via a U.S. client does not count as "intervention." If the Soviet Union or Cuba were to train 1,500 rebels to fight in El Salvador this would be a criminal plot and blatant intervention; whereas the 1,500 El Salvadoran soldiers in training at Fort Benning, Georgia in early 1982 fall into a different class altogether—this is "aid," not "intervention," which we disinterestedly extend to our hemispheric cousins. This purely self serving differentiation between their intrusions and our own is rarely stated outright, but it is always implicit in Free Press discussions of these matters, exactly as Pravda starts out on the premise that Soviet "aid" to Czechoslavakia is inherently justified by the fact that its own state (by definition disinterested and serving larger beneficent ends) is the active party. The Free Press may carp at whether our "aid" is effectual, whether we may be getting bogged down in "another Vietnam"—but this aid is never called by its right name (i.e., indirect aggression by a long-term subversive arming, training, and other support of rightwing military and paramilitary thugs), or castigated as immoral and illegal at the root, even when the entire enterprise of mass killing originated with us and continues mainly as a function of our ongoing decisions and choices.

The same principle is applicable in Guatemala and Chile. In the former, where the United States organized in detail the overthrow of the last democratic government—the last also to show the slightest concern over *either* civil liberties or the basic needs of the majority—[89] and where the U.S. role in creating and training the apparatus of murder was unequivocal, U.S. news reports on the slaughter, and opinion pieces by Flora Lewis, suppress the background and pretend that the struggles and killings are indigenous and inexplicable. But just as the Vietnam war would have been over in 1953 without U.S. intervention, so Guatemalan violence dates from 1954,[90] and Chilean violence dates from 1973 and the U.S. cultivated triumph of the military junta.

In their study of media handling of the Chilean coup, Moraes and Lawton show that, in contrast with the European press, the leading U.S. newspapers took the position that there is not a scintilla of evidence of U.S. participation in the coup.[91] The media achieved this trick by concentrating on the *plans of the last moment*, ignoring the long background of encouragement and support. The evidence that has come to light since 1973 shows that the United States was the *key* factor in the coup as a result of its very extensive destabilization and subversive efforts, which included long-standing incitement of public frenzy through media which it bought and manipulated, training, supply and subversive encouragement of the military, and economic destabilization efforts, that together overwhelmed Chilean democracy. (Moraes and Lawton also show that the U.S. press played down the terror and stressed the "return to normality"—precisely the fascist junta's line, peddled while it was in the throes of torturing and killing.)

9. The U.S. natural right to intervene

This patriotic principle is sometimes in conflict with the preceding and is sometimes a complement to it. Thus, a good propaganda system suppresses inconvenient background facts, like U.S. sponsorship, training and supply of the Guatemalan and El Salvadoran death machines. But these facts, and the large servicing of the El Salvadoran military by ourselves and our clients in the last few years (while we are denouncing alleged Communist supply), rests in part on our natural right to be there. We can ship arms to El Salvador's junta and impose a Vietnam-style land reform on that country because this is our backyard, our property. If the peasants of South Vietnam had no right to stand in the way of our choice of their government, certainly the El Salvadoran peasant doesn't. Schumacher says that "the Reagan administration has made Mr. Duarte the symbol and hope of the American policy of *creating* [sic] a centrist, non-communist government in El Salvador."[92] The "centrist" line has already been shown to be fraudulent, but note how Schumacher admits that the U.S. is completely in charge, molding an image and fixing the de facto government—he doesn't have to hide this; he knows we all take for granted our natural right to intervene.

10. Communist Terror as the Pot of Gold at the End of the Rainbow

As indicated earlier, communist or radical terror, retail or wholesale, is really bad, its victims are worthy, and the systematic bias of the western mass media in attaching themselves to such terror is tremendous. The mass media can pursue communist-radical terror without offending anybody important, valuable lessons can be drawn concerning the merits of private property and the link between it and "freedom," and it provides a wonderful diversion from the escalating violence within the Free World. Refugees from Cambodia, Vietnam and Cuba are of extreme interest to the western mass media. Victims of NSS terror fleeing from Uruguay are not; and the *internal* refugees of the NSSs, "the greatest migratory movement in all history" in the view of former ECLA economist Ernest Feder, is a non-issue in the west. We have already seen that Lech Walesa is newsworthy, but da Silva in Brazil is not. Another interesting contrast is between Sakharov and José Luis Massera, an eminent mathematician and former member of the Uruguyan parliament, arrested in 1975, and accused of "subversive association," "attacking the constitution," and "attacking the morals of the armed forces" of Uruguay.[93] Subjected to torture, he was tried before a military court and sentenced to 20 years in prison. His wife was arrested, and his son-in-law was arrested, tortured, and sentenced to four and a half years in prison for "assistance to subversive association." The physicist Joel Primack states that Massera is ill; and while he writes in prison his writings are confiscated by the authorities.[94] Massera has been offered positions at more than half a dozen major universities in the United States, Canada, France and elsewhere. Committees of scientists in the United States and elsewhere have been pressing his case. It is obvious that the abuses that he and his family have suffered are outrageous—yet the mass media do not give Massera any attention; no campaign emerges; no serious pressures are brought to bear. Massera fails to satisfy this principle.

Table 4-1 provides a graphic display of the fact of systematic mass media bias—which consistently leads them away from NSS (constructive and benign) violence and toward communist (nefarious) terror. The table shows, first, the number of times

Table 4-1

Press Coverage of Abused Persons[1] in the Soviet Sphere and in Eight U.S. Client States

Abused Individuals by Profession and Country	Frequency of Mention in the New York Times[2] 1/1/76-6/30/81	Frequency of Intensive Coverage[3] in the New York Times 1/1/76-6/30/81	Maximum Times Mentioned Where Subject to Intense Coverage
Heri Akhmadi, student leader, Indonesia	0	0	—
Archbishop Dom Helder Camara, Church leader, Brazil	4	0	—
Bishop Dom Pedro Casaldáliga, Church leader, Brazil	0	0	—
Enrique Alvarez Cordova, political leader, El Salvador	2	0	—
Father Luis Espinel, Church leader, Bolivia	0	0	—
Father Carlos Galvez, Church leader, Guatemala	1	0	—
Alexander Ginzburg, writer, Soviet Union	68	2	20
Kim Chi Ha, poet, South Korea		0	—
Muhammed Heikal, journalist, Egypt	8	0	—
Father Francesco Jentel, Church leader, Brazil	0	0	—
José Luis Massera, mathematician, Uruguay	5	0	—
Zelmar Michelini, politician, Uruguay	5	0	—
Yury Orlov, scientist, Soviet Union	70	2	15
Ananta Toer Pramoedya, writer, Indonesia	0	0	—
Archbishop Oscar Romero, Church leader, El Salvador	36	1	8
Father Stanley Rother, Church leader, Guatemala	0	0	—
Andrei Sakharov, scientist, Soviet Union	223	8	19
Anatoly Shcharansky, writer, Soviet Union	138	5	22
Luis Silva, trade union leader, Brazil	3	0	—
Lech Walesa, trade union leader, Poland	81	4	15

[1]Many of these individuals are discussed in the text of this book; most are or were important within their own countries for achievement in substantive fields (Massera, Pramoedya, Sakharov), for leadership in struggles of workers and the poor for social justice (Walesa, Silva, Camara, Casaldáliga, Espinel, Jentel) and for human rights causes within their states (Akhmedi, Ginzburg, Orlov, Romero, Shcharansky). Six names included are of ultimate victims—Michelini tortured and murdered, his daughter "disappeared;" Galvez and Espinel tortured and murdered; Cordova, one of the top leaders of the broadly based FDR party in El Salvador, tortured, murdered and mutilated by government forces, along with five other top FDR leaders; Romero and Rother murdered. Heikal, a longtime distinguished journalist, confidant of Nasser, and member of the Egyptian elite, fell afoul of Sadat for opposition to a number of his policies, including repression, and was himself imprisoned. Kim, a distinguished Korean poet, has been imprisoned, tortured, and threatened with death off and on for some years.

[2]Based on a simple count of number of times mentioned in the New York Times Index.

Intense coverage is defined here, necessarily arbitrarily, as cases where the subject is mentioned six or more times in the Index during any consecutive 30-day period.

various abused individuals were mentioned in the *New York Times* between January 1, 1976, and June 30, 1981; and, secondly, the number of times these individuals attracted *intense* coverage during that period. These are not randomly selected individuals, but the fact clearly observable from the table—that NSS victims are incapable of attracting more than flickering mass media attention in the United States—results not from any bias in selection[95] but rather from their "structural unworthiness," as a group. Most of the NSS victims listed here have been quite well-known in their own countries and have demonstrated high nobility of character (as have the Soviet sphere victims) in the face of severe police state abuse. By and large, the NSS victims on this list have been subject to more extreme violence than those in the Soviet sphere—six were murdered, and at least two others have been severely tortured. The *New York Times* itself has editorialized on the fact that Luis da Silva "is to Brazil what Lech Walesa is to Poland."[96] But Luis da Silva's arrest and conviction by a military tribunal in Brazil for strike activity was virtually ignored by the *Times,* and by the mass media in general, and da Silva has never generated intense coverage, as Walesa has been able to do on four separate occasions (up to March 31, 1981). The table shows that only one of 22 cases of intense coverage involved a NSS victim; the other 21 of 22 were victims within the Soviet sphere. The one exception followed the cold-blooded murder of Archbishop Oscar Romero, the leading Church official in El Salvador; but the coverage here was not only modest in terms of the seriousness of the crime, it petered out quickly, and the connection of Romero's murder with the thug-complex long supported by the United States was downplayed. Romero's death was part of a seamless web in which numerous priests have been abused and killed, nuns have been raped and murdered, and many thousands of innocent civilians have been killed and frequently mutilated. But this enormous bloodbath is U.S.-sponsored, and the mass media therefore provide muted coverage, little indignation, and carefully avoid stress on the "linkages" and role of the superpower, such as those noted between the Soviet Union and the earlier abuse of Cardinal Mindzenty in Hungary[97] and the 1981 imposition of martial law in Poland—nor has there been any suggestion that the local elite of El Salvador should have to "pay dearly" for the murder of the

Archbishop (or any of the thousands of others). The bias displayed by this table is real and massive; its explanation, as I have shown, lies, on the one hand, in the propaganda value of communist terror; on the other hand, in the fact that the NSS is U.S.-sponsored and protected, with its terror serving large U.S. interests.

FIVE

Remedies for Terrorism

Recapitulation

If "terrorism" means "intimidation by violence or the threat of violence," and if we allow the definition to include violence by states and agents of states, then it is these, not isolated individuals or small groups, that are the important terrorists in the world. If terrorist violence is measured by the extent of politically motivated torture and murder, it was shown in chapter 3 that it is in the U.S.-sponsored and protected "authoritarian" states—the real terror network—that these forms of violence have reached a high crescendo in recent decades. In Central America alone, some 60-100 civilians were being murdered by state terrorists *per day* in 1981, and torture was employed on a regular basis and as a "mode of governance" in more than a dozen U.S. client states in Latin America during the 1970s. As a torturer, murderer and intimidator of large numbers, Augusto Pinochet and his Chilean associates by themselves outclass the aggregate of all the members of Claire Sterling's terror network. The CIA's estimate of all deaths attributable to "international terrorists" from 1968-1980 is under 4,000, whereas Pinochet and company exceeded this total by a substantial margin in their first year in power.

More recently, a local human rights report called attention to the following statistics on *state* terrorist acts in the small country of Colombia for the first eight months of 1981:[1]

1,063 illegal arrests
  242 cases of torture
  142 murders
   60 cases of serious injuries
   29 robberies

This list was confined to terror that this group was able to document from press clippings and personal witness, and is very possibly only the tip of an iceberg. In a rare on-the-spot report based on local interviews from Colombia and published in a U.S. newspaper, Tom Wells cites "dozens of peasants" who claim

> That as many as 20 men each day are tortured at the army base [in the Cimitarra region, 110 miles from Bogota] by being kept tied up in the sun and beaten during interrogations. Officers with rank as high as major are present on these occasions...Dozens of other peasants described other means of torture—being burned by cigarettes, slashed with knives and broken bottles, beaten, kicked and hanged in trees by their hands tied behind their backs...Peasants in the Cimitarra region charged that the army executes peasants and then claims they were guerillas killed in combat or that they were executed by guerillas for collaborating with the army.[2]

This assault on the peasantry and peasant movements has been designed to reverse the effect of earlier Colombian land reform legislation and transfers and to allow further seizures of disputed lands for consolidation into agribusiness estates. The use of force to evict small landholders has been widespread in the National Security States (NSSs), and U.S. counterinsurgency warfare training and weaponry has served well to enable estate managers to accumulate lands by defeating peasant "subversion." *Latin America Regional Reports* pointed out in 1979 that

> In the present spate of evictions in Colombia, the police and military have come down strongly on the side of the landowners, who are driving peasants from disputed

land without fear of repercussions. Meanwhile, peasant land invaders are liable to heavy prison sentences under the terms of the security stature.... Since President Julio Cesar Turbay Ayala took power last year, military operations in both rural and urban areas have grown considerably in scale and frequency...The Estatuto de Seguridad ["security" law] introduced by the Turbay government has been widely used and abused in the anti-guerilla war, and as a means of breaking up rural peasant and Indian movements at the same time.... According to ANUC [a peasant union], more than 100 campesinos have been killed by military and civilian armed groups and about 35,000 imprisoned during the organization's lifetime...[3]

Torture was already widespread at the time this account was written in 1979, and violence has escalated greatly since then.

The terror in Colombia is being carried out by a "martial law" regime whose operations make those in Poland look "non-violent" by comparison. This is a government, also, closely linked to the cocaine trade. Yet Turbay Ayala—the Duarte of Colombia—is enthused about Ronald Reagan, and the Reagan administration finds Turbay Ayala a great leader, an asset in the struggle against terrorism.[4] And the mass media of the United States carefully avert their eyes from Colombia and reserve their news and indignation for more worthy objects.

It was shown in chapter 3 that the *direct* terrorism of the NSSs has resulted in scores of thousands of "disappearances" and murders, hundreds of thousands of people tortured, and well over a million political expatriates. The NSSs have also produced many millions of *internal* refugees, as they have encouraged and greatly facilitated a more rapid and ruthless land and capital accumulation process—as in Colombia—at the expense of a politically unprotected majority. The NSS is the antithesis of a welfare state. Not only are the human costs of the massive uprooting of peasants ignored, the dispossession process is subsidized by the state and reinforced by NSS law and the police—with the victimized peasants left to fend for themselves in a steadily replenished reserve army of uncared for people. This is a system *designed* to keep large numbers in a state of serious deprivation while small upper classes, multinational business interests, and elites of military enforcers "develop" these countries without any democratic constraint.

The success of the NSSs in serving their exclusively elite objectives is evident in the huge inequalities in income distribution which prevail among them (see Table 3-1 and the accompanying text), inequalities that have increased even further during recent decades of intensified repression. Their achievements are also displayed in the great increase in luxury consumption and an enlarged consumerist culture, at the same time as scores of millions of people in the NSSs are hungry, severely malnourished and suffering and dying from diseases of poverty and neglect. I have shown that the NSSs fail abysmally to serve their majorities of poor people (Table 3-2 and accompanying text), and that this is based on the deliberate policy choices of the NSS leaders and their external support system (most importantly, foreign multinationals and the U.S. government).

The installation of the NSS has commonly been justified on the ground of the imminent threat of "Communism" and thus the end of both democracy and pluralistic constraints against the abuse of power. As was noted in chapter 1, this is very often a camouflage for opposition to effective trade unions and to the most elementary social-democratic reforms, but the hypocrisy of this ploy runs much deeper. *The NSS itself invariably ends pluralistic constraints*, decimates underclass protective organizations, and unleashes the very "Reign of Terror" allegedly threatened by "Communism," but which, for some strange reason, regularly appears in the real world under the auspices of *anti*communism. In its sponsorship of Somoza, Castillo Armas, Castello Branco, Augusto Pinochet and the assorted other military leaders and mafiosi that have attracted its support, the United States placed a "safety net" under the elites of Latin America (while at the same time serving the interests of its own corporate citizens). In the process, it not only effectively removed any organizational or moral barrier to unrestrained greed, it also helped close out the possibility of peaceful options for change. In countries like Guatemala, the last vestiges of pluralism—that is, a multiplicity of parties and organizations representing many social groupings, free speech, and a free press—ended in the bloodshed of the U.S.-organized coup of 1954.[5] The business-military elite put firmly in the saddle by that U.S. intervention has taken advantage of its safety net, graduating from mere repression of the underclasses (with direct U.S. encouragement and assistance)[6] to the present-day large scale murder of the middle-of-the-road political leadership as well.

The NSS has become widely prevalent in the U.S. sphere of influence because it serves the U.S. business community well. Despite the pretense of U.S. non-involvement, we have seen that the NSS represents a positive choice that has been encouraged and protected by the United States in many ways, direct and indirect.[7] It has been deliberately chosen at numerous "moments of truth" in preference to less controllable and more union-infested constitutional and social democratic regimes, which have been displaced regularly with the tacit approval or active assistance of the United States.[8] Occasionally, murder and torture in the NSSs have reached levels that produce negative reactions at home, sometimes as a result of especially dramatic events, or of domestic political unrest and dissatisfaction seeking an outlet. This should not obscure the fact that both liberal and conservative governments in the United States have sponsored and protected the NSS, with responsibility for some of its ugliest outcroppings quite widely distributed—Franklin D. Roosevelt, Somoza; Harry Truman, Phibun Songkhram of Thailand, "the first pro-Axis dictator to regain power after the war;" John F. Kennedy, General Perelta Azurdia, "decidedly more reactionary than Ydigoras [who he replaced—and, under whom] the Guatemalan dictatorship took on new zeal;"[9] Lyndon Johnson, Balaguer and Mobutu; Nixon, Pinochet, etc. Liberal administrations are more likely to try to curb NSS excesses, but in their most famous manifestation of restraint, the Carter human rights policy, the exceptions were numerous, the corrective measures taken were very modest. They amounted to the temporary cutting off of the allowances of unruly children, still clothed, fed, housed and protected as members of the Free World family.[10]

With the coming into power of the Reagan-Haig-Kirkpatrick team, the veneer of do-goodism has been stripped away from the underlying primary force of economic interest—the basis for the long-standing U.S. acceptance of terror—and the common elements of ideology between the U.S. rightwing and the leaders of the NSSs have become explicit. The new team makes no pretense at support for an enfeebled center (as well as right) or for a pallid reformism, or even for the forms of democracy. It has shown not the slightest interest in bolstering up a floundering Costa Rican democracy, Kirkpatrick even suggesting that what Costa Rica needs is a good dose of militarization, and under Reagan influence the U.S.-dominated Inter-American Development Bank has sharply reduced its aid to Costa Rica.[11] Nicaragua, where for the first time in almost a half century terror has abated and pluralism, participation by the masses, and a concern by the political leadership for the welfare of the "oxen" are on display,[12] the Reagan team is aghast and is not merely destabilizing economically as best it can, but is openly encouraging and threatening military intervention.[13] On the other hand, Garcia, Pinochet, Stroessner, Turbay Ayala, the El Salvador junta, Botha, are all being treated with warm understanding and as prized friends and allies.

In short, with Reagan-Haig-Kirkpatrick U.S. policy has reached this stage: (1) there is indifference *at best* to democratic forms and civil liberties in the Third World; (2) there is active hostility and repugnance toward any manifestations of non-elite and human needs objectives oriented to the majority; (3) there is a pro-fascist bias *in a literal sense*, in which warmth and understanding appear to be roughly but directly proportional to the ruthlessness of the controlling elite and the magnitude of its terroristic behavior as measured by body count. Warm approaches have been extended to Garcia of Guatemala—the Idi Amin of Central America — and the Reagan influence has reshaped lending of the Inter-American Development Bank in 1981 so that, according to the Council on Hemispheric Affairs, all the Southern Cone countries but Argentina got sizable increases, paralleling "an increase of serious human rights violations in the past year." The Council also notes that "the biggest winners by far in the loan sweepstakes were Guatemala and El Salvador....Both were named by COHA and several other regional and international bodies as the worst human rights violators in Latin America for the second consecutive year."[14]

Despite this new, strongly positive tone toward state terror, NSS violence and immiseration of the majority to serve an already affluent elite do not look good, and the western mass media are still working diligently to cover things over as best they can. The Polish case dramatically illustrates how the mass media perform their tasks of averting the public's eyes from relevant and controllable terror, providing effective distractions, and mobilizing the masses in proper directions. Not since Cambodia has the Free Press roused itself to such a frenzy of humanistic concern, once again unfailingly locating worthy victims in the enemy sphere of influence (although the supply in its backyard is not only immense but has been expanding rapidly). The Solidarity movement in Poland has been attempting to wrest concessions and power from a moribund and oppressive Communist state control apparatus. This has been a democratic movement deserving the support of concerned human beings everywhere. The support by the Reagan administration and the U.S. mass media, however, has been corrupt, hypocritical in the extreme, and detrimental to the interests of Solidarity and the Polish working class in general. On these matters I note only the following:

1. *The amazing chutzpah in the pretense of a concern for trade union rights and the bargaining and political power of workers.* The Reagan team has been undermining worker power at home as fast as it can (and has broken the air-controllers' union); but far more telling is the fact that it is aggressively supporting regimes whose *function* has been the dismantling and/or immobilization of trade unions. In every NSS, trade union leaders have been tortured and murdered and trade unions have been crushed. In Guatemala, for example, the Council on Hemispheric Affairs estimates that at least 165 trade union leaders were *murdered or disappeared in 1980 alone,* in addition to which 311 local agricultural union leaders were killed.[15] This mass assassination of union leaders, which was still in progress in 1981 and 1982, was unrecognized in Washington and did not interfere in any way with the warming relationships between the two "antiterrorist" governments. Similarly, although one of the main operations of the martial law government in Colombia for several years, as described above, has been a systematic attack on peasant unions in the countryside, with extensive torture and murder of union organizers, leaders and members well documented, ties between Turbay Ayala and Haig-Reagan have

strengthened as they also have joined together in the fight against terrorism. In another case, after many years of repression by the military dictatorship in Brazil, a well-publicized "abertura" was initiated in the late 1970s. Put to the test by the long pacified labor movement in 1980, it was quickly shown to be fraudulent— a metal workers' strike was crushed by military force and its leaders were tried, barred from further union office, and given prison sentences in 1981.[16] Again the response from Washington (and from the U.S. mass media) was undetectable. Numerous other examples could be cited.

2. *The pretense that the Reagan-Haig team does not like martial law.* The inauguration of martial law in Poland was also greeted in Washington with horror and indignation, and the mass media have also been deeply distressed, conveying the impression that there is nothing the United States abhors more than martial law. Again, the hypocrisy and capacity for segmenting very similar facts into different regions of the brain is remarkable. The United States has sponsored regimes of martial law on a world-wide scale. *The NSS is a system of martial law* in which legal rights are permanently suspended in the fight against "subversion" which, as we have seen, is often equated with effective trade unions. It was shown in chapter 3 that the spread of military dictatorships (martial law regimes) throughout Latin America occurred as a result of a definite U.S. plan of military power enhancement, and that the results were not only predicted but greeted with warm approval (despite occasional tut-tuts and expressions of regret over "excesses"). The imposition of martial law in the Philippines in 1972 was openly welcomed and accompanied by a sharp increase in U.S. aid, and the martial law regime has been protected by Washington ever since. Both Bush and Haig, in visits to the Philippines in 1981, expressed the most perfect contentment with the state of affairs there, Bush, in fact, making a fool of himself with effusive compliments to Marcos on his "dedication" to "democracy." Permanent martial law brought to Brazil with U.S. connivance in 1964 was also greeted with encomiums to triumphant "democracy."

Martial law was imposed in Turkey in 1980, accompanied by the extensive use of torture, at least a dozen "unexplained" deaths of people under arrest, the incarceration of hundreds of trade union leaders, and the suspension of civil and trade union rights. Physical abuse of trade union arrestees was far more severe than anything reported in Poland through 1981. A tiny back page report in the *New York Times* of December 10, 1981, reports that 52 "leftist" trade union leaders are scheduled to go on trial in Turkey for political crimes (not terrorist acts), with the prosecutor asking for death sentences. Western European governments have been putting pressure on the Turkish military junta, trying to mitigate the crackdown on unions, the muzzling of the press, the torturing of political prisoners, and the general collapse of civil and political rights. West Germany and the Scandinavian countries have actually reduced their aid to Turkey and threaten its exclusion from the Council of Europe.[17] The Reagan administration, by contrast, is exercising "quiet diplomacy"—that is, it is selling jet airplanes to the military junta, it has sharply increased military and economic aid (thus partially offsetting any disciplinary effect of the cutbacks by the European powers), and saying in a very muted voice that perhaps something should be done to soothe the feelings of those do-gooders in Northern Europe.[18] During his visit to Turkey in December 1981, Secretary of Defense Weinberger expressed a desire "to be of as much assistance as we can be" to the military regime. Analogous action in Poland would have been an administration offer to rush aid to General Jaruzelski in appreciation of his contribution to the restoration of stability.

In short, for martial law Turkey positive support is extended and not the slightest trace of moral indignation or threat is expressed to a regime that has demonstrated more terroristic violence than the Polish government. The Free Press has moved in exact parallel, focusing on the fearful events in Poland, where trade unionists have actually been arrested and interned, while pretending without explanation that the arrest, torture, and threatened execution of trade unionists in Turkey is a different order of things, legitimately denied newsworthiness and any moral significance.

This differentiation between martial law in the Philippines, Turkey, Colombia and Chile—*good* martial law, conducive to "stability"—and martial law in Poland—"bad" martial law, violating the higher principles, I have explained throughout the book in terms of "the laws of motion of the mass media as a propaganda system." Avert the eyes where the killing of trade union leaders serves U.S. corporate purposes—give maximum attention to, and wax indignant over, abuses in enemy states.

In Poland, an enemy state, "instability" becomes acceptable and can be encouraged in the interest of the higher principles that are entirely ignored in our client states. Still, the hypocrisy level is staggering—leaders of a country actively sponsoring martial law throughout the world, supporting the thugs executing 60-100 civilians per day in Central America, displaying a new warmth toward NSSs that have killed literally thousands of trade union leaders—such leaders are deploring martial law and the subservient mass media go along with them, "playing dumb," avoiding all relevant questions,[19] expressing high indignation at this illustration of Soviet perfidy—and neither the leaders nor media spokesmen are embarrassed or laughed off the stage!

3. *The pretense that Haig-Reagan and company are deeply concerned about the plight of Polish workers and are acting in ways designed to improve their condition.* As the U.S. leadership watches the decimation of trade unionism in Colombia, Guatemala, Turkey and elsewhere in the U.S. sphere of influence with complete unconcern at best, and frequent complicity and positive support, would it not be miraculous if it really cared one whit about the Polish worker? Its indifference *where it would be effective* in helping workers, as in the Philippines or Turkey, is a dead giveaway that the Haig-Reagan concern for the higher values in Poland is a smokescreen for a hidden agenda.

What is the real agenda in Reagan-Haig support of Solidarity and trade union independence and power in Poland? Given their uniform support throughout the entire U.S. sphere of influence of regimes that trample on trade union rights, we must surely start out on the assumption that union rights were not only unsought, but that they were probably looked on with disfavor. This is also suggested by the fact that western bankers have been greatly relieved by the imposition of martial law,[20] reasoning, plausibly enough, that, as in the western sphere, police states bring short-run "stability" and can squeeze interest and principal out of their underlying populations. The U.S. leadership might be willing to sacrifice bank loans in a single country for higher national purposes, but one of them is surely *not* union rights. A slightly more plausible hypothesis is that the Reagan administration hoped that Solidarity might obtain control of the Polish state and begin a process of peaceful withdrawal from the Soviet sphere and integration into the western system. The difficulty with this view is that it is not compatible with the main thrusts of current foreign and domestic policies of the United States. These include the abandonment of detente, a commitment to a renewed arms race and complementary efforts to stir up European and domestic hostility to the Soviet Union. These policies have all tended to make the Solidarity struggle part of a hardening East-West confrontation. Advances by Solidarity and the democratization of Poland and Eastern Europe are not likely to occur in an environment in which the Soviet Union feels acutely threatened.

A far more plausible explanation of the Haig-Reagan devotion to trade unionism in this one spot on the globe, therefore, is as follows: Solidarity and Polish freedom have been employed strictly as an opportunistic instrument of international destabilization—that is, as a device to reestablish cold war tensions, to polarize western Europe by focusing (however hypocritically) on Soviet evil, to justify the prior and already firm Reagan commitment to a renewed arms race, and to obscure an escalated support for South Africa, Chile and the assorted military mafias of the Third World that have now been unleashed. Important elements of the Haig-Reagan team were hoping for an actual Soviet invasion of Poland. Martial law has been, for them, a second best solution, but they are making the most of it. The U.S. is so powerful that the hypocrisy of Haig's "managed anger" at the awfulness of martial law in Poland is effective, even though the European states are perfectly aware of (and even hint at) U.S. cynicism and hypocrisy. They observe the positive U.S. support of the martial law regime in Turkey and the decisive U.S. political backing, subsidization and protection of the on going mass murder of civilians in El Salvador—places where U.S. intervention could alleviate martial law terror if this were the intent. By contrast, U.S. beating of the drums and hysteria over Poland, especially in the context of deteriorating relations with the Soviet Union, *could only serve to weaken the position of Solidarity and the democratic movement in Poland.* But the Polish gambit was entirely successful from the standpoint of *real* U.S. objectives— tensions were heightened and political points were scored against the Soviet Union. It should be clearly recognized, however, that Solidarity and freedom in Poland were planned victims of the cynical ploy of a leadership whose motto might well be: "We had to destroy Solidarity in order to save the arms race."

Solutions

I have distinguished in this book between state (wholesale) terror, and the terror of isolated individuals and small groups (retail terror). It has been argued here, further, that the latter is overrated in relative importance, although many individual acts carried out by these terrorists have caused great pain and suffering and have involved serious injustices to the victims. Retail terror is overblown for political reasons, to distract attention from more substantial terror, and to allow a manipulation of public fears and a more efficient "engineering of consent." Insofar as this is the case, "terrorism" will only recede when the government and mass media decide (or are forced) to terminate their use of the Red Menace. This occurred in 1955, when the political elite decided that Senator Joe McCarthy had satisfactorily completed his job of disrupting the New Deal consensus and was now actually threatening the unity of the Republican Party! All of a sudden, McCarthy and his demagogic red herrings ceased being newsworthy. In the early 1980s, however, retail terror in the form of phantom "Libyan hit squads" and mythical Cuban troops in El Salvador was still serving an elite purpose; but when (and if) the bubble is finally pricked, the inflated balloon of retail terrorism will collapse to very small size.

It is, of course, impossible to eliminate entirely individual acts of terror—they are inescapable in a complex, dynamic world in which means of destruction are readily available to the alienated and oppressed. But a substantial fraction of *real* acts of retail terror arise out of world failures to alleviate widespread misery and injustice and to deal intelligently and humanely with local and regional grievances (Northern Ireland, Israel-Palestine). These more important causes of retail terrorism could be alleviated by responsible policies addressed to sources of endemic conflict and mass distress. A large part of the responsibility for resolving these problems falls to the west, which contains the wealthiest and most dynamic states, who are most closely linked to the poor and troubled enclaves of the world, and whose power of initiative has been maintained up to the present day.[21]

The west has done poorly in addressing world conflict and misery, and the conservative drift of western politics bodes ill for the future. With the advent of the Reagan team, all adverse conflict-misery trends are likely to be accelerated. To a world imperiled by a nuclear arms race, by the impoverished state of the majority and by serious environmental and ecological threats posed by technological advance and uncontrolled growth, the Reagan administration now offers deliberately stoked international tension, remilitarization, the "free market," and an aggressive application of national power to serve parochial U.S. ends. Instead of providing even the beginning of solutions, the United States itself is very much part of the problem. It has become the big bull in the China shop, threatening the shop as well as the china. Under Reagan, in consequence, "terrorism" (retail) is sure to increase. This natural result of greed, short-sightedness and stupidity will then be used to justify greater state violence, which will be wrapped up in an "anti-terrorist" flag. Rightwing ideologues create retail terrorists and are then quite prepared to kill them.

State terrorism, the quantitatively important terrorism, has escalated in scope and violence in recent decades. This is evidenced in the rise of torture as a serious problem, death squad murders, and the use of direct state violence to intimidate millions. While this is a global development, a very sizable proportion of this growth has taken place in the western sphere of influence. I have argued that there is a *system* of terroristic states—the *real* terror network described in chapter 3—that has spread throughout Latin America and elsewhere over the past several decades, and which is deeply rooted in the corporate interest and sustaining political-military-financial-propaganda mechanisms of the United States and its allies in the Free World. The mechanisms that protect this network are extremely potent, combining military force, economic power and coercion, and a vast apparatus serving to engineer consent. The United States has *needed* Polish martial law, Gulag and other Soviet sphere crimes and abuses to distract attention from the escalating reign of terror under its own sponsorship. But the contrast between the actuality of Polish terror and the volume of propaganda outpourings—versus the far more extensive and deadly reality and relative silence and non-indignation as regards terror in Turkey, El Salvador, Guatemala, Colombia and the host of other protected fascist states—should raise questions in the mind of any observer with eyes not closed tightly by nationalistic blinders.

As Alexander Haig says, let us stop using double standards! Let us, for example, apply the principles recently enunciated by the NATO foreign ministers in reference to Poland and the Soviet Union to all countries, including the United States and its client states. Consider the principles at stake:

1. *One must not support martial law governments.* ("The imposition of martial law, the use of force against...workers," demonstrates a lack of "respect for human rights and fundamental freedoms.")[22] The NATO ministers confine their attention to Poland, but following Haig's insistence on a single standard, we must condemn *any* country that sponsors and supports martial law governments. The latter would clearly encompass Argentina, Bolivia, Brazil, Chile, Colombia, El Salvador, Guatemala and quite a few others throughout the system of NSSs. On the basis of this rule of condemnation of support of martial law, there should be special condemnation of any country that maintains a massive training and supply program designed to politicize and activate Third World military elites with the intention of *producing* martial law governments.[23] On this criterion, the United States should be required to terminate its arming, financing and training in the "school of coups" in Panama and in its army bases and police training centers elsewhere, the greatest seedbeds of martial law regimes in human history.

2. *Harsh prison sentences, internments and killings under martial law are to be condemned, and specifically the mistreatment of labor leaders.* ("Internments, the harsh prison sentences and the deaths that have followed, have deprived the...people of their rights and freedoms, in particular in the field of trade

unions.") Excellent. We must remember that the aggregate of deaths under martial law in Poland by the end of 1981 was estimated to fall in the range of 30 to 300—the upper limit, therefore, amounting to fewer than the murder level under martial law in El Salvador or Guatemala in an average month, and less than the 1981 total for operations under the "security law" in tiny Colombia. What is more, the killings in Poland resulted mainly from open fighting; those in the small U.S. clients just mentioned were largely cold-blooded murders of defenseless civilians.[24] Let us, therefore, as believers in a single standard, insist that the NATO foreign ministers and press, and the world at large, follow closely, publicize, and show parallel indignation over the serious mistreatment of trade unionists in Brazil, Chile and Guatemala, where the west has some influence—let us insist that they explain to us openly and clearly why trade unionists *killed* by the score in the NSSs are worth minimal attention and those *arrested* in Poland are uniquely worthy victims. Otherwise, the NATO ministers and the western press stand condemned as agents of U.S. propaganda and protectors of the real terror network.

3. *The right to self-determination.* ("The Soviet Union [United States?] has no right to determine the political and social development of Poland [El Salvador? Chile? Guatemala? Thailand? Zaire?]....The allies call upon the Soviet Union [United States?] to respect Poland's [El Salvador's? etc.] fundamental right to solve its own problems free from foreign interference and to respect the clear desire of the overwhelming majority of the Polish [El Salvadoran? Guatemalan? etc.] people for national renewal and reform. Soviet [U.S.?] pressure, direct or indirect, aimed at frustrating that desire, must cease." Superb. Let us apply this equally to El Salvador and the rest of the NSS empire—U.S. pressure, direct or indirect, must cease, and these small states must be allowed to solve their problems free from foreign interference—*with the United States included as a foreign power.* It would be a truly revolutionary development for the United States to stop bullying and manipulating these tiny states to whom it has brought such pain—as if the United States were (in the words of Simon Bolivar) "destined to plague Latin America with misery in the name of liberty." *But nothing would*

contribute more to a reduction in world terrorism than a U.S. withdrawal from its interventions in Latin America "in the name of liberty."

There are two reasons why active, organized efforts looking toward U.S. restraint and withdrawal are urgently important. The first is purely humanitarian and moral. The United States is actively sponsoring, supporting and protecting narrowly based governments now engaged in local wars against the "enemy within"—against those who General Medici of Brazil referred to as "the people." What is more, this violence threatens to intensify, with a regime now in power in Washington that is not only completely insensitive to human injustice and misery but which displays a positive ideological affinity toward the world's most brutal state terrorists. I have also shown earlier that the scope of the "quiet violence" of systematic mass deprivation and forcible dispossession in the U.S.-sponsored NSSs is enormous. It has been with U.S. business and government connivance that protective organizations and legal rights have been stripped from the lower class majorities in Brazil, Chile, the Dominican Republic, Guatemala, and numerous other Third World states, with terrible human consequences. U.S. citizens therefore bear a special burden of responsibility for the injustice and terror in the NSSs—we are voters, capable of organizing and influencing our own government in ways that abused Brazilian peasants cannot. We should not allow ourselves to hide behind the protective wall of the mass media's deliberate eye aversion, or be gripped by the spirit of apathy in the wake of so many rightwing victories. The "cry of the people" in the NSSs is pressing and a moral imperative calls for giving them aid. We should stand by the great immigrant Bishop Dom Pedro Casaldaliga, living in poverty among the Brazilian peasants, harassed and threatened continuously by local and multinational[25] agribusiness firms as he tries to protect a population stripped of legal rights:[26]

> I cannot be silent and let injustices go uncondemned— injustices that are perpetrated against my people. Whoever fails to speak out against arbitrariness is by his very silence an accomplice of injustice. In today's world there is no longer a place for neutrality...And I will persist in my task until I am called by God or

liquidated by an assassin's bullet in these rude back-lands.

A second reason for serious concern over U.S. support of state terrorism in Latin America (and elsewhere) is the close linkage between the victimization of the masses in the NSSs and the crunch being imposed on the disorganized working class and lower middle class majority at home. Reagan's economic, military and foreign policies have a unity and are each a part of an integrated system that is mutually supportive. At home, Reagan-omics serves the U.S. business community and elite as far as possible by means of "engineered consent" (through huge corporate funding of the media, grass roots organizations, think tanks, and politicans, and the corporate mass media's parallel obfuscation of the issues);[27] whereas in the NSSs the U.S. multinational corporate constituency is helped along by foreign aid—direct and through international agencies—and by means of machine guns and terror.

The lineup of winners and losers in this seamless web of policies is as follows: the winners are the joint venture partners as described in chapter 3—the small multinational corporate elite of business and the wealthy at home, an important segment of the business and latifundist class in Third World client states, and the military "enforcers" in those states, who must be given their cut so that they may provide "stability" in the interests of "develop-ment." The biggest losers are the majorities (the "oxen") in the Third World, but the U.S. majority is a loser as well. The commitment to servicing multinational expansion, with reliance on state terror in the NSSs, affects the domestic economy in a variety of ways. The primary roots through which the two are linked are by the provision to business of both an external "safety valve" against worker advances at home and a conservative ideological climate conducive to the emergence of "supply side economics."

The NSSs are increasingly "monetarist," and their very high interest rates have made them bonanza areas for U.S. multi-national banks, who have become extremely fond of NSS "stability." The low wages, virtual absence of strikes and lack of protection against worker hazards or environmental devastation have stimulated a large influx of capital into the NSSs; they have made the 1960s and 1970s the "golden age" of the runaway shop. This enhanced capital mobility has contributed to chronic and growing structural unemployment and a weakening of labor power at home. Large military budgets and a fervent anticommunism have serviced this multinational expansion based heavily on subsidy and terror. The U.S. investment in training and financing the military enforcers, and the growing multinational stake in the NSSs, have been substitutes for investment and renewal at home. Thus the deteriorating position of the victims within the NSSs, that are brought about with the aid of U.S. resources, feed back with a triple whammy on U.S. workers—their taxes help fund repression and the artificially low wages of Brazil, Chile, El Salvador and the Philippines; the resultant export of capital and loan funds to the NSSs accelerates the rate of "abandonments" and growing structural employment at home; and the victims at home cannot be attended to because the social surplus must be used to finance "defense" and the halting of "Communism" abroad (that is, Luis da Silva and the metal workers in Brazil; ANUC, the peasant union in Colombia, under attack by Turbay Ayala and the military-cocaine mafia in that country; the murder-decimated Guatemalan National Workers Central; Disk, the 600,000 strong trade union federation of Turkey, 500 of whose leaders are under arrest and about to be tried).

Thus the "spiritual values" of anticommunism and militarization, plus the economic pressures stemming from access to cheap and unprotected labor abroad—and the "defense" required to keep that labor cheap—cause the policies put in place at home increasingly to converge with those applied under authoritarian conditions in the NSSs—upward redistribution of income, sharp cuts in social budgets, selective deregulation with subsidies only for the larger business interests, emphasis on the "free market," a new stress on security and arms, and a reliance on extremely tight money as the primary macro-constraint. Reagan's supply side economics lacks only machine guns in active use for complete convergence—but he is putting plenty into a reserve for future "security threats."

In sum, anticommunism, the "terrorist" threat, and militarism are being used to cover over savagely inhumane policies at home and even more scandalous policies abroad. Bank of America, Citibank, General Electric, Westinghouse, ITT and United Technologies may like tight money at home and in Brazil and Chile, and the supportive arms budgets and NSS repression, but what is good for these companies is bad for the majorities of people in Brazil, Chile, the United States, Western Europe and the rest of the world. Insisting on a single standard to be applied to terrorism in Poland, El Salvador, Guatemala, Turkey and Uruguay will quickly demonstrate that the real terror network is white, not red. There is a huge world commonality of interest in containing repression and an arms race designed to keep the home population quiet and to allow Marcos, Pinochet and the rest of the Third World mafia to provide a favorable investment climate for multinational corporate interests.

More immediately, the situation in Central America is strikingly reminiscent of the crisis period 1952-1954, which culminated in the overthrow of the last democratic government of Guatemala by means of armed aggression organized by the Republican administration of that day. That armed attack was preceded and accompanied by a flood of deliberate propaganda fabrications alleging *Guatemala's* threats to its neighbors! During 1981-1982 we have witnessed an almost complete rerun of the earlier scenario in the stream of claims by Alexander Haig on the "Nicaraguan menace," designed to obscure the *real* ongoing efforts by the Reagan administration to subvert Nicaragua. As described earlier, the U.S. termination of Guatemalan democracy in 1954 was followed by 27 years of escalating state violence that reached new heights in the early 1980s. Now, the Nicaraguans having finally thrown off their yoke of Somozan terror—a yoke provided earlier by U.S. intervention in the 1930s—the Reagan team is attempting to do for Nicaragua what we did for Guatemala in 1954. In contrast with the earlier situation, however, the Central American crisis is now wider and deeper, with large numbers struggling against the massive injustices and exceptionally cruel and violent state terrorism in both Guatemala and El Salvador. The Reagan administration is increasing its support for the state terrorists of El Salvador and Guatemala, at the same time reducing aid to the struggling democracy of Costa Rica and escalating its threats of violence against the first non-terrorist government of Nicaragua in 45 years. The Reagan bias toward death and immiseration is highlighted by the fact the Inter-American Development Bank, itself, noted in 1978 that between 1965 and 1975 the extent of child malnutrition rose markedly in all countries in Central America except *Costa Rica*—the average increase in the Reagan favorites was 80%.[28]

The Reagan-Haig team will continue to escalate the violence in Central America to whatever level is required to preserve military mafia/oligarchic control *if they can get away with it.* They have shown themselves to be not only quite comfortable with rule by the most ruthless killers in the hemisphere but entirely unconcerned with the indiscriminate and wholesale murder of civilians. This administration will only be slowed down and reversed in its intervention by a serious and determined opposition. The 1960s demonstrated that ordinary people, organizing and acting at the grassroots, can affect policy. The moral demands and economic and political basis for action were never more clear or of greater urgency.

Footnotes

Preface

1. Charles A. Beard and Mary R. Beard, *The Rise of American Civilization*, Macmillan, 1930, p. 708.
2. The phrase is from David Felix, "Income Distribution and the Quality of Life in Latin America: Patterns, Trends and Policy Implications," Background Paper Prepared for the Aspen Institute Project on Governance in the Western Hemisphere (mimeo, March 1981), p. 7.
3. See chapter 3 below. For a fuller discussion see Miles D. Wolpin, *Military Aid and Counterrevolution in the Third World*, Lexington, 1972.
4. Penny Lernoux, *Cry of the People*, Doubleday, 1980, p. 36.
5. Farrar, Straus, and Giroux, 1975, p. 7.
6. *Ibid.*, p. 184.
7. See Lernoux, *Cry of the People*, pp. 47-50.
8. AI, *Testimony on secret detention camps in Argentina*, 1980, pp. 18-19.
9. Lernoux, *Cry of the People*, pp. 174-175.
10. Lawrence Johnson, "Santiago nights," *Inquiry*, April 27, 1981, p. 11.
11. Lernoux, *Cry of the People*, pp. 3-6.
12. *Human rights and the Phenomenon of Disappearances*, Hearings before the Subcommittee on International Organizations, House Committee on Foreign Affairs, 96th Congress, 1st Session, 1979, p. 48.
13. *Ibid.*
14. AI, *Amnesty International Report 1979*, p. 48.
15. Hannah Arendt, *The Origins of Totalitarianism*, New York, Meridian, 1958, pp. 432-3
16. AI, "'Disappearances,' A Workbook, New York, 1981, p. 1.
17. *Ibid.*, p. 2.
18. *Ibid.*, p. 77.
19. Acta Final Y Resoluciones, 1er Congreso Latinoamericano De Familiares De Desaparecido, San Jose, Costa Rica, 20-24 Enero 1981, p. 5.
20. CIA, *Patterns of International Terrorism: 1980*, June 1981, p. vi.
21. AI, "Amnesty Action," September 1980, p. 3.
22. Warren Hoge, "Repression Increases in Guatemala as U.S. Tries to Improve Relations," *New York Times*, May 3, 1981, p. 2.
23. Council on Hemispheric Affairs, *Washington Report on the Hemisphere*, August 11, 1981, p. 4.

24. "Ministry of death" (Guatemala), *The Economist*, October 17, 1981, p. 43.

25. "The Argentine Pariah," *Foreign Policy*, Winter 1981-1982.

26. *Ibid.*

27. These points, supported in Cook's *The Declassified Eisenhower*, Doubleday, 1981, and in Stephen Kinzer and Stephen Schlesinger, *Bitter Fruit*, Doubleday, 1981, are discussed further below in chapters 1, 3 and 4.

28. Cook, *op. cit.*, p. 222.

29. This is not strictly true—as we shall see in the next chapter, their definitions would include the Garcia regime except that the CIA makes a patriotic assumption that is contrary to fact.

30. Retail terror means terror employed by isolated individuals or small groups; wholesale terror is that used by states. As the words imply, retail terror is usually on a much smaller scale than wholesale terror. See Noam Chomsky and Edward S. Herman, *The Washington Connection and Third World Fascism*, South End Press, Boston, 1979, pp. 6-7, 85-95.

31. See the interview with Kirkpatrick, *New York Times*, December 7, 1980, p. E3.

32. See "Excerpts From State Department Memo on Human Rights," *New York Times*, November 5, 1981.

33. Urban Lehner writes in the *Wall Street Journal* that as "quiet diplomacy" by definition doesn't get much attention, what Washington has been conveying isn't known, but he says in reference to South Korea: "South Korean officials suggest it hasn't been much." Ambassador Walker's reference to the subject of human rights in a speech "was a rarity in the Reagan term." "Koreans Finding a World of Difference Between Carter and Reagan Policies," *Wall Street Journal*, December 15, 1981.

34. The special power of initiative of the United States is nowhere better illustrated in all its perversity than in U.S. leadership in the nuclear arms race. For an excellent statement of the case for overwhelming U.S. dominance in arms race initiatives, see Roy A. Medvedev and Zhores A. Medvedev, "Nuclear Samizdat," *The Nation*, January 16, 1982. The Medvedev brothers say well what many qualified U.S. experts have also said. Herbert F. York, the first Director of Defense Research and Engineering, appointed to that post by President Eisenhower in 1958, is also extremely clear on the question of initiative: "In the large majority of cases the initiative has been in our hands. Our unilateral decisions have set the rate and scale for most of the individual steps in the strategic-arms race. In many cases we started development before they did and we easily established a large and long-lasting lead in terms of deployed numbers and types....In some cases, to be sure, they

started development work ahead of us and arrived first at the stage where they were able to commence deployment. But we usually reacted so strongly that our deployments and capabilities soon ran far ahead of theirs and we, in effect, even here, determined the final size of the operation." *Road to Oblivion, A Participant's View of the Arms Race*, Simon and Schuster, 1970, pp. 230-231.

Chapter One: The Semantics and Role of Terrorism

1. *A Collection of Essays,* Harcourt Brace Jovanovich, 1946, p. 166.
2. *Webster Collegiate Dictionary,* Fifth Edition, 1945, p. 1031.
3. Walter Laqueur, *Terrorism,* Little Brown, 1977, p. 7. Emphasis added.
4. For a further examination of Laqueur's work, see Chomsky and Herman, *The Washington Connection,* pp. 87-91.
5. CIA, *Patterns of International Terrorism, 1980,* June 1981, p. ii.
6. Philip Agee, *Inside the Company: CIA Diary,* Bantam, 1976, p. 372-3.
7. *Transnational Terror,* American Enterprise Institute and Hoover Institution, 1975, p. 3.
8. *Ibid.,* p. 4.
9. J. Bowyer Bell, "Terrorist scripts and live-action spectaculars," *Columbia Journalism Review,* May-June 1978.
10. Chomsky and Herman, *Washington Connection,* p. 91.
11. *Transnational Terror,* p. 14.
12. Quoted by Bill Ryan, "Is Jeremiah Denton Good for America," *Parade,* April 19, 1981, p. 8.
13. *The Origins of Totalitarianism,* pp. 419-479.
14. See "Jose Comblin on National Security Doctrine," *IDOC Monthly,* Jan.-Feb. 1977, pp. 3-9.
15. Compare Comblin, *op. cit.* and Lernoux, *Cry of the People,* pp. 47-50, with Arendt, *Origins of Totalitarianism,* chap. 13.
16. "Chile's 'Neo-Democracy': A Road to Pluralism or the Mystification of Dependent Corporatism?" Paper presented to Conference on Latin American Prospects for the Eighties, Carleton University, Ottawa, Canada, November 13-15, 1980, p. 94.
17. Chomsky and Herman, *Washington Connection,* pp. 253-4.
18. On the propaganda uses of the concept in earlier years, see Herbert Spiro and Benjamin Barber, "The Concept of Totalitarianism as the Foundation of American Counter-Ideology in the Cold War," paper delivered to the 1967 Annual Meeting of the American Political Science Association.
19. See Michael Curtis, "Retreat From Totalitarianism," in Carl J. Friedrich, Michael Curtis, and Benjamin Barber, *Totalitarianism in Perspective: Three Views,* Praeger, 1969.

20. Lernoux, *Cry of the People*, p. 328.

21. *Ibid.,* p. 67.

22. "Christian Requirements of a Political Order," a charter produced at the 15th general assembly of the National Conference of Brazilian Bishops, Feb. 1977, reprinted in *LADOC,* Jan.-Feb. 1978.

23. Quoted in Lernoux, *Cry of the People*, p. 85.

24. Jeane Kirkpatrick, "Dictatorships and Double Standards," *Commentary,* Nov. 1979, p. 35.

25. See Lernoux, *Cry of the People*, chap. 4 for details and citations.

26. See chap. 3 under "U.S. Sponsorship and Support of the System of NSSs."

27. AI, *Report on Torture,* p. 191.

28. Kirkpatrick, *op. cit.,* p. 35.

29. Charles Dickens, *Our Mutual Friend,* E.P. Dutton, 1907 ed., pp. 120-121.

30. Kirkpatrick, *op. cit.,* p. 44.

31. U.S. Committee on Refugees, *1980 World Refugee Statistics*, p. 34; Washington Office on Latin America, "Uruguay: The Plebiscite and Beyond," March 1981; Carlos Maria Gutierrez, *The Dominican Republic: Rebellion and Repression,* Monthly Review, 1972, p. 92; Joel Primack, "Human Rights in the Southern Cone," *Bulletin of Atomic Scientists,* February 1981, pp. 24-29.

32. Hugo Neira, "Guerre totale contre les Elites en Amerique Latine," *Le Monde Diplomatique,* January 1977.

33. "Oppression in Uruguay," *Bulletin of Atomic Scientists,* February, 1981, p. 31.

34. Primack, *op. cit.,* p. 24.

35. Lernoux, *Cry of the People*, p. 21.

36. *Ibid.,* p. 83.

37. *Ibid.*

38. *Ibid.,* p. 84.

39. *Ibid.* p. 145.

40. *Ibid.,* pp.73-79.

41. *Ibid.,* p. 466.

42. Black, *Brazil,* chaps. 1-2.

43. Kinzer and Schlesinger, *Bitter Fruit,* chap. 4-5.

44. *Ibid.,* pp. 106-7, 59-60.

45. According to Kinzer and Schlesinger, "many of the significant figures behind the Guatemalan coup [in Washington] were intimately acquainted with high Fruit Company executives and favored their views" about an area concerning which they knew next to nothing. *Ibid.,* p. 107. Secretary of State Dulles himself had worked earlier for the law firm of United Fruit, and had negotiated one of their 1930s contracts with Dictator Ubico.

46. See Juan Jose Arévalo, *The Shark and the Sardines,* Lyle Stuart, 1961, p. 152; Arévalo, *Anti-Kommunism in Latin America,* Lyle Stuart, 1963, esp. chap. 3.
47. *Bitter Fruit,* pp. 63-64.
48. "Voice from Northeastern Brazil to II Conference of Bishops," Mexico, November 1977, reprinted in *LA DOC,* May/June 1978, p. 15.
49. Murray B. Levin, *Political Hysteria in America,* Basic Books, 1981, p. 3.
50. Matthew Josephson, *The Politicos, 1865-1896,* Harcourt, Brace, 1938, pp. 570-574.
51. *Ibid.,* p. 570.
52. *Red Scare, A Study in National Hysteria, 1919-1920,* University of Minnesota Press, 1955, p. 142.
53. *Ibid.,* p. 155.
54. *Ibid.,* p. 165.
55. *Ibid.*
56. *Ibid.,* p. 121.
57. *Ibid.,* pp. 116-7, 145, 158-9.
58. Levin, *op. cit.* p. 192.
59. *Red Scare,* p. 146.
60. *Ibid.,* p. 219.
61. Quoted in Levin, *op. cit.,* p. 131.
62. *Red Scare,* p. 155.
63. David Caute, *The Great Fear, The Anti-Communist Purge Under Truman and Eisenhower,* Simon and Schuster, 1978, p. 349.
64. Charles J.V. Murphy, "McCarthy and the Businessmen," *Fortune,* April, 1954, p. 180.
65. See Black, *Brazil,* chap 6; Ronald Radosh, *American Labor and United States Foreign Policy,* Random House, 1969.
66. Caute, *op. cit.,* pp. 114-138.
67. *Ibid.,* pp. 136-7.
68. *Ibid.,* pp. 131-2.

Chapter Two: The Lesser and Mythical Terror Networks

1. Simon and Schuster/Conference Board, 1976.
2. Michael T. Klare, *Beyond the Vietnam Syndrome,* Institute for Policy Studies, 1981.
3. A definition of "aggressor," viewed from the standpoint of a pugnacious and militarized superpower, is as follows: "Providing aid and comfort to the side which we oppose." It was in this sense that North

Vietnam, China or the Soviet Union were "aggressors" during the Vietnam War.

4. Levin, *op. cit.*, pp. 178-180.

5. "The grand conspiracy: bad theory, silly book," *Philadelphia Inquirer,* May 3, 1981.

6. *Terror Network,* p. 9.

7. *Ibid.,* p. 8. Characteristically, she quotes a version of Che's speech given in the house organ of the Red Brigades, although there are competent respectable translations that do not use the phrase "violent paroxysms of hatred."

8. *Ibid.,* p. 9.

9. Lernoux, *Cry of the People*, pp. 61-103.

10. A.J. Langguth, *Hidden Terrors*, Pantheon, 1978, pp. 230-31.

11. *Terror Network,* p. 20.

12. *Ibid.,* p. 22.

13. Levin, *op. cit.* p. 122.

14. "The Roots of Terrorism," *The New Republic,* July 25, 1981.

15. *Ibid.*

16. Diana Johnstone, "The 'fright story' of Claire Sterling's tales of terrorism," *In These Times*, May 20-26, 1981.

17. *Ibid.*

18. *Ibid.*

19. *Terror Network,* p. 291.

20. "Roots of Terrorism."

21. *Ibid.*

22. John Stockwell, *In Search of Enemies,* Norton, 1978, p. 172.

23. *Ibid.,* pp. 170-1.

24. "With the Soviets, you deal from strength," *Philadelphia Inquirer,* Sept. 22, 1980.

25. "Documenting the Ties That Bind Terrorists," review of Sterling in *Wall Street Journal*, April 9, 1981.

26. "Carlos-the-Jackal," whose real name is Ilich Ramirez Sanchez, is most famous for his leadership in the successful taking of 42 hostages from a 1975 OPEC meeting in Vienna, for whom a record-shattering ransom, perhaps $50 million, was collected. As J. Bowyer Bell remarks, Carlos, affiliated with a faction of the PLO, and "the man who had shot the three French policemen in 1975...became the media's archetypal terrorist." *A Time of Terror,* Basic Books, 1978, p. 194.

27. William Schapp, "New Spate of Terrorism: Key Leaders Unleashed," *Covert Action Information Bulletin,* Dec. 1980, p. 7.

28. See *Alleged Assassination Plots Involving Foreign Leaders,* Report No. 94-465, Select Committee to Study Government Intelligence Activities, U.S. Senate, 84th Congress 1st Session, Nov. 1975, pp. 75ff.

29. See Warren Hinckle and William Turner, *The Fish is Red*, Harper & Row, 1981.

30. Jeff Stein, "An Army in Exile," *New York*, Sept. 10, 1979.

31. Robin Herman, "'Highest Priority' Given by U.S. To Capture Anti-Castro Group," *New York Times,* March 3, 1980.

32. Ernest Volkman, "CBS says exiles wage war on Cuba," *Philadelphia Inquirer*, June 8, 1977.

33. Schapp, *op. cit.*

34. Stein, *op. cit.* p. 49.

35. Schapp, *op. cit.,* p. 8.

36. Juan deOnis "Anti-Castro Extremists Tolerated, If Not Encouraged by some Latin American Nations," *New York Times,* Nov. 15, 1976.

37. John Dinges and Saul Landau, *Assassination on Embassy Row,* Pantheon, 1980, p. 249.

38. *Ibid.,* p. 251.

39. *Ibid.,* p. 231.

40. Quoted in Black, *op. cit.* p. 211.

41. Juan deOnis, "30 Refugees From Uruguay Reported Abducted in Argentina," *New York Times*, July 20, 1976.

42. "Argentina's Rulers Are There to Help," *New York Times*, August 10, 1980.

43. Dinges and Landau, *Asassination on Embassy Row*, pp. 238-9.

44.. *Ibid.*, p. 160, 162.

45. *Ibid.*, p. 239.

46. *Ibid.*, p. 386.

47. "The Bloody Trail That Leads Back to Pretoria," *The Guardian* (England), February 8, 1981.

48. *Ibid.*

49. June Kronholz, "South Africa Has Reasons for Fighting Rather than Negotiating on Namibia," *Wall Street Journal*, September 10, 1981.

50. *Ibid.*

51. See Joseph Lelyveld, "South African Says Raids in Angola Disrupt Insurgents," *New York Times*, August 1, 1981; "South Africa Says Army Is In Angola," *New York Times*, August 27, 1981; "South Africa Reports Capture of a Soviet Soldier in Angola Raid," *New York Times*, September 10, 1981; Joseph Lelyveld, "South Africans Display the Spoils of Angola Raid," *New York Times*, September 16, 1981.

52. Kronholz, "South Africa Has Reasons..."

53. For many examples, along with documentation of the remarkable double standard of the U.S. media with regard to Arab and Israeli terrorism, see Alfred M. Lilienthal, *The Zionist Connection*, Dodd, Mead, 1978. See also David Hirst, *The Gun and the Olive Branch*, Harcourt Brace Jovanovich, 1977. Much important insight into Israeli state terrorism is provided by the personal diaries of Prime Minister Moshe Sharett; see Livia Rokach, *Israeli's Sacred Terrorism* (Association of Arab-American Graduates, Belmont, Mass., 1980), for extensive

excerpts and commentary. There are other sources, though their impact on the media and general consciousness has been as slight as these.

54. Menahem Begin, letter, *Ha'aretz*, August 4, 1981; translated in *Israleft News Service*, 191, August 20, 1981, POB 9013, 91090 Jerusalem.

55. Abba Eban, "Morality and warfare," *Jerusalem Post*, August 16, 1981.

56. *Ibid.*

57. *Al Hamishmar*, May 10, 1978; Independence Day Supplement.

58. *Ha'aretz*, May 15, 1978. Cited, along with Gur's statements on Israeli practices in South Lebanon, in N. Chomsky, "Armageddon is well-located," *The Nation*, July 22, 1978.

59. A recent Italian court decision based on a nine-year-long investigation of a murder of a Palestinian in Rome on October 16,1972, found this to have been part of a deliberate and efficient operation of a branch of the State of Israel, aimed not at Arab "terrorist groups" (the murdered man was explicitly and vocally opposed to the use of violence) but against any organized pro-Palestinian personage or group anywhere. The investigating court examined five other murders of Palestinians in 1972 and 1973, three in Paris, one in Norway, and one in Cyprus, Neither these murders nor the Italian court investigation and decision have been featured in the Free Press as important instances of the "cold-blooded murder" of a terrorism which so preoccupies them. See "Israeli Secret Agents Behind Killings Rome Court Finds," *Action* (Arab-American), October 26, 1981, p. 3.

60. See Rokach, *Israel's Sacred Terrorism*.

61. *Ibid.*, p. 36.

62. Amos Perlmutter, "Ariel Sharon: Iron Man and Fragile Peace," *New York Times Magazine*, October 18, 1981.

63. Radio broadcast by David Ben-Gurion, October 19, 1953, printed in *Davar*, October 20, 1953; translated in Rokach, *op. cit.*

64. *Ibid.*, p. 16

65. Lesley Hazelton, "The Moderating of Arik Sharon," *The Nation*, November 14, 1981.

66. "Bolivia: Cocaine: the military connection," *Latin America Regional Reports Andean Group*, August 29, 1980.

67. *Ibid.*

68. See Fernando Sanchez, "Bolivian Junta Seeks New Image To Avoid Political Crisis," *Latinamerica Press*, March 26, 1981; "Women of Bolivian Town Report on Military Repression," *Latinamerica Press*, September 4, 1980.

69. Ray Bonner, "Bolivia Becomes a Battleground," *Los Angeles Times*, August 31, 1981.

70. *Ibid.*

71. *Ibid.*

72. See "Lobbyists Target Wolpe For Namibia Stance," *Africa News* October 19, 1981.

73. See "North Africa: Post-Sadat Panic," *Africa News*, October 26, 1981; Claudia Wright, "Enter the Sudan, upstaging the stooges," *New Statesman*, October 16, 1981.

74. "A new force in Central America reported moving against left with U.S. aid," *Philadelphia Inquirer*, February 5, 1982; Council on Hemispheric Affairs, "Argentina, Chile Receive Reaganites To Discuss Relations," *Washington Report on the Hemisphere*, February 9, 1982.

75. Don Oberdorfer and Patrick E. Tyler, "U.S. Latin guerilla plan reported," *Philadelphia Inquirer*, February 14, 1982.

76. *Ibid.*

Chapter Three: The Real Terror Network

1. *Sao Paulo Growth and Poverty*, A Report from the Sao Paulo Justice and Peace Commission, Bowerdean Press and Catholic Institute for International Relations, 1978, p. 54.

2. Quoted in Moyra Ashford, "Committed Bishop Installed in Brazil's New Diocese," *Latinamerica Press*, Sept. 10, 1981, p. 7.

3. Charles Teller et al, "Population and Nutrition: Implications of Sociodemographic Trends and Differentials For Food and Nutrition Policy in Central America and Panama," *Ecology of Food and Nutrition*, 1979, vol. 8, p. 97.

4. Black, *Brazil*, pp. 134-6.

5. Quoted in Larry Rohter, "Brazil's Military, Activist Church Locked in Struggle," *Washington Post*, Jan. 22, 1979.

6. *Politics and Social Structure in Latin America*, Monthly Review, 1970, p. 193.

7. "On the Characterization of Authoritarian Regimes in Latin America," in David Collier, ed., *The New Authoritarianism in Latin America*, Princeton University Press, 1979, p. 36.

8. This is the theoretical model espoused, but in practice the NSS frequently holds on to previously nationalized property, and it sometimes expands these holdings further in bailout operations. One function of nationalized property under the NSS is more effective looting by the military elite. See Chomsky and Herman, *Washington Connection*, especially the discussions of Indonesia and the Philippines.

9. *Op. cit.*, p. 50.

10. A good summary of the aims and ideology of the NSS is given in "Jose Comblin on National Security Doctrine," *IDOC Monthly Bulletin*, Jan.-Feb. 1977, pp. 3-9.

11. "Christian Reflection on the Current Political Situation," Part II, *Latinamerica Press*, Sept. 24, 1981.

12. *Sao Paulo Growth and Poverty*, p. 55.

13. Quoted in *IDOC*, Jan.-Feb. 1977, p. 6.

14. On the expense preference and institutional biases of the military elite, see items cited in note 78 below.

15. Alan Riding, "Guatemala Opening New Lands but the Best Goes to the Rich," *New York Times*, April 5, 1979.

16. *Latin America Regional Reports Southern Cone*, Nov. 13, 1981, p. 3.

17. "Philippines: A Government that Needs U.S. Business," *Business Week*, Nov. 4, 1972, p. 42.

18. "Bolivia: Cocaine, the military connection," *Latin America Regional Reports Andean Group*, Aug. 29, 1980; "The militarization of rural Colombia," *ibid.*, November 30, 1979.

19. See Warren Hoge, "Colombians Combat Cuban Interference," *New York Times*, Aug. 13, 1981.

20. See Chomsky and Herman, *The Washington Connection*, pp. 61-6.

21. On recent looting in the new Chile, see Teofilo Rondon, "Massive Fraud and Corruption Come to Light in Chile," *Latinamerica Press*, Jan. 8, 1981; for Indonesia, see Richard Robison, "Toward a Class Analysis of the Indonesian Military State," *Indonesia*, April 1978; for Zaire see David J. Gould, *Bureaucratic Corruption and Underdevelopment in the Third World*, Pergamon, 1980.

22. Adolfo Figueroa and Richard Weisskoff found inequality positively correlated with per capita incomes in "Viewing Social Pyramids: Income Distribution in Latin America," in Robert Ferber, ed., *Consumption and Income Distribution in Latin America*, OAS, 1980, p. 259. Adelman and Taft's study of 43 LDCs disclosed a strong tendency toward *absolute* decreases in the incomes of the majority under NSS conditions; *Economic Growth and Social Equity in Developing Countries*, Stanford, 1973, pp. 178-9. See also David Felix, "Interrelations Between Consumption, Economic Growth and Income Distribution in Latin America since 1800: A Comparative Perspective," Paper given at Conference on Comparative History of Consumption, University of Groningen, The Netherlands, May 8-12, 1981.

23. See Montek S. Ahluwalia, "Income Distribution: Some Dimensions of the Problem," in Hollis Chenery, et al., *Redistribution with Growth*, Oxford University Press, 1974, pp. 8-9.

24. Teller et al, "Population and Nutrition...", p. 97.

25. See Felix, "Interrelations."

26. *Ibid.* See also Charles Teller et al, "Population and Nutrition,"

27. David Felix, "Income Distribution and the Quality of Life in Latin America: Patterns, Trends and Policy Implications," Background

Paper for Aspen Institute Project on Governance in the Western Hemisphere, March 1981 (mimeo), p. 8.

28. David Felix, "Income Distribution Trends in Mexico and the Kuznets Curves," in Richard S. Weinart and Sylvia Hewlett, eds., *The Political Economy of Brazil and Mexico,* ISHI Press, 1981.

29. David Felix, "Interrelationships...," p. 19.

30. *Ibid.*

31. Joseph R. Ramos, "A Comment to 'Military Government and Real Wages in Chile,'" *Latin America Research Review,* Vol. 12, no. 1, 1977, pp. 173-6; Richard Lagos and Oscar Rufatt, "Military Government and Real Wages in Chile: A Note," *Latin America Research Review,* Vol. 10, no. 2, 1975, pp. 139-146.

32. This is a matter of dispute and hard to establish firmly, but it seems likely given the dispossession of many million peasants, a large fraction now landless and more insecure in a rural surplus labor market; with other millions entering shanty towns of the large cities over the past two decades and eking out a precarious existence under conditions of massive structural unemployment. On conditions in the Rio favelas and bedroom cities, see, Paul Schilling, "'Civil War in Rio De Janeiro'," *Latinamerica Press,* Feb. 12, 1980.

33. See especially, Richard Easterlin, "Does Economic Growth Improve the Human Lot? Some Empirical Evidence," in P.A. David and M.W. Reder, eds., *Nations and Households in Economic Growth: Essays in Honor of Moses Abramovitz,* Stanford University Press, 1975.

34. On the special circumstances affecting income distribution and development in Taiwan and South Korea, see especially Keith Griffin, *Land Concentration and Rural Poverty,* 2nd ed., Holmes and Meier, 1981, chaps 7-8; Irma Adelman and Sherman Robinson, *Income Distribution in Developing Countries,* Stanford, 1978, chaps 3, 7, and 10.

35. David Morawetz, *Twenty-Five Years of Economic Development,* World Bank, 1977, p. 71.

36. On the insecuring effects of the workings of the development model in urban Brazil, see *Sao Paulo Growth and Poverty,* passim. On the effects in the Brazilian countryside, see "I Have Heard the Cry of My People," statement of 18 Catholic Clerics of Northeast Brazil, May 6, 1973.

37. *Development, Reform, and Malnutrition in Chile,* MIT Press, 1974, chaps. 1-2.

38. *Ibid.* pp. 52-53.

39. Quoted in Black, *Brazil,* p. 239.

40. Quoted in Paulo R. Schilling, "Church Proposes Basic Change in Brazil," *Latinamerica Press,* Dec. 25, 1980.

41. Compiled from Ruth Sivard, *World Military and Social Expenditures,* 1981 ed.
42. Aart van de Laar, *The World Bank and the Poor,* Nijoff, 1980, pp. 117-19.
43. World Bank, *Brazil: Human Resources Special Report,* 1979, Annex III, Part II, Table 15.
44. *Ibid.,* p. 1.
45. *Ibid.,* p. 4.
46. *Ibid.,* p. 23.
47. Jan Rohde et al, "Who Dies of What and Why," *Prisma* (Indonesia), March 1978, p. 29.
48. *Op. cit.* p. 85.
49. *Ibid.*
50. World Bank data show a Cuban GNP per capita growth rate of 4.4% for the period 1960-79, which was above the growth rate for all economies of its income class. *Ibid.,* pp. 134-135.
51. Sergio Diaz-Briquets and Lisandro Perez, "Cuba: the Demography of Revolution," *Population Bulletin,* Vol. 36, no. 1, April, 1981, p. 9.
52. *Ibid.,* p. 8.
53. *Ibid.,* p. 9.
54. *Ibid.*
55. *Ibid.*
56. Columns 1-3 and 5, World Bank, *World Development Report 1981.* Columns 4 and 6, computed from Ruth Sivard *World Military and Social Expenditures 1981,* World Priorities, 1981, Table II. Column 7, mainly from World Bank Country Reports with the following exceptions: for Cuba, Carmen Mesa-Lago, *The Economy of Socialist Cuba,* University of New Mexico Press, 1981, especially pp. 122-133; for Brazil, Inter-American Development Bank, *Economic and Social Progress in Latin America,* 1977, p. 130; for Chile, World Bank reports plus Teofilo Rondon. "Minimum Employment Equals Maximum Exploitation in Chile," *Latinamerica Press,* July 24, 1980; for Indonesia, World Bank reports plus G. Jones and B. Supraptilah, "Underutilization of Labor in Palembang and Ujung Pandang," *Bulletin of Indonesian Economic Studies,* July 1976; for the Philippines, Gary Standing and Richard Szal, *Poverty and Basic Needs,* ILO, 1979, pp. 131-135. Column 8, mainly World Bank country reports, with the following exceptions: Cuba, Sergio Diaz-Briquets and Lisandro Perez, "Cuba: The Demography of Revolution," *Population Bulletin,* April 1981; Indonesia, computed from Jan Rohde *et al.,* "Who Dies of What and Why," *Prisma* (Indonesia), March 1978. Column 9, FAO, The Fourth World Food Survey, 1977, Table 5; Columns 10-12, mainly from *World Health Statistics Annual, 1980,* WHO, 1980, except Indonesia. Columns 10-11 computed from Jan Rohde *et al., op. cit.*
57. World Bank, *The Philippines,* 1976, p. 280.

58. This is difficult to prove, because while underemployment in the NSSs may take the form of scouring rubbish, hawking trinkets, and trivial personal service, socialist employment may be of a make-work variety that amounts to a pension with a job designation. This is hard to get data on and evaluate. The World Bank studies of China, Roumania and Yugoslavia suggest that only Yugoslavia has failed to solve the underemployment problem. Mesa-Lago indicates that Cuba created many unproductive state jobs after the revolution, but that a shift to a productivity emphasis in the 1970s markedly reduced this problem (he gives no numbers). Carmen Mesa-Lago, *The Economy of Socialist Cuba*, pp. 124-39. There is little disagreement among serious students that underemployment by all reasonable measures is very substantial in all the U.S. client states included in Table 3-2 with the exception of South Korea. The difference in the objectives of the leaderships as between these two sets is crucial in explaining these huge differentials (as for the others in Table 3-2). With South Korea the relatively low unemployment rates have been a fortuitous result of special circumstances—the land redistribution and the rapid economic growth of an especially well positioned export-platform economy.

59. "With Auto Sales Off and Oil Prices Up, Planners Seek a New 'Economic Miracle'," *Wall Street Journal*, Nov. 17, 1981.

60. The policy significance lies in both the indifference to facts that bear on the welfare of millions, and the desire to cover up evidence of a deleterious human needs impact of the development model in action.

61. "For Justice and Liberation," a statement issued by 20 predominantly lay organizations of Sao Paulo, reprinted in *Latinamerica Press*, Oct. 20, 1977.

62. *Ibid.*

63. Barry Newman, "Mixed Blessing, Do Multinationals Really Create Jobs In the Third World?", *Wall Street Journal*, Sept. 25, 1977.

64. Ingrid Palmer, *The Indonesian Economy Since 1965*, Frank Cass, 1978, p. 164.

65. A large proportion of the reactors now on order are for delivery to countries with repressive rightwing regimes. Large bribes are alleged to have flowed to Marcos and cronies in connection with the Westinghouse reactor being installed there near a volcano and earthquake fault. See Fox Butterfield, "Marcos, Facing Criticism, May End $1 Billion Westinghouse Contract," *New York Times*, Jan. 14, 1978; also "RP Anti-Nuke Campaign Nears Climax," *Phillipine Liberation Courier*, May 28, 1979, pp. 4-5. On the dubious economics and circumstances of Brazil's movement into nuclear energy, see Hartmut Krugman, "The German-Brazilian Nuclear Deal," *Bulletin of Atomic Scientists*, Feb. 1981, pp. 32-37.

66. Ernest Feder, *The Rape of the Peasantry*, Anchor, 1971, p. 38.

67. Gustav Ranis, "Industrial Sector Labor Absorption," *Economic Development and Social Change*, April, 1973; Richard S. Eckhaus, "The Factor Proportions Problem in Underdeveloped Areas," *American Economic Review*, September, 1955; Jacob Viner, *International Trade and Economic Development*, Free Press, 1962; W.W. Rostow, *Stages of Economic Growth*, Oxford, 1955.

68. Marcos Arruda, et al, *Multinationals and Brazil*, Brazilian Studies, 1972; Teofil Rondon, "The Miracle That Never Was," *Latinamerica Press*, Dec. 11, 1980; David Felix, "Monetarism in Latin America," *The IDS Bulletin* (Sussex, England), forthcoming, December, 1981.

69. Felix, *op. cit.*

70. Lernoux, *op. cit.* p. 21.

71. See D. Felix, "The Technology Factor in Socioeconomic Dualism; Toward an Economy of Scale Paradigm for Development Theory," *Economic Development and Culture Change*, Vol. 25, 1977, pp. 180ff.

72. *Ibid.,* pp. 204ff.

73. D. Felix, "The Dilemma of Import Substitution," in G. Papanek, ed., *Development Policy: Theory and Practice*, Harvard University Press, 1968.

74. Chilean industrial output fell by 7.2%, industrial employment by 21.1%, between 1970 and 1978. Felix, "Monetarism in Latin America," Table 1.

75. See Roger Burbach and Patricia Flynn, *Agribusiness in the Americas*, Monthly Review, 1980, Part II; "'I Have Heard the Cry of my People'," Statement signed by 18 Catholic leaders of Northeast Brazil, May 6, 1973.

76. Quoted in *Argentina Outreach*, March-April 1978, p. 3.

77. AI, *Annual Report for 1978*, p. 77.

78. On the material gains to the military from a "security threat," see Merle Kling, "Toward a Theory of Power and Political Instability of Latin America," *Western Political Quarterly*, March 1965, pp. 21-35. On looting by military elites in the NSSs, see Chomsky and Herman, *Washington Connection*, pp. 61-66; Lernoux, *Cry of the People*, passim.

79. Mario Otero, "Oppression in Uruguay," *Bulletin of Atomic Scientists*, Feb. 1981, p. 29.

80. See especially Fred Landis, *Psychological Warfare and Media Operations in Chile, 1970-1973*, Ph. D. Dissertation, University of Illinois at Urbana-Champaign, 1975; Fred Landis, "How 20 Chileans Overthrew Allende for the CIA," *Inquiry*, Feb. 19, 1979, pp. 16-20; *Covert Action in Chile, 1963-1973*, Staff Report of Select Committee to Study Intelligence Activities, U.S. Senate, 1975.

81. International Movement of Catholic Intellectuals and Profes-

sionals, "Voice From Northeastern Brazil To III Conference of Bishops," Mexico, November 1977, reprinted in *LADOC*, May-June 1978, p. 15.

82. The works cited in the footnotes to Table 3-3 below, "The Origin and Spread of the Death Squad in Latin America," especially the reports of AI (virtually suppressed in the United States), and Lernoux's book *Cry of the People*, provide a good introduction.

83. Chomsky and Herman, *Washington Connection*, Frontispiece and associated footnotes.

84. AI, *International Report 1975-1976*, p. 84.

85. *Op. cit.*, p. 205.

86. AI, *Testimony on secret detention camps in Argentina*, 1980, pp. 18-19.

87. AI, *Report on Torture*, p. 199.

88. *Repression in Latin America, A Report of the Russell Tribunal Session in Rome*, Spokesman Books, 1975, p. 114.

89. *Latin America Regional Reports Southern Cone*, November 13, 1981, p. 3.

90. Lernoux, *Cry of the People*, p. 170.

91. See John Dinges and Saul Landau, *Assassination on Embassy Row*, Pantheon, 1980, pp. 70-71; AI, *Report on Torture*, p. 204.

92. "Torture today is essentially a state activity. While the state hardly has a monopoly on the use of violence in today's world...the pre-conditons for torture make it almost the exclusive province of the state." AI, *Report on Torture*, p. 22.

93. AI, *Testimony on secret detention camps in Argentina,* p. i.

94. AI, *"Disappearances,"* 1980, p. 101.

95. "I think that the degree of commitment to moderation and democratic institutions within the Salvadoran military is very frequently underestimated in this country. And I think it's a terrible injustice to the Government and the military when you suggest that they were somehow responsible for terrorism and assassinations." "Cauldron in Central America: What Keeps the Fire Burning?," *New York Times*, December 7, 1980, p. E3.

96. AI, *Report on Torture*, pp. 211-212.

97. AI, *Report 1979*, p. 45.

98. AI, *Report 1975-1976*, p. 84.

99. AI, *Report on Torture*, p. 216.

100. *Ibid.*, p. 222.

101. Lernoux, *Cry of the People*, p. 9.

102. "What is not generally known is that the United States has traditionally opposed and endeavored to subvert social radicals and economic nationalists in other countries. The emergence of such a

pre-cold war posture began with the U.S. decision to occupy Cuba and the Philippines in the 1890s rather than simply grant recognition and military aid to the revolutionary nationalist forces on those islands.... During the early 1930s internal order and the protection of investments but not civil liberties were the objects of U.S. military aid to Latin America." Miles D. Wolpin, *Military Aid and Counterrevolution in the Third World*, Lexington, 1972, p. 5.

103. Quoted in Christopher Knowles, "Strike Wave Grips Argentina," *Guardian*, New York, November 16, 1977.

104. Quoted in Black, *Brazil*, p. 55.

105. "Philippines: A government that needs U.S. business," *Business Week*, November 4, 1972.

106. Obie Whichard, "U.S. Direct Investment Abroad in 1980," *Survey of Current Business*, August 1981, pp. 20-27.

107. See especially Sanjaya Lall, "Transfer-Pricing By Multinational Manufacturing Firms," *Oxford Bulletin of Economics and Statistics*, August 1977, pp. 173-195.

108. Comptroller of the Currency, Federal Deposit Insurance Corporation, Federal Reserve Board, *Country Exposure Lending Survey*, November 1981, Table 2.

109. For a general conspectus, see Lernoux, *Cry of the People*, Part II.

110. Black, *Brazil*, p. 51, n. 39.

111. The most notable exception was U.S. participation in the overthrow (murder) of Trujillo. This may be explained in large part by the fact that Trujillo was seriously restricting opportunities for U.S. capital by swallowing up some two-thirds of the economy in his personal domain (e.g., 63% of sugar production and 71% of cigarettes), and by carrying out a somewhat independent foreign policy. Both divagations were rectified under the successors of Juan Bosch. See "Smoldering Conflict: Dominican Republic 1965-1975," *NACLA*, April 1975.

112. AID adminstrator David Bell, testifying before the Senate Appropriations Committee in 1965, quoted in Black, *Brazil*, p. 139.

113. U.S. Security Assistance Request for Funds for Honduras, For Fiscal 1980.

114. Quoted in Wolpin, *Military Aid*, p. 23.

115. Dr. R.K. Baker testifying before the House Committee on Foreign Affairs in 1970, quoted in *ibid.*, p. 31.

116. *Ibid.*, p. 145.

117. "Military Professionalism and Professional Militarism," quoted in Black, *Brazil*, p. 194.

118. See Wolpin, *Military Aid*, pp. 57-59, 74, 83-85.

119. Quoted from U.S. military personnel in Black, *Brazil*, pp. 208-210.

120. Wolpin, *Military Aid*, pp. 80, 109, 101.

121. Black, *Brazil*, pp. 176-178.
122. Wolpin, *Military Aid*, pp. 57, 128, 136.
123. *The Latin American Military*, Subcommittee on American Republics, Senate Committee on Foreign Relations, October 9, 1967.
124. Michael Klare and Cynthia Arnson, *Supplying Repression*, IPS, 1981, pp. 44-45.
125. *Ibid.*, p. 50.
126. *Ibid.*
127. Lernoux, *Cry of the People*, p. 144.
128. Klare and Arnson, *Supplying Repression*, p. 25.
129. Langguth, *Hidden Terrors*, p. 246.
130. "U.S. Foreign Policy and Human Rights Violations in Latin America: A Comparative Analysis of Foreign Aid Distributions," *Comparative Politics*, January 1981, p. 162.
131. *Washington Connection*, pp. 42-46.
132. Quoted in Delia Miller, Roland Seeman and Cynthia Arnson, "Background Information on Guatemala, The Armed Forces and U.S. Military Assistance," IPS, June 1981, p. 6.
133. *Hidden Terrors*, p. 139.
134. Klare and Arnson, *Supplying Repression*, p. 6.
135. *Hidden Terrors*, pp. 122-3, 244.
136. AI, *Report on Torture*, p. 216.
137. *Ibid.*, p. 81.
138. *Ibid.*, p. 31.
139. There is a great deal of evidence that the El Salvadoran forces were looking for the nuns—that they kept a close and unusual eye on the plane in which one of them was arriving—which is good circumstantial evidence of a planned murder. See Robert Armstrong and Janet Shenk, *El Salvador: The Face of Revolution*, South End Press, 1982, pp. 174-178 and accompanying references.
140. It should be recognized that U.S. intervention in its more violent forms has occurred mainly in democratic societies or those with strong popular movements. Where these have been stifled by state terror, the Godfather rests.
141. Agee, *Inside the Company*, p. 180.
142. Edwin Lieuwen was present at a conference at which David Rockefeller told the assembled group "that it had been decided quite early that Goulart was not acceptable to the U.S. banking community, and that he would have to go." As reported in Black, *Brazil*, p. 78.
143. Described at some length in *ibid.*, passim.
144. See references in footnote 80, above.

Chapter Four: The Role of the Mass Media

1. Notably in Brazil, Chile, El Salvador and Guatemala, but elsewhere as well; see chapter 3 under "U.S. Sponsorship and Support of the National Security States."

2. *Foreign Assistance, 1966*, Hearings Before the Senate Committee on Foreign Relations, 89th Congress, 2nd Session, 1966, p. 693.

3. *New York Times*, June 19, 1966.

4. The most authoritative presentation of the official U.S. government view is the CIA Research Paper *Kampuchea: A Demographic Catastrophe*, National Technical Information Service, May 1980. Noting that its "assumptions are highly speculative," the CIA alleges that in addition to deaths from inadequate food, lack of medical care, harsh labor, etc., "50,000 to 100,000 former military personnel, bureaucrats, teachers, and educated people may have been executed." The CIA assumes that the population declined by about 700,000 in 1979, after the fall of the Pol Pot regime, that the population in April 1975 was about 7.1 million, and that the December 1979 population was about 5.2 million. Relief agencies, basing themselves on their own investigations and on population figures from provincial authorities, estimate that the current population is considerably higher, in the neighborhood of 6.5 million (Cf., e.g., *Report of the FAO Food Assessment Mission, Kampuchea*, Office for Special Relief Operations, Rome, November 1980; also *Asia Record*, December 1980, May 1981). Scholarship has in general been cautious and skeptical. See, e.g., Carlyle A. Thayer (Department of Government, University of New South Wales and Royal Military College, Canberra, Australia), "New Evidence on Kampuchea," *Problems of Communism*, May-June 1981, reviewing a series of books on Cambodia, who concludes that the extrapolations in the best-publicized accounts "do not seem to be anywhere near the correct order of magnitude" and were "highly inflated," overlooking much variety from area to area. As one indication of the general unreliability of statistics, compare the estimates of the *Asia 1979 Yearbook* of the *Far Eastern Economic Review* (January 1979) and the *Asia 1980 Yearbook*: the former, allegedly relying on CIA estimates, gives a population figure of 8.2 million, well above the estimated 1975 figure; the latter gives a population estimate of 4.2 million. For a critical analysis of these and other sources and much new evidence based on extensive refugee studies, see Michael Vickery, *Cambodia*, South End Press, forthcoming.

5. Quoted in Tad Szulc, "The CIA and Chile," *Washington Post*, October 21, 1973.

6. Chomsky and Herman, *Washington Connection*, pp. 129-204.

7. See note 4. In the case of Timor, estimates of deaths resulting from the Indonesian aggression are generally in the range of 100,000 to

200,000, with the higher estimates (some considerably higher than this) coming generally from Church sources, including priests who lived in the mountains through the worst period of the Indonesian attack in 1977-1978 or who work closely with Timorese refugees. Indonesian Foreign Minister Adam Malik estimated the number killed at 50,000 to 80,000 by early 1977 (Melbourne *Age*, April 1, 1977), well before the major Indonesian offensives launched with new armaments dispatched by the Human Rights Administration, which, according to Church and other sources, led to something approaching genocide. The prewar population was perhaps close to 700,000.

8. Porter and Hildebrand have described in detail the long erosion of the Cambodian economy before 1975—the great decline in agricultural output, the serious increase in hunger and malnutrition, the complete dependence of the Lon Nol government on a U.S. dole (which comprised 95% of government revenues) and the fact that the war continued into the mass starvation phase only because of U.S. unwillingness to terminate its support of a totally corrupt and completely isolated government. They argued that in that crucial period of the early to mid-1970s,

> Only the United States could make and enforce a decision that Cambodians would not starve to death. But the United States did not have sufficient concern for the problem of starvation to sacrifice interests that loomed larger in U.S. policy. The overriding U.S. aim was to avoid a humiliating defeat by forcing the NUFK to negotiate a settlement with the Lon Nol regime.

(George C. Hildebrand and Gareth Porter, *Cambodia: Starvation and Revolution*, Monthly Review Press, 1976, p. 33.) This view of events, which I consider entirely reasonable, has been swept aside in the propaganda tide (noted briefly in the text below).

9. See Chomsky and Herman, *Washington Connection*, p. 151.

10. The "line" desired was not merely the fact of cruel violence, but that there was a centralized, countrywide *policy* of political murder. The evidence that much of the killing was local, uncontrolled from above, and concentrated in regions of intense conflict and large-scale prior official murder and U.S. bombings, was submerged. See Chomsky and Herman, *After the Cataclysm*, South End Press, 1979, pp. 204-234.

11. *Public Opinion Quarterly*, Summer 1972, pp. 176-187.

12. Although there are many forms of media in the United States and a large number of firms operating in the country at large, there is a fairly small layer of very powerful organizations at the top that are capable of setting trends. In connection with the Nixon effort to bring the mass media into undeviating conformity, H.R. Haldeman wrote a confidential memo to Jeb Magruder urging that the Silent Majority be

mobilized against "the few places which count, which would be NBC, *Time*, *Newsweek* and *Life*, the *New York Times*, and the *Washington Post*." David Paletz and Robert Entman, who quote this memo, would add CBS, ABC and the wire services (A.P., U.P.I. and perhaps Reuters), and they would delete *Life* (*Media • Power • Politics*, Basic Books, 1981, p. 7). I would add to these the *Readers Digest* and *TV Guide*, with circulations approaching 20 million each, and the *Wall Street Journal*, a nationally circulated quality newspaper with the largest daily sales. These are the media institutions with the greatest capacity for news initiatives that are not easy to ignore, which may generate further explorations along the same line and a gradual spread of their preoccupations into the other media layers. The second level of firms comprising the mass media would include the ten newspaper chains with the largest circulation, with 6 to 78 papers per chain and an aggregate circulation of about 39% of the national daily total, the dozen largest multistation TV groups that fall just below the top three networks, and the additional score of consumer and farm magazines with circulations of 2 million of more. See Benjamin M. Compaine, *Who Owns the Media, Concentration of Ownership in the Mass Communications Industry*, Harmony Books, 1979, pp. 23, 82-83, 147.

13. Eric Barnouw, *The Sponsor*, Oxford University Press, 1978, p. 158.
14. *Ibid.*, pp. 85-86.
15. *Ibid.*, p. 57.
16. *Ibid.*, p. 151.
17. *Ibid.*, pp. 164, 168.
18. Over this ten year span the ratio of articles devoted to Communist-left-campus violence to articles critical of rightist terror regimes was almost exactly 10 to 1.
19. See Table 4-1 below and associated text.
20. Leon V. Sigal, *Reporters and Officials: The Organization and Politics of Newsmaking*, Heath, 1973, p. 124.
21. Quoted in Paletz and Entman, *Media• Power• Politics*, p. 15.
22. Edouard Bailby, "Terror in El Salvador's Countryside," *Le Monde Diplomatique*, January 1981 (translation by the present writer).
23. Robert Armstrong and Philip Wheaton, "Reform and Repression: U.S. Policy in El Salvador: 1950 Through 1981," Testimony on the Role of the United States presented to the Permanent People's Tribunal, Mexico City, February 10, 1981, p. 34.
24. *Latinamerica Press*, September 3, 1981.
25. See Chomsky and Herman, *Washington Connection*, pp. 61-66, 210-215 for an introduction to managed looting, and references.
26. Guy Sacerdoti, "The power of one man's pen," *Far Eastern Economic Review*, October 24, 1980.

27. Richard Arens, ed., *Genocide in Paraguay*, Temple University Press, 1976, p. 5.

28. Maria Teresa Moraes and George A. Lawton, "Images of Chile in the U.S. Press," *Brazilian Studies* (undated mimeo), p. 11.

29. Ivna Gusmao and Alan Benjamin, "The New York Times' Coverage of El Salvador," January 1981 (mimeo).

30. Jonathan Evan Maslow and Ana Arana, "Operation El Salvador," *Columbia Journalism Review*, May/June, 1981, pp. 56-57.

31. Ralph McGehee, "The C.I.A. and The White Paper on El Salvador," *The Nation*, April 11, 1981.

32. Jonathan Kwitney, "Tarnished Report? Apparent Errors Cloud U.S. 'White Paper' on Reds in El Salvador," *Wall Street Journal*, June 8, 1981.

33. "U.S. Officials Concede Flaws in Salvador White Paper but Defend Its Conclusion," *New York Times*, June 10, 1981.

34. James Petras, "The White Paper," *The Nation*, March 26, 1981; John Dinges, "Wide Disparity Between Haig's White Paper and Salvadoran Documents," *Latinamerica Press*, March 26, 1981.

35. Maslow and Arana, *op. cit.*, pp. 54-55.

36. *Ibid.*, p. 56.

37. "A Reply To The White Paper," reprinted in I.F. Stone, *In A Time of Torment*, Random House, 1967, pp. 212-218.

38. Center for International Policy Aid Memo, "Total Aid Package for El Salvador May Reach $532 Million," April 1981.

39. Chomsky and Herman, *After the Cataclysm*, p. 84.

40. World Bank, *Indonesia*, 1980, p. 63.

41. *Ibid.*, p. 91.

42. Guy Standing and Richard Szal, *Poverty and Basic Needs*, ILO, 1979, pp. 86-89, 101-105.

43. World Bank, *Indonesia*, p. 91; Standing and Szal, *Poverty and Basic Needs*, pp. 86-89.

44. Chomsky and Herman, *Washington Connection*, pp. 61-66 and 205-251.

45. Ingrid Palmer, *The Indonesian Economy Since 1965,* Frank Cass, 1978, p. 164.

46. "In Guatemala, A Debilitating and Inept War," *New York Times,* May 10, 1981.

47. AI, *Guatemala, A Government Program of Political Murder*, 1981, p. 5.

48. *Ibid.*, p. 6.

49. *Ibid.*

50. See especially, *ARC Newsletter*, June 1981 including Thomas Melville's "Guatemala: The Indian Awakening;" and "An Indian Voice: The Suppression of Native Leadership."

51. Flora Lewis, "Ambassador Extraordinary: John Peurifoy," *New York Times Magazine*, July 18, 1954.

52. Kinzer and Schlesinger, *Bitter Fruit*, pp. 206-208.

53. *Ibid.*, pp. 222-223.

54. *Ibid.*, p. 244.

55. *Ibid.*, p. 246.

56. Ronald Schneider, *Communism in Guatemala 1944-49*, Praeger, 1959.

57. Kinzer and Schlesinger, *Bitter Fruit*, pp. 54-63, 79-97.

58. *Ibid.*, p. 106.

59. "El Salvador Struggles to Reduce Its Noncombatant Killings," *New York Times*, February 27, 1981.

60. Alan Riding, "The Cross and Sword," *New York Review of Books,* May 28, 1981, p. 8.

61. Private correspondence with this Church official.

62. Quoted in "Salvadoran Archdiocese Denounces Thousands of Political Killings," *Latinamerica Press*, November 12, 1981.

63. AI, *Guatemala*, p. 8.

64. "Guatemala: 30 killed, 14 abducted," *Philadelphia Inquirer*, October 29, 1981, p. 22-A.

65. Quoted in Gusmao and Benjamin, "The New York Times' Coverage of El Salvador," July 1981 (mimeo), p. 2.

66. *Solidaridad*, May 12, 1981, pp. 1-2.

67. Gusmao and Benjamin, *op. cit.*, pp. 4-5.

68. Armstrong and Wheaton, *op. cit.*, pp. 23-24.

69. Armstrong and Wheaton, *op. cit.*, p. 30.

70. "Populist Figure For Argentines," *New York Times*, October 6, 1980.

71. Penny Lernoux, "Bishops hit governments' acts," *National Catholic Reporter,* August 28, 1981.

72. Quoted in Karl Dietrich Bracher, *The German Dictatorship*, Praeger, 1970, p. 423.

73. Quoted in Lernoux, "Bishops hit governments' acts."

74. Quoted in June Carolyn Erlick, "Argentina's Military Influence Affects Colombia," *Latinamerica Press*, October 2, 1980, p. 8.

75. For another illustration of de Onis' tendency to look at the NSS world from the standpoint of its managers, see Chomsky and Herman, *Washington Connection*, p. 269.

76. For a discussion of the role of the United States in the Chilean counterrevolutionary process, see the works cited in chapter 3, note 80.

77. Teofilo Rondon, "Reversal of Chile's Land Reform Benefits Agribusiness," *Latinamerica Press*, November 6, 1980.

78. Cristina Hurtado Beca, "Ocupacion, Salario y Consumo de los Trabajodores," *Chile-America*, October-December 1981, Table 1, p. 33.

79. David Felix, "Monetarism in Latin America," *The IDS Bulletin* (Sussex, England), December 1981.

80. Norman Gall, "How the 'Chicago boys' fought 1,000% inflation," *Forbes*, March 31, 1980 (interview with Harberger), p. 80.

81. Felix, "Monetarism in Latin America."

82. "Anyone in Argentina Can Give You Lessons On Beating Inflation," *Wall Street Journal*, July 16, 1979.

83. Everett Martin, in *Wall Street Journal*, October 6, 1981.

84. Warren Hoge, in *New York Times*, March 29, 1981.

85. Warren Hoge, in *New York Times*, May 9, 1979.

86. Kirk Felsman, "Street Urchins of Colombia," *Natural History*, April 1981.

87. Penny Lernoux, "Notes on a Revolutionary Church: Human Rights in Latin America," Alicia Patterson Foundation, 1978, pp. 40-41.

88. Paul R. Schilling, "Civil War In Rio De Janeiro," *Latinamerica Press*, February 12, 1980.

89. Kinzer and Schlesinger, *Bitter Fruit*, pp. 59-63.

90. This is not strictly true—there was significant violence under the Ubico dictatorship, which the United States found entirely unobjectionable; see *ibid.*, chapter 2.

91. Moraes and Lawton, "Images of Chile," pp. 6-8.

92. "Duarte, Three Months in Power, Bringing Change to El Salvador," *New York Times*, March 30, 1981.

93. Eric Stover, "Human Rights Conditions in the Americas," in AAAS Workshop Report, *Human Rights and Scientific Cooperation,* AAAS, 1981, pp. 88-89.

94. Joel Primack, "Human Rights in the Southern Cone," *Bulletin of Atomic Scientists*, February 1981, pp. 24-29.

95. The only omissions of note are Timerman and Letelier: the former because of the complication of the Jewish and antisemitism questions; the latter because he was an expatriate, living and murdered in the United States. Also omitted from this table is Solzhenitzyn, an expatriate.

96. "Making Trouble on Human Rights," *New York Times* (editorial), November 30, 1981.

97. Cardinal Archbishop Mindszenty was a cause celebre during the early surge of the cold war. A conservative leader of a conservative Catholic Church in Hungary, he furiously opposed the actions of the postwar Communist government, including the ending of compulsory religious education, land reform (including confiscation of Church lands), the nationalization of schools, more liberal divorce laws, and the like. After on and off bouts of conflict, Cardinal Mindszenty was sentenced to life imprisonment in 1949. See D.F. Fleming, *The Cold War and Its Origins, 1917-1960*, Doubleday, 1961, vol. I, p. 260.

Chapter Five: Remedies for Terrorism

1. *Latin America Regional Reports Andean Group*, December 11, 1981, pp. 3-4.

2. "Tales of Jungle Death Squad: Colombia Peasants Claim Soldiers Torture, Murder Them; Army Generals Deny It," *Los Angeles Times*, October 18, 1981.

3. "The militarisation of rural Colombia," *Latin America Regional Reports Andean Group*, November 30, 1979.

4. Warren Hoge, "Colombians Combat Cuban Interference," *New York Times*, Aug. 13, 1981.

5. See Kinzer and Schlesinger, *Bitter Fruit*, pp. 59-63, chapters 14 and 15.

6. *Ibid.*, chapters 14-15; AI, *Guatemala, A government program of political murder*, 1981. According to Francisco Villagran Kramer, the vice president of Guatemala who resigned in September 1980: Guatemala has established a "new form of government, based on terrorism employed by the military and other ultraright groups. The conservative groups in the private sector approve of and are comfortable with this pattern. We have arrived at a system in which the military and the business community have completely come to terms on all issues." Stephen Kinzer, "No. 2 man in Guatemala quits, citing terror," *Boston Globe*, September 4, 1980.

7. The principal indirect mode of encouragement has been the military aid and training program, discussed in chapter 3, and more fully in Miles Wolpin, *Military Aid and Counterrevolution in the Third World*, Heath, 1972.

8. The most important moments of truth where there was a tilt away from constitutional government toward the NSS were: Guatemala, 1954; Brazil, 1964; Dominican Republic, 1965; and Chile, 1973, but there have been others.

9. Kinzer and Schlesinger, *Bitter Fruit*, p. 244.

10. In no case were relations with a terror state broken, an Embassy closed down, a boycott put in place, or pressure put on private banks, firms or international institutions, to terminate business dealings with countries like Argentina and Chile. Such serious actions have been reserved for countries threatening or violating property rights. See Chomsky and Herman, *Washington Connection*, pp. 32-37.

11. See "Technocracy and Repression in IDB Policies," *Washington Report on the Hemisphere*, January 26, 1982.

12. Warren Hoge, "Nicaraguan Poor Get Sidewalks, Buses and Dialect," *New York Times*, January 2, 1981. Hoge writes: "There are schools and clinics and vaccination programs against measles, dengue and polio. 'One of the striking differences,' said a nurse, 'is that they

aren't always having funerals for children like before. There used to be a lot of baby boxes around here.'"

13. In addition to continuous bluster and threats by Haig and the State Department, exiles are training in Florida and California for the explicit purpose of invading Nicaragua, and in violation of the U.S. Neutrality Act: see e.g., Jo Thomas, "Latin Exiles Focus on Nicaragua As They Train Urgently in Florida," *New York Times,* December 23, 1981; Ronnie Lowler, "U.S. Ignores Plot Against Nicaragua," *Philadephia Inquirer,* January 31, 1982.

14. "Technocracy and Repression in IDB Policies," *Washington Report on the Hemisphere,* January 26, 1982.

15. Council on Hemispheric Affairs, "The Travail of the Guatemalan Trade Union Movement," February 18, 1981 (research memo by Michael Carman).

16. Council on Hemispheric Affairs, "Major Brazilian Trade Union Leaders Convicted By Military," Press Release, February 27, 1981; Warren Hoge, "Brazil Cracks Down on Its One Strong Union," *New York Times,* April 19, 1981, p. E-5.

17. Metin Demirsar, "Europe's Tiff With Turkey Worsens," *Wall Street Journal,* December 29, 1981.

18. *Ibid.* Also, "U.S. sales of jets soothes Turkey," *Philadephia Inquirer,* April 12, 1981.

19. Relevant questions would include: 1) why moral indignation as regards Poland and not Turkey, etc.? 2) Why is the instability brought about by labor conflict justification for martial law in Turkey, Chile and the Philippines but not Poland. 3) In the light of deteriorating relations with the Soviet Union and increased tension, could U.S. support of Solidarity fail to be counterproductive from the viewpoint of Solidarity's aims? 4) Since these above points are all pretty obvious, what are the *real* motives of Haig-Reagan?

20. Jeff Frieden, "Why The Big Banks Love Martial Law," *The Nation,* January 12, 1981.

21. The view expressed earlier in this book (Preface and chapter 2) is that the Soviet Union has done poorly also, behaving in opportunistic and parochial fashion, but that it has been largely on the defensive and is only a regional great power.

22. "Text of NATO Foreign Ministers Declaration," *New York Times,* January 12, 1981.

23. See references in note 7 above.

24. See *Solidaridad,* May 12, 1981, pp. 1-2; AI, *Guatemala, a government program of political murder,* 1981.

25. According to Bishop Casaldaliga, "the majority" of attacks he has suffered for his work on behalf of the peasantry "have been ordered by the administrators and technocrats of the multinational latifundios." "Brazilian Bishop Casaldaliga: The Gospel Is My Weapon," *Latinamerica Press,* November 6, 1975.

26. *Ibid.*
27. See Thomas Ferguson and Joel Rogers, eds., *The Hidden Election, Politics and Economic in the 1980 Presidential Campaign,* Pantheon, 1981; Edward S. Herman, *Corporate Control, Corporate Power*, Cambridge University Press, 1981, chapters 5 and 7.
28. Inter-American Development Bank, *Economic and Social Progress in Latin America*, Washington, D.C., 1978, pp 140-141.

Index